The Nestlé Cookbook

The Nestlé Cookbook

Hundreds of triple-tested, easy recipes
for breakfast, lunch, dinner, and dessert from
the largest food company in the world

contents

introduction

Many people associate Nestlé with chocolate, but, in fact, it's the largest food company in the world. With its global reach, Nestlé is also known for having one of the finest test kitchens. Fueled by its ever-growing array of brands, such as BUITONI, STOUFFER'S, NESTLÉ TOLL HOUSE, CARNATION, NESQUIK, NESCAFÉ, NESTEA, MAGGI, and others, Nestlé's state-of-the-art kitchens are continually testing and retesting hundreds of recipes each year. From breakfasts to lunches to dinners, and yes, desserts, Nestlé's team of culinary experts works tirelessly to help food lovers resolve their disparate tastes—always creating new award-winning combinations and ingredients.

In this cookbook, the editors of Nestlé's popular website Meals.com have chosen over 300 of their favorite, easy-to-prepare recipes. So whether you're whipping up something fast, or taking your time to make something special, consider this book a guide to everyday meal strategizing. With this in mind, we are confident that *The Nestlé Cookbook* will become a valuable addition to your kitchen. Bon Appetite!

an amazing history …

Today, Nestlé is the world's largest food company. But in 1867, "Nestlé" was but Henri Nestlé, a pharmacist looking to develop a food for babies who were unable to breastfeed. His first success was with a premature infant who could not tolerate his mother's milk or any of the usual substitutes. As word spread about Mr. Nestlé's new baby formula that helped save a child's life, Nestlé the corporation was born.

In 1905, Nestlé merged with the Anglo-Swiss Condensed Milk Company, and by the early 1900s, the company was operating factories in the United States, Britain, Germany, and Spain. World War I created new demand for dairy products in the form of government contracts. By the end of the war, Nestlé's production had more than doubled.

After the war, government contracts dried up and consumers switched back to fresh milk. However, Nestlé's management responded quickly, and in the 1920s expanded into new products, with chocolate becoming Nestlé's second most important product.

With the onset of World War II, Nestlé felt the effects. Profits dropped from $20 million in 1938 to $6 million in 1939. Ironically, the war helped with the introduction of the Company's newest product, Nescafé, which was a staple drink of the US military.

The end of World War II was the beginning of a dynamic phase for Nestlé. Growth accelerated and companies were acquired, thus positioning Nestlé to expand into a variety of food groups. In 1947 came the merger with Maggi seasonings and soups. Libby's followed in 1971, as did Stouffer's (1973), Carnation (1984), and others.

As the Company continued to expand into additional food groups, its investment in test kitchens increased dramatically. Today, the Nestlé Research Center is the hub of a worldwide research community. The role of the research center is to help fulfill Nestlé's vision of making good food central to enjoying a healthy life for consumers everywhere. With its main headquarters located in the rolling hills above Lausanne in Switzerland, and close to Lake Geneva, the Nestlé Research Center is recognized by its scientific peers as one of the leaders today in food research and nutritional sciences.

breakfast basics

breakfast basics

While it's true that the morning meal is the most important of the day, it is also true that breakfast meals are not just for breakfast any more. All of the following recipes kick-start your morning, but many of them can do double- or triple-duty as healthy afternoon snacks or even lunch or dinner items. Go ahead. Serve an egg casserole for dinner or savory muffins with soup for lunch, and don't forget to put out a plate of fruit or nut bread slices for hungry afterschool snackers. With our easy-to-make breakfast basics, you can keep your family and guests revved the whole day through. And for more great breakfast recipes visit Meals.com.

Apple Banana Breakfast Crunch

Looking for a change of pace from your regular breakfast? Break away from your boxed cereal and turn your morning into something truly unique.

MAKES 4 SERVINGS

INGREDIENTS

2 packages (12 ounces each)
  STOUFFER'S frozen Harvest Apples,
  defrosted*, divided
2 containers (8 ounces each)
  banana yogurt
1 cup banana crunch-style cereal

DIRECTIONS

COMBINE yogurt and cereal in small bowl.

DIVIDE 1 package of harvest apples into 4 dessert dishes; top with one-half of yogurt mixture. Repeat layers with remaining harvest apples and remaining yogurt mixture.

*DEFROST harvest apples in microwave on MEDIUM (50%) power for 6 to 7 minutes.

Estimated Time
Preparation: 15 mins

Apple Banana Breakfast Crunch

Apple Bran Muffins

A healthy and delicious snack—these muffins make a great everyday breakfast or lunchbox treat.

MAKES 12 MUFFINS

INGREDIENTS

1 cup all-purpose flour

⅓ cup packed brown sugar

2 teaspoons baking powder

½ teaspoon salt

½ teaspoon ground cinnamon

¼ teaspoon ground nutmeg

1 cup (1 medium) peeled, finely chopped tart apple

¾ cup water

½ cup dry NESTLÉ CARNATION Instant Nonfat Dry Milk

¼ cup vegetable oil

1 large egg

2 cups bran flake cereal

DIRECTIONS

PREHEAT oven to 400° F. Grease or paper-line 12 muffin cups.

COMBINE flour, sugar, baking powder, salt, cinnamon, and nutmeg in medium bowl. Mix apple, water, dry milk, oil, and egg in small bowl. Add to flour mixture; stir until moistened. Stir in cereal. Spoon into prepared muffin cups, filling about two-thirds full.

BAKE for 12 to 15 minutes or until wooden pick inserted in center comes out clean. Remove to wire rack; cool slightly. Serve warm.

Estimated Times

Preparation: 15 mins

Cooking: 12 mins

Cooling: 10 mins

Banana Nut Bread

Banana Nut Bread is a great way to start the morning. Save your ripe bananas for this recipe by peeling and storing them in the freezer.

MAKES 2 LOAVES

INGREDIENTS

4 cups all-purpose flour

1¼ cups dry NESTLÉ CARNATION Instant Nonfat Dry Milk

4 teaspoons baking powder

1 teaspoon ground cinnamon

4 large eggs

3½ cups (about 7 medium) mashed, ripe bananas

2 cups granulated sugar

1 cup vegetable oil

1 cup chopped walnuts

DIRECTIONS

PREHEAT oven to 350° F. Grease two 9 x 5-inch loaf pans.

COMBINE flour, dry milk, baking powder, and cinnamon in medium bowl. Beat eggs, bananas, sugar, and oil in large mixer bowl on medium speed. Gradually beat in flour mixture; stir in nuts. Spoon into prepared pans.

BAKE for 60 to 65 minutes or until wooden pick inserted in centers comes out clean. Cool in pans on wire racks for 10 minutes; remove to wire racks to cool completely.

Estimated Times

Preparation: 15 mins

Cooking: 1 hr

Cooling: 30 mins

Eggs

Most recipes typically assume use of eggs known commercially as "Grade A-Large." Our Nestlé kitchens always develop recipes using large eggs.

"Grade A-Large" eggs generally weigh 2 ounces each. Two "Large" eggs or 3 "Medium" eggs equal ½ cup. One dozen "Large" whole eggs equal approximately 2⅓ cups. Thirteen large eggs equal 2½ cups.

Blueberry Muffins

Nothing beats warm muffins made with fresh blueberries.

MAKES 12 MUFFINS

INGREDIENTS

MUFFINS

1½ cups fresh or frozen blueberries
⅓ cup butter, melted
⅓ cup warm water
¼ cup Original NESTLÉ COFFEE-MATE
  Powdered Coffee Creamer
1 large egg
1 large egg yolk
¾ teaspoon vanilla extract
½ teaspoon grated lemon or orange peel
1½ cups all-purpose flour
¾ cup granulated sugar
1½ teaspoons baking powder
¾ teaspoon salt

TOPPING

⅓ cup all-purpose flour
¼ cup granulated sugar
3 tablespoons cold butter, cut into pieces

DIRECTIONS

PREHEAT oven to 375° F. Grease or paper-line 12 muffin cups. Wash and drain fresh blueberries or thaw frozen blueberries and drain.

FOR MUFFINS:

COMBINE butter, water, Coffee-mate, egg, egg yolk, vanilla extract, and lemon peel in medium bowl; whisk until blended.

COMBINE flour, sugar, baking powder, and salt in large bowl. Stir in Coffee-mate mixture just until combined. Fold in blueberries.

DIVIDE batter between 12 prepared muffin cups.

FOR TOPPING:

COMBINE flour, sugar, and butter in medium bowl. Mix with fork or fingers until crumbly. Sprinkle evenly over batter in muffin cups.

BAKE for 23 to 25 minutes or until golden. Cool in pan on wire rack for 10 minutes.

Estimated Times
Preparation: 15 mins
Cooking: 23 mins
Cooling: 10 mins

Brunch Sausage Casserole

You can put this hearty egg, cheese, and sausage casserole into the oven early on a weekend morning and it will be ready by the time the whole family is up. An easy holiday brunch recipe!

MAKES 8 TO 10 SERVINGS

INGREDIENTS

1 package (16 ounces) bulk pork sausage,
  cooked, drained, and crumbled
4 cups cubed day-old bread
2 cups (8 ounces) shredded sharp
  cheddar cheese
2 cans (12 fluid ounces each) NESTLÉ
  CARNATION Evaporated Milk
10 large eggs, lightly beaten
1 teaspoon dry mustard
¼ teaspoon onion powder

DIRECTIONS

GREASE 13 x 9-inch baking dish. Place bread in prepared baking dish. Sprinkle with cheese.

COMBINE evaporated milk, eggs, dry mustard, and onion powder in medium bowl. Pour evenly over bread and cheese. Sprinkle with sausage. Cover; refrigerate overnight.

PREHEAT oven to 325° F. Uncover casserole.

BAKE for 55 to 60 minutes or until cheese is golden brown. Cover with foil if top browns too quickly. Season with ground black pepper.

Estimated Times
Preparation: 15 mins
Refrigerating: 8 hrs
Cooking: 55 mins

Brunch Sausage Casserole

Cheesy Bacon Muffins

**A great change of pace from a BLT!
Serve with watermelon wedges.**

MAKES 6 SERVINGS

INGREDIENTS

2 packages (10 ounces each)
    STOUFFER'S frozen Welsh Rarebit,
    prepared according to package
    directions, kept hot
12 strips bacon, cooked and drained
2 medium tomatoes, cut into
    ½-inch-thick slices
6 tablespoons vegetable oil
⅔ cup all-purpose flour
6 English muffins, split and toasted

DIRECTIONS

SPRINKLE tomatoes with salt and
ground black pepper to taste. Heat oil
in medium skillet over medium heat.
Dip tomatoes in flour; cook on both
sides until browned.

PLACE 2 muffin halves on each plate;
top each with a fried tomato slice, hot
Welsh rarebit, and bacon.

Estimated Times
Preparation: 10 mins
Cooking: 10 mins

The Carnation Story

Over 100 years ago, a grocer
named E.A. Stuart and a fellow
business partner founded the
Pacific Coast Condensed Milk
Company. It was based solely on
the little-understood, relatively
new process of evaporation.

In 1901 his partner sold out,
leaving Stuart the company and a
large debt. But Stuart pressed on
believing that there was value in
sanitary milk at a time when fresh
milk was neither universally available
nor always drinkable. He believed
that his product would soon join
other staples on the grocer's shelves,
such as salt and sugar.

Today, NESTLÉ CARNATION
Evaporated Milk is virtually the same
high-quality product it has been
since its introduction in 1899. It truly
has become the American staple
that E. A. Stuart envisioned many
years ago. NESTLÉ CARNATION
Evaporated Milk is a product that
we have all come to know and trust.

Chocolate Brunch Waffles

Make Sunday brunch special with these chocolatey waffles. Topped with fruit and whipped cream, they're perfect for company or as a dessert.

MAKES 10 BELGIAN WAFFLES

INGREDIENTS

2¼ cups all-purpose flour
½ cup granulated sugar
1 tablespoon baking powder
¾ teaspoon salt
1 cup (6 ounces) NESTLÉ TOLL HOUSE
   Semi-Sweet Chocolate Morsels
¾ cup (1½ sticks) butter or margarine
1½ cups milk
3 large eggs, lightly beaten
1 tablespoon vanilla extract
Toppings (e.g., whipped cream,
   chocolate shavings, sifted powdered
   sugar, fresh fruit, ice cream)

DIRECTIONS

COMBINE flour, sugar, baking powder, and salt in large bowl.

MICROWAVE morsels and butter in medium, uncovered, microwave-safe bowl on HIGH (100%) power for 1 minute; STIR. The morsels may retain some of their original shape. If necessary, microwave at additional 10- to 15-second intervals, stirring just until melted. Cool to room temperature. Stir in milk, eggs, and vanilla extract. Add chocolate mixture to flour mixture; stir (batter will be thick).

COOK in Belgian waffle maker* according to manufacturer's directions. Serve warm with your choice of toppings.

*Can also be cooked in standard waffle maker (makes about 20 standard-size waffle squares).

Estimated Times
Preparation: 10 mins
Cooking: 15 mins

Coffee Cake

This warm coffee cake with crumb topping is perfect for those special mornings.

MAKES 8 SERVINGS

INGREDIENTS

CRUMB TOPPING
1 cup chopped walnuts or pecans
½ cup granulated sugar
½ cup packed brown sugar
¼ cup all-purpose flour
1 teaspoon ground cinnamon
6 tablespoons cold butter, cut into pieces

CAKE
⅔ cup warm water
⅓ cup Original NESTLÉ COFFEE-MATE
   Powdered Coffee Creamer

2 cups all-purpose flour
½ cup granulated sugar
⅓ cup butter, softened
2 teaspoons baking powder
1 teaspoon ground cinnamon
½ teaspoon salt
1 large egg

DIRECTIONS

PREHEAT oven to 375° F. Grease 9-inch-square baking pan.

FOR CRUMB TOPPING:
COMBINE nuts, granulated sugar, brown sugar, flour, cinnamon, and butter in medium bowl. Mix with fork until mixture resembles coarse crumbs.

FOR CAKE:
WHISK together water and Coffee-mate in small bowl until smooth. Combine flour, sugar, butter, baking powder, cinnamon, and salt in large mixer bowl. Beat by hand or on low speed with an electric mixer until flour is coated with the butter. Stir egg into butter-flour mixture. Gradually stir in Coffee-mate mixture.

SPOON half of batter into prepared pan. Sprinkle half of crumb topping over batter; spoon remaining batter over crumb topping. Sprinkle with remaining crumb topping.

BAKE for 30 minutes or until wooden pick inserted near center comes out clean. Cool in pan on wire rack for 15 minutes before cutting. Best served warm.

Colossal Chocolate Cinnamon Rolls

Scrumptious and easy to make. Baked exactly how you like them and finished off with a heavenly glaze. A great alternative to traditional holiday bread.

MAKES 12 SERVINGS

INGREDIENTS

2 loaves (1 pound each) frozen white
    yeast bread dough, thawed, divided
¼ cup granulated sugar
1 tablespoon ground cinnamon
2 cups (12-ounce package) NESTLÉ
    TOLL HOUSE Semi-Sweet
    Chocolate Morsels
1 cup chopped nuts, divided
1 cup powdered sugar, sifted
3 tablespoons milk

DIRECTIONS

GREASE two 9-inch-round baking pans.

ROLL 1 bread loaf into 16 x 10-inch rectangle on lightly floured surface. Combine granulated sugar and cinnamon in small bowl; sprinkle 2 tablespoons over dough leaving ½-inch border around sides. Sprinkle with 1 cup morsels and ½ cup nuts.

ROLL up dough starting at short end; seal edges. Cut into 6 slices; place cut-side-up in prepared baking pan. Repeat with remaining bread loaf, sugar mixture, morsels, and nuts; place in second prepared baking pan. Cover; let rise in warm place until dough almost fills pans.

PREHEAT oven to 350° F.

BAKE for 25 to 30 minutes or until deep golden brown. Cool slightly in pans on wire racks.

COMBINE powdered sugar and milk in small bowl to make a stiff glaze. Drizzle over cinnamon rolls.

Estimated Times
Preparation: 20 mins
Standing: 1 hr
Cooking: 25 mins

Colossal Chocolate Cinnamon Rolls

About Nestlé Toll House

Back in 1930, Kenneth and Ruth Wakefield purchased a Cape Cod-style Toll House located in Massachusetts. The Wakefield's converted the house to a lodge, calling it the Toll House Inn.

One day, while preparing a batch of cookies, Ruth cut a bar of our NESTLÉ TOLL HOUSE Semi-Sweet Chocolate into tiny bits and added them to her dough, expecting them to melt.

Instead, the chocolate held its shape and softened to a delicately creamy texture. Ruth eventually approached Nestlé and together we reached an agreement that allowed us to print what would become the Nestlé Toll House Cookie recipe on the wrapper of our Semi-Sweet Chocolate Bar. Part of this agreement included supplying Ruth with all of the chocolate she could use to make her delicious cookies for the rest of her life.

Corn Meal Pancakes

Liven up your breakfast or brunch with these hearty corn meal pancakes.

MAKES 8 TO 10 PANCAKES

INGREDIENTS

1 cup ALBERS Yellow Corn Meal
1 tablespoon honey
1 teaspoon salt
1 cup boiling water
½ cup all-purpose flour
2 teaspoons baking powder
1 teaspoon ground cinnamon (optional)
1 large egg
½ cup NESTLÉ CARNATION Evaporated Milk
Maple syrup or applesauce

DIRECTIONS

COMBINE corn meal, honey, and salt in medium bowl. Slowly stir in boiling water. Cover; let stand for 10 minutes. Stir in flour, baking powder, and cinnamon just until blended.

PREHEAT griddle or skillet. Lightly grease griddle or skillet.

COMBINE egg and evaporated milk in small bowl; add to corn meal mixture. Spoon ⅓ cup batter for each pancake onto prepared griddle or skillet; cook for about 1 minute or until bubbles appear. Turn; continue to cook for 1 to 2 minutes or until golden. Repeat with remaining batter. Serve warm with maple syrup.

FOR CHEESE AND ONION CORN MEAL PANCAKES:
ADD ½ cup (2 ounces) shredded cheddar or mozzarella cheese and ¼ cup finely chopped onions to batter; stir just until blended. Proceed as above.

Estimated Times
Preparation: 10 mins
Standing: 10 mins
Cooking: 10 mins

Down-Home Sausage Gravy

Savory breakfast sausage adds a ton of flavor to this simple biscuits 'n' gravy recipe. It's practically a meal in itself but don't be shy about adding eggs and hash browns for a hearty brunch.

MAKES 10 SERVINGS

INGREDIENTS

1 package (16 ounces) breakfast sausage
2 tablespoons finely chopped onion
6 tablespoons all-purpose flour
2 cans (12 fluid ounces each) NESTLÉ CARNATION Evaporated Milk
1 cup water
¼ teaspoon salt
⅛ to ¼ teaspoon hot pepper sauce
10 hot biscuits, split

DIRECTIONS

COMBINE sausage and onion in large skillet. Cook over medium-low heat, stirring occasionally, until sausage is no longer pink. Stir in flour; mix well. Stir in evaporated milk, water, salt, and hot pepper sauce. Cook, stirring occasionally, until mixture comes to a boil. Cook for 1 to 2 minutes.

SERVE immediately over hot biscuits.

Estimated Times
Preparation: 10 mins
Cooking: 15 mins

Easy Cheesy Bacon, Eggs, and Potatoes

Reinvent your breakfast with this morning treat. Serve with cantaloupe wedges and orange juice and start your day with a smile. This also makes a great lunch or dinner surprise for your family.

MAKES 6 SERVINGS

INGREDIENTS

2 packages (11.5 ounces each) STOUFFER'S frozen Potatoes au Gratin, defrosted*
6 strips bacon, cooked, drained, and crumbled
5 large eggs, lightly beaten
⅔ cup (about 2½ ounces) shredded cheddar cheese
¼ cup chopped green onions

DIRECTIONS

PREHEAT oven to 350° F.

COMBINE potatoes au gratin, bacon, eggs, cheese, and green onions in large bowl; transfer to 8-inch-square baking pan.

BAKE for 40 to 45 minutes or until knife inserted near center comes out clean. Season with ground black pepper.

*DEFROST potatoes au gratin in microwave on MEDIUM (50%) power for 5 to 6 minutes.

Estimated Times
Preparation: 15 mins
Cooking: 40 mins

Easy Cheesy Bacon, Eggs, and Potatoes

Eggs

Always beat eggs at room temperature (65° to 75° F) for best results. Beat until pale yellow in color and add to the recipe as directed. Do not beat in or with aluminum or plastic, which will discolor eggs and may also inhibit volume development.

Grits and Sausage Bake

Surprise your family with this Southern favorite!

MAKES 6 SERVINGS

INGREDIENTS

1 package (16 ounces) breakfast sausage, cooked, drained, and crumbled

3 cups water

¾ cup ALBERS Quick Grits

2 cups (8 ounces) shredded sharp cheddar cheese, divided

⅔ cup (5 fluid-ounce can) NESTLÉ CARNATION Evaporated Milk

¼ teaspoon garlic powder

⅛ teaspoon hot pepper sauce (optional)

2 large eggs, lightly beaten

DIRECTIONS

PREHEAT oven to 350° F. Grease 8-inch-square baking dish.

BRING water to a boil in medium saucepan; slowly stir in grits. Cover; reduce heat to low. Cook, stirring occasionally, for 5 to 6 minutes. Add 1½ cups cheese, evaporated milk, garlic powder, and hot pepper sauce; stir until cheese is melted. Add sausage and eggs; stir well. Pour into prepared baking dish.

BAKE for 1 hour. Top with remaining cheese. Bake for an additional 5 to 10 minutes or until cheese is melted and golden brown. Let cool for 10 minutes before serving. Season with ground black pepper.

NOTE: Batter can be made the day before. Cover and refrigerate. Let stand at room temperature for 30 minutes before baking.

Estimated Times
Preparation: 15 mins
Cooking: 1 hr, 15 mins
Cooling: 10 mins

Ham and Swiss Quiche

Perfect for any meal of the day, this quiche is a deep-dish pie shell filled with delicious ingredients, including savory ham, Swiss cheese, and evaporated milk.

Contrary to popular belief, real men do eat quiche…

MAKES 8 SERVINGS

INGREDIENTS

1 unbaked 9-inch (4-cup volume) deep-dish pie shell

1 cup (4 ounces) shredded Swiss cheese, divided

1 cup finely chopped, cooked ham

2 green onions, sliced

1 can (12 fluid ounces) NESTLÉ CARNATION Evaporated Milk

3 large eggs

¼ cup all-purpose flour

¼ teaspoon salt

⅛ teaspoon ground black pepper

Grits and Sausage Bake

Ham and Swiss Quiche

DIRECTIONS

PREHEAT oven to 350° F.

SPRINKLE ½ cup cheese, ham, and green onions into pie shell. Whisk together evaporated milk, eggs, flour, salt, and pepper in large bowl. Pour mixture into pie shell and sprinkle with remaining cheese.

BAKE for 45 to 50 minutes or until knife inserted near center comes out clean. Cool on wire rack for 10 minutes before serving.

VARIATION: For a lattice-top quiche, use ready-made pie pastry for single crust pie. Cut pastry into ½-inch-wide strips. Lay pastry strips over filling in lattice-fashion, turning pastry over outside edge of dish. Bake as directed above.

Estimated Times
Preparation: 20 mins
Cooking: 45 mins
Cooling: 10 mins

Hash-Brown Casserole

Satisfy all of your breakfast needs with this all-in-one, hash-brown casserole.

MAKES 12 SERVINGS

INGREDIENTS

6 large eggs, well beaten
1 can (12 fluid ounces) NESTLÉ CARNATION Evaporated Milk
1 teaspoon salt
½ teaspoon ground black pepper
1 package (30 ounces) frozen shredded hash-brown potatoes
2 cups (8 ounces) shredded cheddar cheese
1 medium onion, chopped
1 small green bell pepper, chopped
1 cup diced ham (optional)

DIRECTIONS

PREHEAT oven to 350° F. Grease 13 x 9-inch baking dish.

COMBINE eggs, evaporated milk, salt, and black pepper in large bowl. Add potatoes, cheese, onion, bell pepper, and ham; mix well. Pour mixture into prepared baking dish.

BAKE for 60 to 65 minutes or until set.

Hash-Brown Casserole

NOTE: For a lower-fat version of this recipe, use 3 cartons (4 ounces each) cholesterol-free egg product, substitute NESTLÉ CARNATION Evaporated Fat Free Milk for Evaporated Milk, and 10 slices turkey bacon, cooked and chopped, for the diced ham. Follow recipe directions.

Estimated Times
Preparation: 15 mins
Cooking: 1 hr

Evaporated Milk

To make evaporated milk, we take fresh milk and remove half the water. When there's less water, the milk fat, protein, and calcium are concentrated. That means there is more milk fat, protein, and calcium per cup. Along with the special process, these are the key components of milk that give evaporated milk its creaminess, full-body, and nutrition.

Evaporated milk has more creaminess than regular milk, so it makes a perfect lower-fat substitute for cream products. With less than one-half the fat of light cream and heavy cream, it also has more than double the calcium and protein!

Italian Pumpkin Strata

Dense and creamy, this vegetable-filled strata blends bread, cheese, milk, pumpkin, and eggs together to create a moist and delicious casserole. Cut into squares or wedges and serve with a platter of fresh fruit for a smashing brunch!

MAKES 12 SERVINGS

INGREDIENTS

1 tablespoon vegetable oil
1 pound sweet Italian sausage, casings removed
1 small onion, chopped
½ cup chopped green bell pepper
½ cup chopped red bell pepper
2 cloves garlic, finely chopped
About 1 pound loaf Italian or French bread, cut into 1½-inch cubes (12 cups)
2 cups (8 ounces) shredded mozzarella cheese
2 cans (12 fluid ounces each) NESTLÉ CARNATION Evaporated Milk
1 can (15 ounces) LIBBY'S 100% Pure Pumpkin
4 large eggs
1 teaspoon salt
½ teaspoon ground black pepper
½ teaspoon dried oregano, crushed
½ teaspoon dried basil, crushed
½ teaspoon dried marjoram, crushed

DIRECTIONS

PREHEAT oven to 350° F. Grease 13 x 9-inch baking pan.

HEAT oil in large skillet over medium-high heat. Add sausage, onion, bell peppers, and garlic. Cook, stirring to break up sausage, for 7 to 10 minutes or until sausage is no longer pink; drain.

COMBINE bread cubes, cheese, and sausage mixture in large bowl. Beat evaporated milk, pumpkin, eggs, salt, black pepper, oregano, basil, and marjoram in medium bowl. Pour over bread mixture, stirring gently to moisten bread. Pour into prepared baking pan.

BAKE for 30 to 35 minutes or until set. Serve warm.

Estimated Times
Preparation: 30 mins
Cooking: 40 mins

Libby's Pumpkin Cranberry Bread

A moist and delectable pumpkin bread with tart fresh cranberries. Have a slice for breakfast or enjoy as an afternoon snack.

Libby's Pumpkin Cranberry Bread

MAKES 2 LOAVES

INGREDIENTS

3 cups all-purpose flour

1 tablespoon, plus 2 teaspoons
    pumpkin pie spice

2 teaspoons baking soda

1½ teaspoons salt

3 cups granulated sugar

1 can (15 ounces) LIBBY'S 100%
    Pure Pumpkin

4 large eggs

1 cup vegetable oil

½ cup orange juice or water

1 cup sweetened dried, fresh,
    or frozen cranberries

DIRECTIONS

PREHEAT oven to 350° F. Grease and
flour two 9 x 5-inch loaf pans.

COMBINE flour, pumpkin pie spice,
baking soda, and salt in large bowl.
Combine sugar, pumpkin, eggs, oil, and
orange juice in large mixer bowl; beat
until just blended. Add pumpkin mixture
to flour mixture; stir just until moistened.
Fold in cranberries. Spoon batter into
prepared loaf pans.

BAKE for 60 to 65 minutes or until
wooden pick inserted in center comes
out clean. Cool in pans on wire racks
for 10 minutes; remove to wire racks
to cool completely.

FOR THREE 8 x 4-INCH LOAF PANS:
PREPARE as above. Bake for 55 to
60 minutes.

**FOR FIVE OR SIX 5 x 3-INCH
MINI-LOAF PANS:**
PREPARE as above. Bake for 50 to
55 minutes.

Estimated Times
Preparation: 15 mins
Cooking: 1 hr
Cooling: 30 mins

Old-Fashioned Nut Loaf Bread

**Wrap up a loaf and give it as a gift!
Pumpkin, evaporated milk, and, of
course, nuts make each slice moist
and flavorful.**

MAKES 1 LOAF

INGREDIENTS

2 cups all-purpose flour

2 teaspoons pumpkin pie spice

2 teaspoons baking powder

1 teaspoon salt

½ teaspoon baking soda

1 can (15 ounces) LIBBY'S 100%
    Pure Pumpkin

½ cup granulated sugar

½ cup packed brown sugar

½ cup NESTLÉ CARNATION
    Evaporated Fat Free Milk

1 large egg

1 large egg white

1 tablespoon vegetable oil

¼ cup chopped nuts

DIRECTIONS

PREHEAT oven to 350° F. Grease
9 x 5-inch loaf pan.

COMBINE flour, pumpkin pie spice,
baking powder, salt, and baking soda
in medium bowl. Blend pumpkin,
granulated sugar, brown sugar,
evaporated milk, egg, egg white, and oil
in large mixer bowl. Add flour mixture;
mix just until moistened. Pour into
prepared loaf pan; sprinkle with nuts.

BAKE for 60 to 65 minutes or until
wooden pick inserted in center comes
out clean. Cool in pan on wire rack for
10 minutes; remove to wire rack
to cool completely.

Estimated Times
Preparation: 15 mins
Cooking: 1 hr, 5 mins
Cooling: 30 mins

Puffy Baked Apple Pancake

Puffy Baked Apple Pancake

Baked apple pancakes are a special treat for a festive brunch. Try this delicate pancake sprinkled with a little cinnamon-sugar and frosty glasses of orange juice.

MAKES 6 TO 8 SERVINGS

INGREDIENTS

Nonstick cooking spray

½ cup NESTLÉ CARNATION Evaporated Milk

⅓ cup all-purpose baking mix

2 tablespoons granulated sugar, divided

3 large eggs, separated

2 tablespoons orange juice

¼ teaspoon ground cinnamon

1 medium apple, cored and thinly sliced

1 tablespoon cinnamon-sugar

DIRECTIONS

PREHEAT oven to 375° F. Spray 10-inch ovenproof skillet lightly with nonstick cooking spray. Place in oven for 10 minutes.

PLACE evaporated milk, baking mix, 1 tablespoon sugar, egg yolks, orange juice, and cinnamon in blender; blend until smooth. Beat egg whites in large mixer bowl until soft peaks form; gradually add remaining sugar. Beat until stiff peaks form. Fold milk mixture into egg whites.

POUR batter into hot skillet. Gently push each apple slice about ½ inch into batter, peel-side-up, to form a spoke-like pattern around batter. Sprinkle with cinnamon-sugar.

BAKE for 10 to 15 minutes or until set. Serve immediately.

Estimated Times
Preparation: 15 mins
Cooking: 10 mins

Pumpkin Apple Streusel Muffins

Our cinnamon streusel topping makes these muffins memorable!

MAKES 24 MUFFINS

INGREDIENTS
MUFFINS
2½ cups all-purpose flour
2 cups granulated sugar
1 tablespoon pumpkin pie spice
1 teaspoon baking soda
½ teaspoon salt
1¼ cups LIBBY'S 100% Pure Pumpkin
2 large eggs
¼ cup vegetable oil
2 cups peeled and finely chopped apples

STREUSEL TOPPING
¼ cup granulated sugar
2 tablespoons all-purpose flour
½ teaspoon ground cinnamon
2 tablespoons butter or margarine

DIRECTIONS
PREHEAT oven to 350° F. Grease or paper-line 24 muffin cups.

FOR MUFFINS:
COMBINE flour, sugar, pumpkin pie spice, baking soda, and salt in large bowl. Combine pumpkin, eggs, and oil in medium bowl; mix well. Stir into flour mixture just until moistened. Stir in apples. Spoon batter into prepared muffin cups, filling about three-fourths full.

FOR STREUSEL TOPPING:
COMBINE sugar, flour, and cinnamon in medium bowl. Cut in butter with pastry blender or two knives until mixture is crumbly. Sprinkle over muffin batter.

BAKE for 30 to 35 minutes or until wooden pick inserted in center comes out clean. Cool in pans for 5 minutes; remove to wire racks to cool slightly.

Estimated Times
Preparation: 20 mins
Cooking: 30 mins
Cooling: 5 mins

LIBBY'S Pumpkin

LIBBY'S Pumpkin first found its way to grocers' shelves in 1929, when a food canning company in Chicago expanded its product line to include America's unique fruit. Unlike the average field pumpkin, Libby's only uses a pumpkin known for its rich, golden color, creamy texture, and pure pumpkin flavor—the Dickinson. LIBBY'S 100% Pure Pumpkin is exactly that—with no additives or preservatives. We wouldn't want anything to interfere with our unique, delicious pumpkin flavor. Libby's has always been a producer of canned pumpkin, planting approximately 4,000 acres of pumpkin each year. LIBBY'S Pumpkin is used to create more than 50 million pies every Thanksgiving as well as used year round in many delicious pumpkin recipes.

Pumpkin Pancakes

Pumpkin Pancakes

Wake up to spicy Pumpkin Pancakes hot from the griddle! Serve with Pumpkin Maple Sauce and broiled grapefruit halves sprinkled with brown sugar and cinnamon for a wintertime treat.

MAKES 8 SERVINGS

INGREDIENTS

2 cups all-purpose flour
2 tablespoons packed brown sugar
1 tablespoon baking powder
1¼ teaspoons pumpkin pie spice
1 teaspoon salt
1¾ cups milk
½ cup LIBBY'S 100% Pure Pumpkin

1 large egg
2 tablespoons vegetable oil
Pumpkin Maple Sauce (recipe follows)
Chopped nuts (optional)

DIRECTIONS

COMBINE flour, sugar, baking powder, pumpkin pie spice, and salt in large bowl. Combine milk, pumpkin, egg, and oil in small bowl; mix well. Add to flour mixture. Stir just until moistened; batter may be lumpy.

HEAT griddle or skillet over medium heat; brush lightly with oil. Pour ¼ cup batter onto hot griddle; cook until bubbles begin to burst. Turn; continue cooking for 1 to 2 minutes. Repeat with remaining batter. Serve with Pumpkin Maple Sauce and nuts.

FOR PUMPKIN MAPLE SAUCE:

HEAT 1¼ cups LIBBY'S 100% Pure Pumpkin, 1 cup maple syrup, and ¼ teaspoon ground cinnamon or pumpkin pie spice in small saucepan until warm.

Estimated Times
Preparation: 15 mins
Cooking: 20 mins

Pumpkin Pear Strudel

Wrap pears, pumpkin, and chopped nuts sweetened with brown sugar and spices in puff pastry sheets and pop them into the oven for a few minutes. Out will come a light and flaky pastry bursting with sweet, juicy flavor.

MAKES 10 SERVINGS

INGREDIENTS

2 sheets (17¼-ounce package) frozen puff pastry, thawed according to package directions, divided
2 cups peeled and diced pears
1 cup LIBBY'S 100% Pure Pumpkin
¾ cup packed brown sugar
¾ cup chopped walnuts
1 teaspoon ground cinnamon
⅛ teaspoon ground cloves
⅛ teaspoon ground ginger
1 large egg, lightly beaten
Cinnamon-sugar

Pumpkin Pear Strudel

DIRECTIONS

PREHEAT oven to 375° F.

COMBINE pears, pumpkin, sugar, nuts, cinnamon, cloves, and ginger in medium bowl. Spoon half of filling in center third of 1 pastry sheet.

MAKE downward slanting strips in outer sections of pastry (¾-inch apart), starting about 1 inch away from top of pastry and side of filling, cutting to outside edges. Starting at top, alternately fold left and right side pastry strips over filling forming a braid. Seal at top and bottom of strudel. Place on ungreased rimmed baking sheet. Repeat with remaining filling and pastry sheet. Brush strudels with egg; sprinkle with cinnamon-sugar.

BAKE for 25 to 30 minutes or until golden brown and puffy. Serve warm.

Estimated Times
Preparation: 25 mins
Cooking: 25 mins

Quiche Lorraine

This easy, elegant quiche makes a delicious brunch, lunch, or dinner served with a fresh fruit salad. This quiche can be prepared two to four hours in advance of baking and chilled until ready to bake.

MAKES 6 SERVINGS

INGREDIENTS
1 package (10 ounces) STOUFFER'S
    frozen Welsh Rarebit, defrosted*
1 unbaked 9-inch pie shell
4 large eggs, lightly beaten
¼ teaspoon ground black pepper

5 strips bacon, cooked, drained,
    and crumbled
½ cup (2 ounces) shredded Swiss cheese
1 tablespoon sliced green onion

DIRECTIONS

PREHEAT oven to 350° F.

COMBINE Welsh rarebit, eggs, and pepper in medium bowl. Add bacon, cheese, and green onion; stir. Pour mixture into pie shell.

BAKE for 40 minutes or until knife inserted near center comes out clean.

*DEFROST Welsh rarebit in microwave on MEDIUM (50%) power for 5 to 6 minutes.

Estimated Times
Preparation: 10 mins
Cooking: 50 mins

Quiche Lorraine

Sausage Potato Pancakes

Sausage Potato Pancakes

The aroma of these pancakes will bring everyone running to the kitchen. Serve for breakfast with warm maple syrup and fresh fruit, or surprise your family with an unexpected dinner treat.

MAKES 8 SERVINGS

INGREDIENTS

2 packages (11.5 ounces each) STOUFFER'S frozen Potatoes au Gratin, defrosted*

1 pound bulk sausage, cooked, drained, and crumbled

1½ cups all-purpose baking mix

⅔ cup milk

2 large eggs, lightly beaten

¼ teaspoon ground black pepper

1 cup (4 ounces) shredded cheddar cheese

¼ cup chopped green onions

Vegetable oil

DIRECTIONS

COMBINE baking mix, milk, eggs, and pepper in medium bowl; stir until moistened. Add potatoes au gratin, sausage, cheese, and green onions; gently stir until combined.

COAT bottom of medium skillet with oil; heat over medium heat until hot. Pour ¼ cup batter into skillet for each pancake. Cook until small bubbles appear on top of pancakes. Turn; continue cooking until undersides are golden brown.

*DEFROST potatoes au gratin in microwave on MEDIUM (50%) power for 5 to 6 minutes.

Estimated Times

Preparation: 20 mins

Cooking: 15 mins

Seasoned Tomato and Garlic Quiche

This easy-to-make dish features a mouth-watering topping of bouillon-infused tomatoes, seasoned bread crumbs, Parmesan cheese, and a sprinkling of chopped garlic.

MAKES 8 SERVINGS

Seasoned Tomato and Garlic Quiche

Southwestern Quiche

INGREDIENTS

1 unbaked 9-inch (4-cup volume)
    deep-dish pie shell

2 medium tomatoes, chopped

2 MAGGI Chicken Flavor or Vegetarian
    Vegetable Flavor Bouillon Cubes

1 container (16 ounces) sour cream

3 large eggs

½ cup (2 ounces) freshly grated
    Parmesan cheese, divided

¼ cup seasoned bread crumbs

2 cloves garlic, finely chopped

DIRECTIONS

PREHEAT oven to 350° F.

COMBINE tomatoes and bouillon in small saucepan. Cook over medium-high heat, stirring frequently, just until bouillon is dissolved. Remove from heat.

COMBINE sour cream, eggs, and ¼ cup cheese in medium bowl; pour into pie shell. Combine bread crumbs, remaining cheese, and garlic in small bowl; sprinkle over sour cream mixture. Spoon tomato mixture over cheese mixture.

BAKE for 50 to 60 minutes or until filling is set.

Estimated Times
Preparation: 15 mins
Cooking: 55 mins

Southwestern Quiche

Breakfast, lunch, or dinner, this combination of eggs, cheese, chiles, and salsa will be a hit! As a dinner entrée, finish it off with a side of refried beans.

MAKES 12 SERVINGS

INGREDIENTS

½ cup chopped green or red bell pepper

1 can (4 ounces) diced green chiles

2 green onions, chopped

2 cups (8 ounces) shredded cheddar or
    Monterey Jack cheese, divided

12 large eggs, lightly beaten

1 container (8 ounces) sour cream

½ cup NESTLÉ CARNATION
    Evaporated Milk

Toppings (e.g., chopped fresh
    cilantro, salsa)

DIRECTIONS

PREHEAT oven to 350° F. Grease 13 x 9-inch baking dish.

SPRINKLE bell pepper, chiles, and green onions onto bottom of baking dish. Top with 1½ cups cheese.

WHISK eggs, sour cream, and evaporated milk in medium bowl. Pour over vegetables and cheese in baking dish. Sprinkle with remaining cheese.

BAKE for 35 to 45 minutes or until knife inserted near center comes out clean. Cool on wire rack for 5 minutes. Top with toppings; season with salt.

Estimated Times
Preparation: 15 mins
Cooking: 35 mins
Cooling: 5 mins

Brown Sugar

This sugar is a moister beet or cane sugar. It comes in light or dark varieties. Dark brown sugar is more strongly flavored with molasses. Brown sugar hardens and lumps more easily. Store it in airtight containers in a cool, moist place. Sprinkle lumpy brown sugar lightly with a few drops of water and heat in a low oven for a few minutes or microwave for a few seconds. You may substitute 1 cup firmly packed brown sugar for 1 cup granulated sugar, but this will produce a different flavor in the finished product.

Stuffed French Toast with Fresh Berry Topping

Your favorite strawberry preserves mixed with creamy ricotta cheese comprise the delectable filling in these French toast 'sandwiches.' Fresh berries and a dusting of powdered sugar top them off for an attractive and colorful presentation.

MAKES 6 SERVINGS

INGREDIENTS

2 cups mixed fresh berries
   (e.g., strawberries, raspberries, blueberries, blackberries)
2 tablespoons granulated sugar
⅔ cup lowfat ricotta cheese
¼ cup strawberry preserves
3 large eggs
⅔ cup (5 fluid-ounce can) NESTLÉ CARNATION Evaporated Fat Free Milk
2 tablespoons packed brown sugar
2 teaspoons vanilla extract
12 slices French bread (about ¾-inch-thick)
Vegetable oil, butter, or margarine
Powdered sugar (optional)
Maple syrup, heated (optional)

DIRECTIONS

COMBINE berries and granulated sugar in small bowl. Combine ricotta cheese and preserves in separate small bowl; mix well. Combine eggs, evaporated milk, brown sugar, and vanilla extract in pie plate or shallow bowl; mix well.

SPREAD ricotta-preserve mixture evenly over 6 bread slices. Top with remaining bread slices to form sandwiches.

HEAT small amount of oil in large, nonstick skillet or griddle over medium heat. Dip sandwiches in egg mixture, coating both sides. Cook on each side for about 2 minutes or until golden brown.

SPRINKLE with powdered sugar and top with berries. Serve with maple syrup.

Estimated Times
Preparation: 15 mins
Cooking: 12 mins

Stuffed French Toast with Fresh Berry Topping

Toll House Crumbcake

This sour cream crumbcake is topped with a mixture of brown sugar, butter, nuts, and mini chocolate morsels. A special treat for morning, noon, or night.

MAKES 12 SERVINGS

INGREDIENTS

TOPPING

⅓ cup packed brown sugar

2 tablespoons butter or
   margarine, softened

1 tablespoon all-purpose flour

½ cup chopped nuts

2 cups (12-ounce package) NESTLÉ
   TOLL HOUSE Semi-Sweet
   Chocolate Mini Morsels, divided

CAKE

1¾ cups all-purpose flour

1 teaspoon baking powder

1 teaspoon baking soda

¼ teaspoon salt

¾ cup granulated sugar

½ cup (1 stick) butter or
   margarine, softened

1 teaspoon vanilla extract

3 large eggs

1 cup sour cream

DIRECTIONS

PREHEAT oven to 350° F. Grease
13 x 9-inch baking pan.

Toll House Crumbcake

FOR TOPPING:
COMBINE sugar, butter, and flour in small bowl with pastry blender or two knives until mixture is crumbly. Stir in nuts and ½ cup morsels.

FOR CAKE:
COMBINE flour, baking powder, baking soda, and salt in small bowl. Beat sugar, butter, and vanilla extract in large mixer bowl until creamy. Add eggs one at a time, beating well after each addition. Gradually add flour mixture alternately with sour cream. Fold in remaining morsels. Spread into prepared baking pan; sprinkle with topping.

BAKE for 25 to 35 minutes or until wooden pick inserted in center comes out clean. Cool in pan on wire rack.

Estimated Times
Preparation: 20 mins
Cooking: 25 mins
Cooling: 10 mins

Evaporated Milk

NESTLÉ CARNATION Evaporated Milk has become indispensable in many kitchens because of its versatility, convenience, and its creamy taste. Use in place of cream to reduce fat or when you want to add richness to recipes that use milk. It is available in 12 or 5 fluid-ounce cans.

Tortilla Scramble with Salsa

A scramble for a crowd or breakfast for the family. Farm-fresh eggs, broken tortilla chips, and shredded cheese all work together in this robust dish good for serving any time of the day or night.

MAKES 4 SERVINGS

INGREDIENTS

2 tablespoons butter or margarine

10 large eggs

½ cup NESTLÉ CARNATION Evaporated Milk

½ teaspoon ground cumin

2 cups (about 4 ounces) coarsely broken tortilla chips

1 cup (4 ounces) shredded cheddar cheese

2 tablespoons chopped fresh cilantro (optional)

Salsa, warmed

DIRECTIONS

MELT butter in large skillet over medium-high heat. Beat eggs, evaporated milk, and cumin in large bowl; pour into skillet.

COOK, stirring frequently, until eggs start to set. Sprinkle egg mixture with chips and cheese. Cook, stirring frequently, until eggs are cooked through. Sprinkle with cilantro; serve with salsa. Season with salt and ground black pepper.

Estimated Times

Preparation: 10 mins

Cooking: 10 mins

Tortilla Scramble with Salsa

Upside-Down Apple Coffee Cake

A 'coffee cake' in the most literal sense of the term, this java-infused treat is embellished with a warm apple topping.

MAKES 8 SERVINGS

Upside-Down Apple Coffee Cake

INGREDIENTS

CAKE

⅓ cup packed brown sugar

⅓ cup chopped pecans, toasted

3 tablespoons all-purpose flour

2 tablespoons butter or margarine, melted

2 cups all-purpose baking mix

½ cup granulated sugar

2 teaspoons ground cinnamon

⅔ cup Original NESTLÉ COFFEE-MATE Liquid Coffee Creamer

¼ cup vegetable oil

1 large egg, lightly beaten

2 tablespoons hot water

1 tablespoon NESCAFÉ TASTER'S CHOICE 100% Pure Instant Coffee Granules

1 teaspoon vanilla extract

APPLE TOPPING

1 package (12 ounces) STOUFFER'S frozen Harvest Apples, defrosted*

¼ cup packed brown sugar

¼ cup chopped pecans, toasted

2 tablespoons butter or margarine

DIRECTIONS

PREHEAT oven to 350° F. Lightly grease 9-inch-round cake pan.

FOR CAKE:

COMBINE brown sugar, nuts, flour, and butter in small bowl; mix well. Sprinkle over bottom of prepared cake pan. Stir together baking mix, granulated sugar, and cinnamon in medium bowl. Combine Coffee-Mate, oil, egg, water, coffee granules, and vanilla extract in small bowl; stir into baking mix mixture. Pour over nut mixture in cake pan.

BAKE for 30 to 35 minutes or until wooden pick inserted in center comes out clean. Cool in pan on wire rack for 10 minutes. Run knife around edge to loosen side; invert onto serving platter. Top with Apple Topping.

FOR APPLE TOPPING:

COMBINE harvest apples, brown sugar, nuts, and butter in medium skillet. Cook over medium heat until warm.

*DEFROST harvest apples in microwave on MEDIUM (50%) power for 6 to 7 minutes.

Estimated Times
Preparation: 25 mins
Cooking: 30 mins
Cooling: 10 mins

Nuts

If you need large nut pieces, simply break nuts like pecans or walnuts with your fingers. For finer pieces, use a knife or chopping bowl. Nuts may be chopped in a blender or food processor, ½ cup at a time, for 30 seconds on high speed.

party starters and fun snacks

party starters and fun snacks

Whether you are hosting an adult cocktail party, a get-together for the

whole family, a fun and frenzied fiesta for the kids, or just an afternoon

snack, we've got the recipe for you. We've included our favorite dips,

party mixes, and sweet and savory finger foods—from Hot Spinach Dip

to Mini Pizza Rolls to Cereal Snacking Mix and lots more. With their

no-fuss preparation and delicious results, they'll be favorites of yours, too.

And for even more favorite snack

recipes visit Meals.com.

Morsel Facts

Chocolate morsels keep best in constant temperatures. It's best to store them in a cool, dry place. When they've been exposed to temperature changes, the surface of the morsels can develop a whitish film which is called the "bloom." It's actually just fine traces of melted cocoa butter that have hardened again and it won't affect the flavor or performance of the chocolate. Morsels can also get scuffed sometimes in handling and shipping. These scuffs or scratches have no bearing on the freshness of the chocolate.

Blizzard Party Mix

Blizzard Party Mix

Don't wait for the next football game to enjoy a handful of this party mix.

MAKES 8 APPETIZER SERVINGS

INGREDIENTS

Nonstick cooking spray
2 cups oven-toasted cereal squares
2 cups small pretzel twists
1 cup dry-roasted peanuts
1 cup coarsely chopped caramels (about 20)
2 cups (12-ounce package) NESTLÉ
   TOLL HOUSE Premier White Morsels

DIRECTIONS

SPRAY 13 x 9-inch baking pan with nonstick cooking spray.

COMBINE cereal, pretzels, peanuts, and caramels in large bowl.

MICROWAVE morsels in medium, uncovered, microwave-safe bowl on MEDIUM-HIGH (70%) power for 1 minute; STIR. The morsels may retain some of their original shape. If necessary, microwave at additional 10- to 15-second intervals, stirring just until smooth. Pour over cereal mixture; stir to coat evenly.

SPREAD mixture into prepared baking pan; let stand for 20 to 30 minutes or until firm. Break into bite-sized pieces.

Estimated Times
Preparation: 10 mins
Cooking: 2 mins
Standing: 20 mins

Breaded Ravioli with Dipping Sauces

These cheese-filled pasta pillows turn crispy when cooked and are a perfect complement to the pasta sauces.

INGREDIENTS
1 package (9 ounces) BUITONI
   Refrigerated Four Cheese Ravioli
1¾ cups plain, dry bread crumbs
1½ teaspoons salt
1 teaspoon garlic powder
1 teaspoon Italian seasoning
⅔ cup milk
1 large egg
Vegetable oil
1 container (15 ounces) BUITONI
   Refrigerated Marinara Sauce
1 container (10 ounces) BUITONI
   Refrigerated Alfredo Sauce

DIRECTIONS
LINE baking sheet with wax paper.

PREPARE ravioli according to package directions. Rinse and drain.

COMBINE bread crumbs, salt, garlic powder, and Italian seasoning in small bowl. Whisk milk and egg together in separate small bowl until well blended. Dip ravioli into milk mixture, coating both sides, then into bread crumb mixture. Place on prepared baking sheet.

ADD oil to 2-inch depth in electric skillet or large skillet; heat to 350° F.

FRY ravioli, 5 to 6 at a time, on each side for 20 to 30 seconds or until golden brown. Remove with slotted spoon; drain.

HEAT sauces. Serve with ravioli.

Estimated Times
Preparation: 20 mins
Cooking: 20 mins

Bumps on a Log

Here's a quick, healthful snack kids are sure to love.

INGREDIENTS
1 celery stalk, washed and ends trimmed
2 tablespoons creamy or chunky
   peanut butter

10 NESTLÉ RAISINETS Milk Chocolate-
   Covered Raisins or NESTLÉ GOOBERS
   Milk Chocolate-Covered Peanuts

DIRECTIONS
FILL celery with peanut butter. Press Raisinets into peanut butter.

LITTLE KITCHEN HELPER HINTS:
Even the littlest hands can press Raisinets into the log.

Help the children count out the raisin and peanut pieces or make little piles of 5 each. It's fun math!

For those who are still hungry, spread peanut butter on small round crackers and have the kids make eyes, nose, and mouths with Raisinets.

Have small baby carrots and apple wedges on hand for hungry kids to dip in peanut butter.

Estimated Time
Preparation: 5 mins

Bumps on a Log

Cereal Snacking Mix

Shake up the troops with this good and good-for-you snack.

MAKES 6 APPETIZER SERVINGS

INGREDIENTS

2 cups toasted whole grain oat cereal
½ cup dried cranberries
2 tablespoons granulated sugar
½ teaspoon ground cinnamon
1 tablespoon butter, melted
1 cup (7-ounce package)
   NESTLÉ RAISINETS Milk Chocolate-
   Covered Raisins or NESTLÉ GOOBERS
   Milk Chocolate-Covered Peanuts

DIRECTIONS

COMBINE cereal and cranberries in large, resealable plastic bag.

COMBINE sugar and cinnamon in small bowl.

Cereal Snacking Mix

POUR cinnamon-sugar mixture and butter over cereal mixture; seal bag. Shake well to combine. Add Raisinets; shake well.

Estimated Time
Preparation: 10 mins

Cheesy Tortilla Spirals

Wrapped tortillas filled with tasty chipped beef are great for parties.

MAKES 10 APPETIZER SERVINGS

INGREDIENTS

1 package (11 ounces) STOUFFER'S
   frozen Creamed Chipped Beef,
   defrosted*
2 packages (3 ounces each) cream
   cheese, at room temperature
⅓ cup shredded cheddar cheese
2 teaspoons lime juice
1 teaspoon ground chili powder
½ teaspoon ground cumin
2 tablespoons chopped fresh cilantro
2 tablespoons chopped green onion
10 (8-inch) soft taco-size flour tortillas
¼ cup (1 ounce) shredded cheddar
   cheese

DIRECTIONS

PREHEAT oven to 400° F.

Cheesy Tortilla Spirals

COMBINE cream cheese, ⅓ cup cheddar cheese, lime juice, chili powder, and cumin in medium bowl; stir in creamed chipped beef, cilantro, and green onion. Evenly divide mixture among tortillas, spreading to cover each tortilla.

ROLL up each tortilla. Place rolled tortillas seam-side-down on baking sheet; sprinkle with ¼ cup cheddar cheese.

BAKE for 7 minutes or until cheese is melted. Let stand for 3 to 5 minutes; slice into 1-inch pieces. Serve hot.

NOTE: This recipe can also be prepared without baking. Omit ¼ cup cheddar cheese topping and refrigerate filled and rolled tortillas for at least 1 hour to set filling before slicing.

*DEFROST creamed chipped beef in microwave on MEDIUM (50%) power for 5 to 6 minutes.

Estimated Times
Preparation: 30 mins
Cooking: 15 mins
Standing: 3 mins

Crab Curry Dip

Try this reduced-fat dip with a curry twist!

MAKES 8 APPETIZER SERVINGS

INGREDIENTS

1 package (8 ounces) light cream cheese
(Neufchâtel), at room temperature
½ cup NESTLÉ CARNATION Evaporated
Fat Free Milk
¾ cup (4 ounces) fresh, cooked, or
chopped imitation crabmeat
2 tablespoons thinly sliced green onion
2 tablespoons finely chopped red
bell pepper
½ teaspoon curry powder
¼ teaspoon garlic salt
Assorted cut fresh vegetables

DIRECTIONS

BEAT cream cheese and evaporated
milk in small mixer bowl until creamy.
Stir in crabmeat, green onion, bell
pepper, curry powder, and garlic salt.
Cover; refrigerate for 30 minutes.
Serve with vegetables.

Estimated Times
Preparation: 10 mins
Refrigerating: 30 mins

Creamy Garlic Dip with Crudités

**Dry milk helps thicken this sour
cream-based dip. Cut up some carrots,
broccoli, bell peppers, mushrooms,
and green beans for a healthy and
colorful snack.**

MAKES 6 APPETIZER SERVINGS

INGREDIENTS

1 container (8 ounces) sour cream
½ cup dry NESTLÉ CARNATION Instant
Nonfat Dry Milk
2 tablespoons sliced green onion
1 tablespoon cider vinegar
1 clove garlic, finely chopped
½ teaspoon salt
¼ teaspoon ground black pepper
Assorted fresh vegetables for dipping

DIRECTIONS

COMBINE sour cream, dry milk, green
onion, vinegar, garlic, salt, and pepper
in small bowl; stir until smooth. Serve
with vegetables.

NOTE: For a dip lower in fat, substitute
8-ounce container lowfat or fat free
sour cream.

Estimated Time
Preparation: 10 mins

About Stouffer's

Stouffer's guiding principle of
serving families started in 1922
when Mr. and Mrs. A.E. Stouffer
opened their small, stand-up dairy
counter in downtown Cleveland's
now famed "old" Arcade.

Good food, good service, clean
surroundings, and a fair price value
were the products then. And they
still are. But one special ingredient
has been the key to Stouffer's
success—a keen intuition about
the American family, its appetites,
and its eating likes and dislikes
as well as how to serve them.

Now Stouffer's is much, much
larger. But it's not much different.
Careful attention to the needs and
wants of the American family has
helped the home cooked meals
grow from a family of four to
a family of millions. For more
delicious Stouffer's meals visit
us at Stouffers.com.

Hot Spinach Dip with Cheesy Chips

Hot Spinach Dip with Cheesy Chips

Nothing quite beats the combination of rich and creamy spinach dip and crunchy warm tortilla chips. Serve this at your next party or as a midday snack on a cool afternoon.

MAKES 6 APPETIZER SERVINGS

INGREDIENTS

1 package (9 ounces) STOUFFER'S frozen Spinach Soufflé, prepared according to package directions

1 package (3 ounces) cream cheese, at room temperature

½ cup, plus 1 tablespoon (about 2½ ounces) grated Parmesan cheese, divided

¼ cup mayonnaise

2 tablespoons chopped green onion

Tortilla chips

Toppings (e.g., diced tomatoes, chopped green onions, shredded Monterey Jack cheese)

DIRECTIONS

PREHEAT oven to 350° F.

COMBINE spinach soufflé, cream cheese, ½ cup Parmesan cheese, mayonnaise, and 2 tablespoons green onion in medium bowl. Transfer to small baking dish; sprinkle with 1 tablespoon Parmesan cheese. Place baking dish in center of baking sheet or ovenproof platter.

ARRANGE tortilla chips around dip. Sprinkle chips with tomatoes, chopped green onions, and Monterey Jack cheese.

BAKE for 20 to 25 minutes or until dip is hot and Monterey Jack cheese is melted.

Estimated Times
Preparation: 15 mins
Cooking: 20 mins

Mini Beef and Pepperoni Pizza Rolls

These mini pizza appetizers are the perfect party finger food for your next get-together with friends and family.

MAKES 36 APPETIZER SERVINGS

INGREDIENTS

1 container (15 ounces) BUITONI Refrigerated Tomato Herb Parmesan Sauce
8 ounces ground beef, cooked and drained
¼ cup diced pepperoni
1 cup (4 ounces) shredded mozzarella cheese
3 packages (8 ounces each) refrigerated crescent rolls

DIRECTIONS

PREHEAT oven to 350° F. Lightly grease baking sheet.

COMBINE sauce, beef, pepperoni, and cheese in medium bowl.

SEPARATE dough into 12 rectangles and press seams together. Spoon about 2 tablespoons filling onto dough along the long side of the rectangle. Roll the dough lengthwise, like a jelly roll. Cut each roll into 3 pieces. Place seam-side-down on prepared baking sheet.

BAKE for 12 to 15 minutes or until hot and golden brown.

Estimated Times
Preparation: 25 mins
Cooking: 15 mins

About Buitoni

The story begins with Mamma Giulia Buitoni, an Italian woman from the town of Sansepolcro. For Mamma Giulia, wheat semolina was the best raw material to preserve "al dente" pastas after cooking.

Mamma Giulia's pastas were so famous in her region that she decided to manufacture them. The small factory increased quickly thanks to the efforts of her five sons who in 1907 decided to build a factory in Perugia.

In 1937, during the International Fair in Paris, Giovanni Buitoni, descendant of Giulia, made people taste the Buitoni pastas under the Eiffel Tower. The fame of Casa Buitoni expanded in France in 1949 when Buitoni started selling raviolis in cans.

Nestlé acquired Buitoni in 1988. Known for its dry pasta, you can also find Buitoni sauces, cheese, frozen meals, and pasta at Buitoni.com.

Mini Beef and Pepperoni Pizza Rolls

Mini Corn Quiches

Looking for a special appetizer for your next party? Look no further than these easy yet elegant mini corn quiches. Quick to fix, and a surefire hit with all your guests.

MAKES 36 MINI QUICHES

INGREDIENTS

1 refrigerated 9-inch double-crust
    pie pastry, rolled to ⅛-inch thickness
1 package (12 ounces) STOUFFER'S
    frozen Corn Soufflé, defrosted*
¾ cup (3 ounces) shredded Swiss
    cheese, divided
⅓ cup diced ham
¼ cup sour cream
1 large egg, lightly beaten
2 tablespoons chopped green onion
1 tablespoon all-purpose flour
⅛ teaspoon ground black pepper
Sliced green onions (optional)
Diced red bell pepper (optional)

DIRECTIONS

PREHEAT oven to 375° F. Grease mini-muffin pans.

CUT pastry into 36 two-inch squares. Place squares in prepared mini-muffin pans, pressing down to form shells.

COMBINE corn soufflé, ½ cup cheese, ham, sour cream, egg, chopped green onion, flour, and black pepper in medium bowl; mix well. Spoon mixture into shells, filling three-fourths full. Sprinkle with remaining cheese.

BAKE for 30 to 35 minutes or until golden brown. Cool in pans on wire racks for 5 minutes. Garnish with sliced green onions and bell pepper. Serve warm.

*DEFROST corn soufflé in microwave on MEDIUM (50%) power for 6 to 7 minutes.

Estimated Times
Preparation: 25 mins
Cooking: 30 mins
Cooling: 5 mins

Pecan-Crusted Spinach Artichoke Dip

How can you describe this remarkable dip? Warm, rich, and irresistible comes to mind. Serve this at your next get-together with a variety of crackers or chips and everyone will want to be on your guest list.

MAKES 12 APPETIZER SERVINGS

INGREDIENTS

2 packages (9 ounces each) STOUFFER'S
    frozen Creamed Spinach, defrosted*
1 package (8 ounces) cream cheese,
    at room temperature
½ cup mayonnaise
1 can (14 ounces) artichoke hearts,
    drained and coarsely chopped
½ cup (2 ounces) grated Parmesan cheese
⅓ cup chopped onion
⅛ teaspoon cayenne pepper
⅓ cup crushed herb stuffing
½ cup chopped pecans

DIRECTIONS

PREHEAT oven to 400° F.

COMBINE cream cheese and mayonnaise in large bowl; add creamed spinach, artichoke hearts, Parmesan cheese, onion, and pepper. Place in 2-quart baking dish. Combine stuffing and nuts in small bowl; sprinkle over dip.

BAKE for 20 to 25 minutes or until hot and lightly browned on top.

*DEFROST creamed spinach in microwave on MEDIUM (50%) power for 5 to 6 minutes.

Pecan-Crusted Spinach Artichoke Dip

Pesto Party Dip

Spice up your veggies with a pesto-flavored dip from Buitoni. This indulgent dip uses only a few ingredients but packs a full-flavored punch.

MAKES 14 APPETIZER SERVINGS

INGREDIENTS

1 container (7 ounces) BUITONI
   Refrigerated Pesto with Basil

4 ounces cream cheese, at
   room temperature

½ cup sour cream

2 tablespoons grated Parmesan cheese

Fresh vegetables and/or shrimp

DIRECTIONS

PLACE pesto, cream cheese, sour cream, and Parmesan cheese in food processor or blender; cover. Process until creamy.

SERVE with fresh vegetables and/or shrimp.

Estimated Time

Preparation: 10 mins

Risotto-Stuffed Mushrooms

Risotto-Stuffed Mushrooms

Try this appetizer the next time you are entertaining or for that special occasion.

MAKES 18 TO 20 APPETIZER SERVINGS

INGREDIENTS

1 package (5.5 ounces) BUITONI
   Risotto with Portobello Mushrooms,
   prepared according to package
   directions, kept warm

¾ cup (3 ounces) shredded Monterey
   Jack cheese, divided

3 tablespoons grated Romano or
   Parmesan cheese, divided

1 tablespoon finely chopped chives
   or green onion

1 tablespoon finely chopped red
   bell pepper

1 large clove garlic, finely chopped

18 to 20 jumbo whole white
   mushrooms (about 1¾ pounds
   total), stems removed

DIRECTIONS

PREHEAT oven to 375° F.

COMBINE risotto, ½ cup Monterey Jack cheese, Romano cheese, chives, bell pepper, and garlic in medium bowl. Arrange mushrooms on baking sheet. Fill mushrooms with risotto mixture, mounding slightly. Sprinkle with remaining Monterey Jack cheese.

BAKE for 20 to 25 minutes or until mushrooms are golden brown and cheese is melted.

Estimated Times

Preparation: 25 mins

Cooking: 25 mins

Svelte Blue Cheese Dressing and Dip

Your guests will appreciate this healthy alternative to their favorite dip. It makes an easy holiday appetizer.

MAKES 8 APPETIZER SERVINGS

INGREDIENTS

½ cup plain fat free yogurt

¼ cup dry NESTLÉ CARNATION Instant Nonfat Dry Milk

½ cup chopped green onions

2 ounces blue cheese, crumbled

1 small clove garlic, finely chopped

¼ teaspoon crushed dried basil

¼ teaspoon crushed dried rosemary

⅛ teaspoon salt

DIRECTIONS

COMBINE yogurt and dry milk in small bowl. Add green onions, cheese, garlic, basil, rosemary, and salt; mix well.

COVER; refrigerate for 30 minutes before serving.

Estimated Times

Preparation: 10 mins

Refrigerating: 30 mins

Svelte Blue Cheese Dressing and Dip

Sweet Pumpkin Dip

Sweet Pumpkin Dip

Serve this luscious dip with a tray of gingersnaps, vanilla wafers, or lemon wafers. Spread this mixture on crustless white bread and cut out shapes with cookie cutters to create delicate party sandwiches.

MAKES 15 APPETIZER SERVINGS

INGREDIENTS

2 packages (8 ounces each) cream
   cheese, at room temperature
1 can (15 ounces) LIBBY'S 100%
   Pure Pumpkin
2 cups sifted powdered sugar
1 teaspoon ground cinnamon
1 teaspoon ground ginger
Sliced fruit, bite-sized cinnamon graham
   crackers, gingersnap cookies, toasted
   mini-bagels, toast slices, muffins, or
   English muffins

DIRECTIONS

BEAT cream cheese and pumpkin in large mixer bowl until smooth. Add sugar, cinnamon, and ginger; mix thoroughly. Cover; refrigerate for 1 hour. Serve as a dip or spread.

COOKING TIP

Sweet Pumpkin Dip can also be served as a spread or used to make dessert sandwiches. Spread on thin slices of cinnamon raisin bread or vanilla or chocolate pound cake, and cut sandwiches into small neat triangles or use a favorite cookie cutter.

NOTE: For a dip lower in fat, substitute light cream cheese (Neufchâtel) for cream cheese.

Estimated Times
Preparation: 5 mins
Refrigerating: 1 hr

Nonfat Dry Milk

Introduced as "magic crystals" by Carnation in 1954, nonfat dry milk was an immediate hit for its fresh milk flavor when mixed with ice-cold water.

Ready instantly for cereals, cooking, and baking, NESTLÉ CARNATION Instant Nonfat Dry Milk is rich in protein, calcium, and vitamins just like fresh milk. Reconstituted, this milk will remain fresh for 5 to 7 days when stored in the refrigerator.

In dry form or reconstituted, with zero fat and as an excellent source of calcium, it's easy to add extra calcium to all your recipes.

Thai Pumpkin Satay

Thai Pumpkin Satay

Skewered morsels of succulent grilled chicken served with a zippy peanut pumpkin sauce make for a taste-tempting appetizer or main dish.

MAKES 30 APPETIZER SERVINGS

INGREDIENTS

1 cup LIBBY'S 100% Pure Pumpkin
⅔ cup milk
⅓ cup creamy or chunky peanut butter
2 green onions, chopped
2 cloves garlic, peeled
2 tablespoons chopped fresh cilantro
2 tablespoons lime juice
1 tablespoon soy sauce
2 teaspoons granulated sugar
¼ teaspoon salt

⅛ to ¼ teaspoon cayenne pepper
4 boneless, skinless chicken breast halves (about 1 pound total), cut into 1-inch pieces
2 large red bell peppers, cut into 1-inch pieces
2 bunches green onions (white parts only), cut into 1-inch pieces
30 (4-inch) skewers

DIRECTIONS

PLACE pumpkin, milk, peanut butter, chopped green onions, garlic, cilantro, lime juice, soy sauce, sugar, salt, and cayenne pepper in blender or food processor; cover. Blend until smooth. Combine ½ cup pumpkin mixture and chicken in medium bowl; cover. Reserve remaining pumpkin mixture. Marinate in refrigerator, stirring occasionally, for 1 hour.

ALTERNATELY thread chicken, bell peppers, and green onion pieces onto skewers. Discard any remaining marinade.

PREHEAT grill or broiler.

GRILL or broil, turning once, for 10 minutes or until chicken is no longer pink. Heat remaining pumpkin mixture; serve with satay.

NOTE: If using wooden skewers, soak in water for 30 minutes before threading.

Estimated Times
Preparation: 20 mins
Marinating: 1 hr
Cooking: 10 mins

Warm Spinach Dip in Bread Bowl

Here's a warmed-up version of the traditional spinach dip that is always a crowd-pleaser. STOUFFER'S frozen Spinach Soufflé makes it easier than ever to prepare.

MAKES 10 APPETIZER SERVINGS

INGREDIENTS

2 packages (9 ounces each) STOUFFER'S frozen Spinach Soufflé, prepared according to package directions
4 ounces cream cheese, at room temperature
¾ cup, plus 2 tablespoons (about 3½ ounces) grated Parmesan cheese, divided
⅓ cup mayonnaise
¼ cup chopped green onions
1 pound round bread loaf

DIRECTIONS

PREHEAT oven to 400° F.

COMBINE spinach soufflé, cream cheese, ¾ cup Parmesan cheese, mayonnaise, and green onions in large bowl.

SLICE top off bread loaf; carefully remove soft bread from inside, leaving ½-inch-thick shell. Cut top piece and soft bread into bite-sized pieces. Spoon spinach mixture into shell and sprinkle with remaining 2 tablespoons Parmesan cheese. Wrap loaf in foil, leaving filling exposed.

BAKE for 35 to 40 minutes or until heated through. Serve warm with bread pieces for dipping.

Estimated Times
Preparation: 20 mins
Cooking: 35 mins

Warm Spinach Dip in Bread Bowl

Pumpkin

When you think of pumpkin, what comes to mind? Would you be surprised to learn that along with its culinary virtues, pumpkin offers significant nutritional benefits that are surprisingly high compared with other foods? Naturally low in calories and fat, pumpkin contains a wide variety of vitamins and minerals, is rich in vitamin A, and is an excellent source of fiber. Pumpkin is rich in carotenoids, which have been linked to a host of health-promoting activities. Besides their antioxidant activity, carotenoids have been shown to help maintain eye health. Pumpkin's deep orange color is the clue to its rich amounts of these important carotenoids.

One of the most studied antioxidants, beta-carotene, converts to vitamin A in the body to promote good circulation, a healthy heart, eyes, and lungs.

salads, soups, and sandwiches

salads, soups, and sandwiches

Our collection of salad, soup, and sandwich recipes range from traditional, comfort food basics, such as Chicken Noodle Soup and Hearty Beef Stew, to more exotic fare, such as Thai-Style Pumpkin Soup and Oriental Ramen Salad. And we've added a few twists to old stand-bys, such as Maggi Potato Salad. Whether traditional or exotic, however, they're all simple to make in your own kitchen. And they're also ideal to serve as a snack, lunch, or dinner, depending on your family's appetite. We've provided plenty of serving suggestions, and even more easy and creative tasty combinations at Meals.com.

Evaporated Milk

NESTLÉ CARNATION Evaporated Milk is your secret ingredient for making quick meals creamier and more like homemade. Just substitute an equal amount of NESTLÉ CARNATION Evaporated Milk in place of the regular milk called for on the can or box. It's the easy way to add your personal touch!

For a lowfat or fat free alternative, you can also substitute NESTLÉ CARNATION Evaporated Milk with Evaporated Lowfat 2% or Evaporated Fat Free Milk to cut calories. These alternatives can also be used in place of regular milk to make any recipe richer, while providing your family with more tasty and nutritional meals!

Ambrosia

Try this salad for the holidays or anytime. Sweet and fruity, yet low in fat, this mixture of succulent fruits will delight guests.

MAKES 6 SERVINGS

INGREDIENTS

3 cans (15 ounces each) chunky
    fruit cocktail, drained
1 can (11 ounces) Mandarin
    oranges, drained
1 cup miniature marshmallows
1 cup flake coconut
2 bananas, thinly sliced
⅔ cup (5 fluid-ounce can) NESTLÉ
    CARNATION Evaporated Milk
1 cup sliced fresh strawberries

DIRECTIONS

COMBINE fruit cocktail, oranges, marshmallows, coconut, bananas, and evaporated milk in large bowl. Refrigerate for 30 minutes. Stir in strawberries before serving.

NOTE: Try substituting NESTLÉ CARNATION Evaporated Fat Free Milk.

Estimated Times
Preparation: 10 mins
Refrigerating: 30 mins

Ambrosia

Beef Tenderloin over Greens

There's no better way to top a salad than with melt-in-your-mouth beef tenderloin.

MAKES 4 SERVINGS

INGREDIENTS

1 cup boiling water
1 MAGGI Beef Flavor Bouillon Cube
¼ cup balsamic vinegar
2 tablespoons light brown sugar
1 teaspoon olive oil
12 ounces beef tenderloin, fat trimmed, cut into 4 pieces
8 cups baby salad greens
1 cup cherry tomatoes, cut in half

DIRECTIONS

COMBINE water and bouillon in small bowl; stir to dissolve. Stir in vinegar and sugar.

HEAT oil in large skillet over medium-high heat. Add beef; cook on each side for 3 to 5 minutes or until desired doneness. Remove from skillet. Slice beef into strips. Divide baby greens and tomatoes among plates and top with beef.

ADD sauce mixture to skillet; stir to loosen brown bits from bottom of skillet. Cook over medium-high heat, without stirring, for 5 minutes or until reduced by half. Pour over salad.

Estimated Times
Preparation: 10 mins
Cooking: 15 mins

Crunchy Orange Chicken Salad

This gourmet salad has a sweet and creamy dressing and the crunchy flavors of almonds and celery. For a summertime lunch party or just a light dinner, serve this delicious salad with whole wheat rolls and chilled iced tea.

MAKES 6 SERVINGS

INGREDIENTS

2 tablespoons granulated sugar
1 tablespoon all-purpose flour
1 teaspoon salt (optional)
⅔ cup (5 fluid-ounce can) NESTLÉ CARNATION Evaporated Milk
⅓ cup orange juice
1 large egg, well beaten
3 cups cooked, chopped, boneless, skinless chicken breast meat
3 large stalks celery, thinly sliced
¾ cup sliced almonds, toasted
2 tablespoons sliced green onion
1 can (11 ounces) Mandarin oranges, drained
½ head lettuce leaves (optional)

DIRECTIONS

COMBINE sugar, flour, and salt in medium, heavy-duty saucepan; gradually stir in evaporated milk, orange juice, and egg. Cook over medium heat, stirring constantly, until dressing comes just to a boil and begins to thicken. Remove from heat. Cover; refrigerate until cool.

COMBINE chicken, celery, nuts, dressing, and green onion in large bowl. Gently stir in oranges. Cover; refrigerate for 2 hours. Serve over lettuce.

NOTE: Try substituting NESTLÉ CARNATION Evaporated Fat Free Milk.

Estimated Times
Preparation: 15 mins
Cooking: 5 mins
Refrigerating: 2 hrs, 20 mins

Crunchy Orange Chicken Salad

Cooking Tip

Remember these tips the next time you are cooking fresh vegetables. It's important to maintain the great taste of fresh vegetables while preventing nutrient loss during cooking.

Try using quick-cooking techniques such as stir-frying or steaming to keep cooking time to a minimum. Make sure to leave the preparation until just before cooking and do not leave vegetables soaking in water for long periods of time. And always leave the vegetables whole or cut into large pieces to limit the surface area.

Fettuccine Tomato Basil Salad

Fettuccine Tomato Basil Salad

Here's a pasta dish that's a breeze to prepare! Serve with crunchy breadsticks.

MAKES 4 SERVINGS

INGREDIENTS

1 package (9 ounces) BUITONI
   Refrigerated Fettuccine
¼ cup (1 ounce) grated Parmesan cheese
1 tablespoon olive oil
1 tablespoon red wine vinegar
1 pound fresh tomatoes, chopped
¼ cup chopped fresh basil (or
   1 tablespoon dried basil, crushed)

DIRECTIONS

PREPARE pasta according to package directions.

TOSS pasta with cheese, oil, and vinegar. Add tomatoes and basil. Season with salt and ground black pepper.

Estimated Times
Preparation: 15 mins
Cooking: 5 mins

Garden Pasta Salad

Crisp bell pepper and broccoli florets are combined with tender three-cheese tortellini in a tangy Italian dressing, tossed with chopped tomatoes and sliced olives.

MAKES 8 SERVINGS

INGREDIENTS

1 package (20 ounces) BUITONI
   Refrigerated Family Size Three
   Cheese Tortellini
1 cup Italian salad dressing
2 cups broccoli florets
2 medium tomatoes, chopped
1 large green bell pepper, chopped
¾ cup (3 ounces) shredded
   Parmesan-Romano cheese
1 can (2.25 ounces) sliced ripe olives

DIRECTIONS

PREPARE pasta according to package directions. Drain; rinse in cold water.

POUR dressing into large bowl. Add pasta, broccoli, tomatoes, bell pepper, cheese, and olives; toss well to coat. Refrigerate or serve immediately.

Estimated Time
Preparation: 15 mins
Cooking: 7 mins

Garden Pasta Salad

Maggi Potato Salad

MAGGI bouillon brings a savory twist to this colorful potato salad just in time for your next picnic or barbecue.

MAKES 8 SERVINGS

INGREDIENTS

9 medium boiling potatoes (about 3 pounds), peeled and cut into 1-inch chunks
2 MAGGI Chicken Flavor Bouillon Cubes
1 small onion, finely chopped
1 small green bell pepper, finely chopped
⅔ cup olive oil
⅓ cup red wine vinegar
3 cloves garlic, finely chopped
1 teaspoon lemon juice
1 can (8½ ounces) sweet green peas, drained
1 jar (4 ounces) sliced pimientos
2 tablespoons sliced Spanish olives
1 tablespoon diced jalapeños (optional)

DIRECTIONS

PLACE potatoes and bouillon in large saucepan. Cover with water; bring to a boil. Cook over medium-high heat for 20 to 25 minutes or until tender; drain. Place in large bowl.

COMBINE onion, bell pepper, oil, vinegar, garlic, and lemon juice in small bowl; pour over potatoes. Gently stir in peas, pimientos, olives, and jalapeños. Season with salt and ground black pepper; stir gently. Refrigerate until ready to serve.

Estimated Times
Preparation: 30 mins
Cooking: 25 mins

About Maggi

Convenience foods—packaged soups, frozen meals, prepared sauces, and flavorings—date back more than a century. In 1882, Julius Maggi had taken over his father's mill near Zurich and had the reputation as an inventive and capable businessman. He was commissioned by the Swiss Public Welfare Society to create a vegetable food product that would be nutritious, affordable, quick to prepare, and easy to digest to help with the problem of women having less time to prepare meals, as more women worked outside the home. The results—two instant pea soups and an instant bean soup—were a huge success.

By the turn of the century, Maggi & Company was producing not only powdered soups, but also bouillons, sauces, and flavorings. Maggi merged with Nestlé in 1947, continuing a tradition of providing families with great-tasting products. Known worldwide for innovation and quality, Maggi is today a leading culinary brand within the Nestlé family.

Orange and Grape Tortellini Salad

Mandarin oranges and grapes pair perfectly with cheese tortellini in this cool and refreshing pasta salad. Serve with crunchy breadsticks.

MAKES 4 SERVINGS

INGREDIENTS

1 package (9 ounces) BUITONI Refrigerated Three Cheese Tortellini
1 cup red seedless grapes
1 cup green seedless grapes
1 can (11 ounces) Mandarin oranges, drained
¼ cup finely chopped red onion
¼ cup chopped walnuts, toasted
1 cup honey Dijon salad dressing

DIRECTIONS

PREPARE pasta according to package directions; refrigerate.

COMBINE pasta, grapes, oranges, onion, and nuts in medium bowl. Add dressing; toss to coat.

Estimated Times
Preparation: 10 mins
Cooking: 7 mins
Refrigerating: 15 mins

Orange and Grape Tortellini Salad

Oriental Ramen Salad

Crunchy noodles and crisp greens combine for a quick and delicious salad. To make this salad a meal, simply add sliced roasted chicken breast and Mandarin oranges.

MAKES 8 SERVINGS

INGREDIENTS

2 tablespoons butter or margarine

1 package (3 ounces) dry oriental-flavor ramen noodle soup, noodles crumbled and seasoning packet reserved

½ cup sliced almonds

⅔ cup (5 fluid-ounce can) NESTLÉ CARNATION Evaporated Milk

⅔ cup vegetable oil

3 tablespoons white vinegar

2 tablespoons granulated sugar

2 packages (10 ounces each) romaine-radicchio salad greens

4 green onions, sliced diagonally

DIRECTIONS

MELT butter in large skillet over medium heat. Add crumbled ramen noodles and nuts; cook, stirring constantly, until noodles are golden. Remove from pan; cool.

PLACE evaporated milk, oil, ramen seasoning packet, vinegar, and sugar in blender; cover. Blend until smooth.

Oriental Ramen Salad

COMBINE salad greens, noodle mixture, green onions, and dressing in large bowl; toss to coat well. Serve immediately.

NOTE: Try substituting NESTLÉ CARNATION Evaporated Fat Free Milk.

Estimated Times
Preparation: 10 mins
Cooking: 5 mins
Cooling: 5 mins

Ranch Salad Dressing

This ranch dressing is easy to make and so delicious, you'll always want to have some on hand. Coffee-mate also makes it great for those with lactose intolerance.

MAKES 2 CUPS

INGREDIENTS

¾ cup water

⅓ cup Original NESTLÉ COFFEE-MATE Powdered Coffee Creamer

1 cup mayonnaise

1 packet (1 ounce) ranch salad dressing mix

DIRECTIONS

WHISK together water and Coffee-mate in medium bowl until smooth. Whisk in mayonnaise and dressing mix. Store covered in refrigerator for up to 1 week.

Estimated Time
Preparation: 5 mins

Tortellini and Shrimp Caesar Salad

Tortellini and Shrimp Caesar Salad

Here's a salad for the seafood lovers in your family. Shrimp and tortellini take the classic Caesar salad to new heights. Perfect for lunch or add warm rolls for a complete dinner.

MAKES 4 SERVINGS

INGREDIENTS

1 package (9 ounces) BUITONI Refrigerated Spinach Cheese Tortellini

1 package (10 ounces) romaine salad greens

12 ounces cooked medium shrimp

¾ cup Caesar salad dressing

1 cup Italian-style croutons

¼ cup (1 ounce) grated Parmesan cheese

DIRECTIONS

PREPARE pasta according to package directions; refrigerate.

COMBINE pasta, salad greens, and shrimp in large bowl. Add dressing; toss until evenly coated.

TOP with croutons and cheese. Season with ground black pepper.

Estimated Times

Preparation: 20 mins

Cooking: 7 mins

Refrigerating: 15 mins

Tuna Tortellini Pasta Salad

This is a delicious change of pace from a standard tuna salad. Line your serving bowl with salad greens and garnish with Parmesan cheese curls.

MAKES 6 SERVINGS

INGREDIENTS

1 package (20 ounces) BUITONI
  Refrigerated Family Size Three
  Cheese Tortellini
½ pound green beans, cut into
  1-inch pieces and cooked
2 cans (6 ounces each) solid white
  tuna packed in water, drained
1 large tomato, chopped
¾ cup sliced ripe black olives
4 green onions, sliced
¾ cup mayonnaise
3 tablespoons balsamic vinegar
¾ teaspoon celery salt

DIRECTIONS

PREPARE pasta according to package directions; rinse and drain.

COMBINE pasta, green beans, tuna, tomato, olives, and green onions in large bowl. Combine mayonnaise, vinegar, and celery salt in small bowl. Stir mayonnaise mixture into pasta mixture. Season with salt and ground black pepper.

Estimated Times
Preparation: 10 mins
Cooking: 7 mins

Healthy Eating Mediterranean-Style

Many researchers around the world have supported the benefits of traditional Mediterranean-style eating, which has been proven to lower the risk of heart disease and many types of cancer. The diet is based on high amounts of whole grains, fruits, nuts, vegetables and, of course, olive oil. This style of eating blends together foods from 14 countries surrounding the Mediterranean Sea. So learn from these cultures and prepare foods in a fresh and simple way, relax and socialize with friends and family, and go for a stroll, as part of a regular exercise program!

Tuna Tortellini Pasta Salad

Baked Potato Soup

This soup is sure to warm you up on a cold day.

MAKES 4 SERVINGS

INGREDIENTS

¼ cup (½ stick) butter or margarine

¼ cup chopped onion

¼ cup all-purpose flour

1 can (14.5 fluid ounces) chicken broth

1 can (12 fluid ounces) NESTLÉ CARNATION Evaporated Milk

2 large or 3 medium baking potatoes, baked or microwaved

Cooked and crumbled bacon

Shredded cheddar cheese

Sliced green onions

Baked Potato Soup

Evaporated Milk Cooking Tip

A simple can of condensed soup becomes restaurant quality with the addition of NESTLÉ CARNATION Evaporated Milk. Substitute an equal amount of NESTLÉ CARNATION Evaporated Milk for regular milk or water called for on the label. It makes soups, such as tomato, mushroom, potato, and seafood chowders full, rich, and delicious.

DIRECTIONS

MELT butter in large saucepan over medium heat. Add onion; cook, stirring occasionally, for 1 to 2 minutes or until tender. Stir in flour. Gradually stir in broth and evaporated milk. Scoop potato pulp from 1 potato (reserve potato skin); mash. Add mashed pulp to broth mixture.

COOK over medium heat, stirring occasionally, until mixture comes just to a boil. Dice remaining potato skin and potato(es); add to soup. Heat through.

Season with salt and ground black pepper. Top each serving with bacon, cheese, and green onions.

NOTE: For a different twist to this recipe, omit the bacon, cheddar cheese, and green onions. Cook 2 tablespoons shredded carrot with the onion and add ¼ teaspoon dried dill to the soup when adding the broth. Follow recipe above for cooking directions.

Estimated Times

Preparation: 25 mins

Cooking: 10 mins

Cheddar Cheese Soup

Thick and creamy with a dash of Worcestershire sauce for zest, this cheddar cheese soup is certain to please on a blustery day. Serve with hot, crusty bread and a leafy green salad.

MAKES 4 SERVINGS

INGREDIENTS

¼ cup (½ stick) butter or margarine

¼ cup all-purpose flour

2 cans (12 fluid ounces each) NESTLÉ CARNATION Evaporated Milk

1 cup beer or water

2 teaspoons Worcestershire sauce

½ teaspoon dry mustard (optional)

¼ teaspoon cayenne pepper

2 cups (8 ounces) shredded sharp cheddar cheese

Toppings (e.g., crumbled cooked bacon, sliced green onions, croutons)

DIRECTIONS

MELT butter in large saucepan over medium heat. Add flour; cook, stirring constantly, until bubbly. Add evaporated milk; bring to a boil, stirring constantly. Reduce heat. Stir in beer, Worcestershire sauce, mustard, and cayenne pepper.

COOK for 10 minutes. Remove from heat. Stir in cheese until melted. Season with salt. Serve with toppings.

Estimated Times

Preparation: 10 mins

Cooking: 15 mins

Cheese Tortellini in Savory Broth

Tortellini is a warming, homey dish just right for cold days. Serve with fresh focaccia bread for a complete meal.

MAKES 4 SERVINGS

INGREDIENTS

7 cups water

6 MAGGI Chicken Flavor Bouillon Cubes

1 package (9 ounces) BUITONI Refrigerated Three Cheese Tortellini

1 medium zucchini, shredded

1 medium tomato, chopped

Grated Parmesan cheese

DIRECTIONS

BOIL water and bouillon in stockpot. Stir in pasta; cook for 5 to 6 minutes. Reduce heat to low; stir in zucchini and tomato. Cook until vegetables are heated through. Sprinkle with cheese before serving. Season with ground black pepper.

Estimated Times

Preparation: 10 mins

Cooking: 15 mins

Cheese Tortellini in Savory Broth

About Buitoni

With Buitoni's refrigerated pastas, an Italian meal can be prepared in less than eight minutes. Buitoni has been making Italian food for over 170 years. With Nestlé acquiring the company in 1988, Nestlé's vision of applying its technical know-how to expand the range of Buitoni's products has continued the Buitoni legacy of creating high quality foods with only the finest ingredients.

Along with pastas, you can also find sauces like Roasted Garlic Marinara Sauce or the classic Alfredo, to name a few. So if you're wondering how long it takes to cook delicious Italian food—here's the answer—directly from Casa Buitoni in Tuscany, Italy to your home kitchen.

Chicken and Wild Rice Soup

When you're craving comfort, but not its bulk, try this home-style soup. It's light-tasting, yet nourishes the soul. Serve with sliced French bread.

MAKES 6 SERVINGS

INGREDIENTS

1 package (6 ounces) long-grain and wild rice mix, prepared according to package directions
1 tablespoon vegetable oil
2 boneless, skinless chicken breast halves (about 8 ounces total), chopped
2 cups (8 ounces) sliced fresh mushrooms
1 medium onion, chopped
2 cloves garlic, finely chopped
2 cans (14.5 fluid ounces each) chicken broth
½ teaspoon dried tarragon, crushed
¼ teaspoon dried thyme, crushed
¼ teaspoon salt
⅛ teaspoon ground black pepper
1 can (12 fluid ounces) NESTLÉ CARNATION Evaporated Milk
3 tablespoons cornstarch
2 tablespoons dry white wine (optional)
Sliced green onions (optional)
Toasted slivered almonds (optional)

DIRECTIONS

HEAT oil in large saucepan over medium heat. Add chicken, mushrooms, chopped onion, and garlic. Cook, stirring occasionally, for 5 to 8 minutes or until vegetables are tender and chicken is no longer pink.

ADD rice, broth, tarragon, thyme, salt, and pepper; bring to a boil over medium-high heat. Combine small amount of evaporated milk and cornstarch in small bowl; stir until smooth. Add to saucepan with remaining evaporated milk and wine. Cook, stirring occasionally, for 3 to 5 minutes or until soup is thickened. Garnish with green onions and nuts.

FOR FREEZE AHEAD:
PREPARE as above; do not top with green onions and nuts. Cool soup completely. Place in airtight container; freeze for up to 2 months. Thaw overnight in refrigerator.

HEAT in large saucepan over medium heat, stirring occasionally, for 15 to 20 minutes or until heated through. Garnish with green onions and nuts.

Estimated Times
Preparation: 30 mins
Cooking: 15 mins

Chicken Noodle Soup

The ultimate comfort food made easy!

MAKES 4 SERVINGS

INGREDIENTS

7 cups water

1 cup sliced carrots

½ cup sliced celery

7 teaspoons MAGGI Instant Chicken
   Flavor Bouillon

2 boneless, skinless chicken breast halves
   (about 8 ounces total), cooked and
   cut into 1-inch strips

2 cups egg noodles, uncooked

1 tablespoon finely chopped parsley

DIRECTIONS

PLACE water, carrots, celery, and
bouillon in large stockpot. Cook over
medium heat, stirring occasionally, for
20 to 22 minutes or until vegetables
are tender. Stir in chicken and noodles.
Cook for 8 to 10 minutes or until
noodles are tender. Stir in parsley
before serving.

Estimated Times
Preparation: 15 mins
Cooking: 30 mins

Chorizo and Potato Stew

Chorizo and Potato Stew

**Serve this hearty stew on a cold, chilly
day accompanied by hot corn muffins
spread with honey, and hot cocoa
with a cinnamon stick for stirring.**

MAKES 6 SERVINGS

INGREDIENTS

12 ounces pork chorizo, cooked,
   drained, and crumbled

1 jar (16 ounces) mild salsa

1¾ cups water

1 can (14.5 ounces) diced tomatoes,
   undrained

1 MAGGI Chicken Flavor Bouillon Cube

2 cups diced potatoes

2 cups frozen cut green beans, thawed

1 can (15 ounces) black beans, rinsed
   and drained

Toppings (e.g., sliced green onions,
   shredded cheddar cheese, sour cream)

DIRECTIONS

HEAT salsa, water, tomatoes with
juice, and bouillon in medium saucepan
over medium-high heat until gently
boiling. Add potatoes. Cover; cook for
15 minutes. Add chorizo, green beans,
and black beans. Cook for 10 minutes
or until potatoes are tender. Top
with toppings.

Estimated Times
Preparation: 15 mins
Cooking: 30 mins

Cooking Tip

Use the pulse feature of a food
processor to prepare a large
quantity of chopped onions.
Pack up three tablespoons of
chopped onion, approximately
one-quarter medium onion, in
freezer bags. Seal well and store in
the freezer until needed. Use the
onion directly from the freezer. The
onions will defrost quickly in the pan
for quick use in your next recipe.

Clam Chowder

What could be better than a big bowl of creamy clam chowder?

MAKES 4 SERVINGS

INGREDIENTS

2 tablespoons butter or margarine

1 cup peeled and finely chopped potato

¼ cup peeled and finely chopped carrot

¼ cup finely chopped celery

¼ cup finely chopped onion

1 can (12 fluid ounces) NESTLÉ CARNATION Evaporated Milk

¼ cup all-purpose flour

1½ cups milk

1 can (6.5 ounces) chopped or minced clams, undrained

½ cup water

½ teaspoon salt

¼ teaspoon Worcestershire sauce

¼ teaspoon ground white pepper

DIRECTIONS

MELT butter in medium saucepan over medium heat. Add potato, carrot, celery, and onion. Cook, stirring frequently, for 7 to 8 minutes or until potato is tender.

COMBINE evaporated milk and flour in small bowl until blended; add to vegetable mixture. Stir in milk, clams and juice, water, salt, Worcestershire sauce, and pepper. Reduce heat to medium-low. Cook, stirring frequently, for 15 to 20 minutes or until creamy and slightly thick.

Estimated Times

Preparation: 20 mins

Cooking: 25 mins

Clam Chowder

Corn Chowder

Corn Chowder

Simple to prepare, this chowder has a rich flavor and interesting texture that make it enormously satisfying. Serve it with a crisp green salad, plus fresh fruit for dessert.

MAKES 4 SERVINGS

INGREDIENTS

1 tablespoon vegetable oil

1 small onion, coarsely chopped

2 packages (16 ounces each) loose-pack frozen whole-kernel corn, thawed, divided

2 cups water

3 MAGGI Chicken Flavor Bouillon Cubes

1 can (12 fluid ounces) NESTLÉ CARNATION Evaporated Milk

½ cup chopped red bell pepper

½ teaspoon chopped fresh rosemary

1 tablespoon chopped fresh basil (optional)

DIRECTIONS

HEAT oil in large saucepan over medium-high heat. Add onion; cook, stirring occasionally, until tender. Add 4 cups corn; cook, stirring occasionally, until tender. Add water and bouillon; cook, stirring frequently, for 15 minutes or until corn is very soft.

PLACE corn mixture in blender or food processor; blend until smooth. Return to saucepan. Stir in remaining corn, evaporated milk, bell pepper, and rosemary. Cook, stirring frequently, until chowder is thick and bell pepper is tender. Season with salt and ground black pepper. Garnish with basil.

NOTE: For a Southwestern-style twist to this recipe, add 1 can (4 ounces) diced green chiles with the bell pepper. Eliminate rosemary; stir in 1 teaspoon chopped fresh cilantro. Garnish with cilantro leaves instead of basil.

Estimated Times

Preparation: 10 mins

Cooking: 30 mins

Evaporated Milk

The process of evaporating milk will give a slightly off-white color, caused by a carmelization of the natural milk sugars. As the product ages or is left in a warm environment, the product will continue to yellow. Under these conditions the carmelization of the natural milk sugars will continue. In addition, these conditions can also cause the product to separate, altering the color.

We do not recommend using the product beyond its shelf life, as it may not meet quality standards.

Corn Chowder with Bacon, Leeks, and Potatoes

This corn chowder makes a hearty meal with leeks and chunks of potatoes. Perfect on a cold winter's night with some crusty bread.

MAKES 4 SERVINGS

INGREDIENTS
4 strips turkey bacon, diced
1 teaspoon olive oil
6 cups sliced leeks (white and green parts)
¼ cup dry white wine
3 cups diced red potatoes
2 cans (12 fluid ounces each) NESTLÉ CARNATION Evaporated Milk
2 cups water
4 teaspoons MAGGI Instant Chicken Flavor Bouillon
¼ teaspoon ground black pepper
1 tablespoon water
2 teaspoons all-purpose flour
2 cups whole-kernel corn

DIRECTIONS
PLACE bacon and oil in stockpot. Cook over medium heat, stirring frequently, for 2 to 4 minutes or until bacon is crisp. Add leeks and wine. Cook, stirring occasionally, for 4 to 6 minutes or until leeks are tender.

ADD potatoes, evaporated milk, 2 cups water, bouillon, and pepper; bring to a boil. Reduce heat to medium-low. Cook, stirring occasionally, for 15 to 18 minutes or until potatoes are tender.

MIX 1 tablespoon water and flour in small bowl. Add corn and flour mixture to stockpot. Cook, stirring occasionally, for about 10 minutes.

PLACE about 3 cups soup in blender; cover. Carefully blend until smooth. Return blended soup to stockpot; stir well.

Estimated Times
Preparation: 20 mins
Cooking: 35 mins

Cream of Broccoli Soup

The homemade goodness of this creamy soup will satisfy any appetite.

MAKES 6 SERVINGS

INGREDIENTS
3 cans (14.5 fluid ounces each) chicken or vegetable broth
9 cups (about 1½ pounds) broccoli florets
1 small onion, coarsely chopped
2 cloves garlic, finely chopped

Cream of Broccoli Soup

1½ cups dry NESTLÉ CARNATION Instant Nonfat Dry Milk

½ cup water

¼ cup all-purpose flour

¼ teaspoon salt

¼ teaspoon ground black pepper

DIRECTIONS

BOIL broth in large saucepan. Add broccoli, onion, and garlic. Bring to a boil; reduce heat to low. Cover; cook for 5 to 7 minutes or until broccoli is tender. Remove from heat; cool slightly.

TRANSFER half of vegetable-broth mixture to blender or food processor (in batches, if necessary); cover. Blend until desired consistency. Return to saucepan.

COMBINE dry milk, water, and flour in medium bowl; mix well. Stir into soup; add salt and pepper. Heat to serving temperature.

FOR BROCCOLI CHEESE SOUP:

PREPARE Cream of Broccoli Soup and add 1 cup (4 ounces) shredded cheddar cheese. Stir over low heat until melted.

FOR FREEZE AHEAD:

PREPARE as above. Cool soup completely. Place in airtight container; freeze for up to 2 months. Thaw overnight in refrigerator.

HEAT in medium saucepan over medium heat, stirring occasionally, for 15 to 20 minutes or until heated through.

Estimated Times

Preparation: 15 mins

Cooking: 20 mins

Cream of Chicken and Vegetable Soup

This silky-rich chicken soup is a terrific main dish on a cold winter's night.

MAKES 6 SERVINGS

INGREDIENTS

¼ cup (½ stick) butter or margarine

¼ cup all-purpose flour

1 can (12 fluid ounces) NESTLÉ CARNATION Evaporated Milk

1 package (16 ounces) frozen mixed vegetables, prepared according to package directions

2 boneless, skinless chicken breast halves (about 8 ounces total), cooked and cubed

1 can (14.5 fluid ounces) chicken broth

¼ teaspoon onion salt

DIRECTIONS

MELT butter in medium saucepan over medium heat. Stir in flour. Gradually stir in evaporated milk. Cook, stirring constantly, until mixture comes to a boil. Add vegetables, chicken, broth, and onion salt. Heat through.

NOTE: For a lower-fat version of this recipe, substitute NESTLÉ CARNATION Evaporated Lowfat 2% Milk and light or fat free chicken broth. Follow recipe directions above.

Estimated Times

Preparation: 15 mins
Cooking: 10 mins

Cream of Mushroom Soup

You can never go wrong with this recipe of a classic soup.

MAKES 4 SERVINGS

INGREDIENTS

2 cans (7 ounces each) mushroom stems and pieces, drained and liquid reserved

¼ cup (½ stick) butter or margarine

2 tablespoons chopped onion

¼ cup all-purpose flour

1 teaspoon seasoned salt

1 can (12 fluid ounces) NESTLÉ CARNATION Evaporated Milk

DIRECTIONS

CHOP mushrooms. Add water to mushroom liquid to make 2 cups.

MELT butter in large saucepan over medium heat. Add onion; cook for 1 to 2 minutes or until tender. Remove from heat. Stir in flour and seasoned salt; return to heat. Stir in mushroom liquid mixture, evaporated milk, and mushrooms. Cook over medium heat, stirring constantly, until mixture comes to a boil.

Estimated Times

Preparation: 15 mins
Cooking: 15 mins

Cream of Chicken and Vegetable Soup

Cream of Pumpkin Curry Soup

Pumpkin and chicken broth are beautifully blended with sautéed garlic and onions to form the base of this fabulous soup. Curry, coriander, and crushed red pepper add zest, flavor, and liveliness to this creamy combination.

MAKES 4 SERVINGS

INGREDIENTS

3 tablespoons butter

1 small onion, finely chopped

1 clove garlic, finely chopped

1 teaspoon curry powder

½ teaspoon salt

⅛ to ¼ teaspoon ground coriander

⅛ teaspoon crushed red pepper

3 cups water

3 MAGGI Chicken Flavor Bouillon Cubes

1 can (15 ounces) LIBBY'S 100% Pure Pumpkin

1 to 1½ cups Original NESTLÉ COFFEE-MATE Half & Half

Sour cream (optional)

Chopped chives (optional)

DIRECTIONS

MELT butter in large saucepan over medium-high heat. Add onion and garlic; cook for 3 to 5 minutes or until tender. Stir in curry powder, salt,

Cream of Pumpkin Curry Soup

coriander, and crushed red pepper. Cook for 1 minute. Add water and bouillon; bring to a boil. Reduce heat to low; cook, stirring occasionally, for 15 to 20 minutes to develop flavors. Stir in pumpkin and Half & Half; cook for 5 minutes or until heated through.

TRANSFER mixture to blender or food processor (in batches, if necessary); cover. Blend until creamy. Serve warm or reheat to desired temperature. Serve with sour cream and chives.

NOTE: Soup may be prepared the day ahead. Cool to room temperature after adding pumpkin and Half & Half. Cover and refrigerate. Just before serving, blend then reheat to serving temperature, but do not boil.

FOR FREEZE AHEAD:

PREPARE as above; do not top with sour cream and chives. Cool soup completely. Place in airtight container; freeze for up to 2 months. Thaw overnight in refrigerator.

Pumpkins

Where were the first pumpkins grown?
Pumpkins are believed to have been first cultivated in Central America. Spanish and Portuguese explorers carried pumpkin seeds back to Europe in the 14th century. In North America, Native Americans grew pumpkins for food long before the first Europeans arrived on the continent in the 1600s.

Why are pumpkins orange?
The vivid orange color of pumpkin indicates a high content of carotene pigments such as lutein, alpha-carotene, and beta-carotene (which turns into vitamin A in the body).

Is the pumpkin a vegetable or a fruit?
Surprise! The pumpkin is actually a fruit, a member of the Cucurbitaceae family of plants with trailing vines.

HEAT in large saucepan over medium heat, stirring occasionally, for 20 to 25 minutes or until heated through. Serve with sour cream and chives.

Estimated Times
Preparation: 15 mins
Cooking: 30 mins

Creamy Tomato Tortellini Soup

Creamy Tomato Tortellini Soup

Team with crusty bread or a grilled cheese sandwich made with mozzarella or provolone cheese.

MAKES 4 SERVINGS

INGREDIENTS

1 package (9 ounces) BUITONI
    Refrigerated Three Cheese Tortellini

2 cans (10.75 fluid ounces each)
    condensed tomato soup

2 soup cans milk

½ teaspoon crushed basil

Grated Parmesan cheese

DIRECTIONS

PREPARE pasta according to package directions.

COMBINE pasta, soup, milk, and basil in medium saucepan. Bring to a boil over medium heat; reduce heat to low. Cook, stirring occasionally, for 10 minutes. Serve with cheese.

Estimated Times

Preparation: 5 mins

Cooking: 15 mins

Curried Cream of Vegetable Soup

The curry powder imparts a classic taste of India to this soup. Pair with warm, crusty rolls and crisp green salad.

MAKES 4 SERVINGS

INGREDIENTS

4 cups water

2 large carrots, peeled and chopped

½ head cauliflower, chopped

1 medium potato, peeled and chopped

1 small onion, chopped

5 MAGGI Chicken Flavor Bouillon Cubes

1½ teaspoons curry powder

¼ teaspoon ground white pepper

¼ teaspoon Worcestershire sauce

1 can (12 fluid ounces) NESTLÉ
    CARNATION Evaporated Milk

2 tablespoons finely chopped
    chives (optional)

DIRECTIONS

PLACE water, carrots, cauliflower, potato, onion, bouillon, curry powder, pepper, and Worcestershire sauce in stockpot. Bring to a boil. Reduce heat to medium. Cook, stirring occasionally, for 20 to 25 minutes or until vegetables are tender.

TRANSFER mixture to blender or food processor (in batches, if necessary); cover. Blend until almost smooth. Return to stockpot; stir in evaporated milk. Cook over low heat, stirring occasionally, for 10 to 12 minutes or until heated through. Sprinkle with chives before serving.

FOR FREEZE AHEAD:

PREPARE as above; do not sprinkle with chives. Cool soup completely. Place in airtight container; freeze for up to 2 months. Thaw overnight in refrigerator.

HEAT in medium saucepan over medium heat, stirring occasionally, for 15 to 20 minutes or until heated through. Sprinkle with chives before serving.

Estimated Times

Preparation: 20 mins

Cooking: 35 mins

Curried Cream of Vegetable Soup

Double Chicken Tortellini Soup

Double Chicken Tortellini Soup

A simmering pot of soup is a guarantee that everyone will be on time for dinner. This is a fantastic first course for your next get-together, or add garlic bread and a ready-to-serve salad for a quick and satisfying meal.

MAKES 8 SERVINGS

INGREDIENTS

5 cans (14.5 fluid ounces each) chicken broth

1½ cups frozen whole-kernel corn

1 can (14.5 ounces) Italian-style diced tomatoes, undrained

1 package (9 ounces) BUITONI Refrigerated Herb Chicken Tortellini

2½ cups cooked shredded chicken

Grated Parmesan cheese

Sliced green onions

DIRECTIONS

PLACE broth, corn, and tomatoes and juice in large saucepan. Bring to a boil over medium-high heat.

ADD pasta and chicken; reduce heat to medium. Cook, stirring occasionally, for 10 minutes or until pasta is tender. Season with salt and ground black pepper. Serve with cheese and green onions.

Estimated Times

Preparation: 10 mins

Cooking: 15 mins

French Onion Soup

Perfect for chilly nights!

MAKES 6 SERVINGS

INGREDIENTS

3 tablespoons butter or margarine
4 small onions, thinly sliced
5½ cups warm water
½ cup dry white wine
6 MAGGI Beef Flavor Bouillon Cubes
1 teaspoon Worcestershire sauce
¾ cup (3 ounces) diced Swiss cheese
6 slices French bread, toasted
½ cup (2 ounces) shredded Swiss cheese
¼ cup (1 ounce) grated Parmesan cheese

DIRECTIONS

PREHEAT oven to 425° F.

MELT butter in large saucepan over medium heat. Add onions; cook for 15 to 17 minutes or until golden brown and tender. Stir in water, wine, bouillon, and Worcestershire sauce; bring to a boil. Reduce heat to low. Cover; cook for 20 minutes.

LADLE soup into 6 oven-proof bowls. Top soup with diced Swiss cheese and toasted bread. Sprinkle with shredded Swiss and Parmesan cheeses.

BAKE for 10 to 15 minutes or until cheese is golden.

Estimated Times
Preparation: 20 mins
Cooking: 50 mins

Hearty Beef Stew

A hearty stew will warm chilled bones on a chilly winter day. Serve up steaming bowls of this simple yet nutritious and satisfying combination to anyone looking for a hearty meal.

MAKES 4 SERVINGS

INGREDIENTS

2 tablespoons all-purpose flour
½ teaspoon salt
¼ teaspoon ground black pepper
1 pound beef stew meat, cut into
    1-inch pieces
2 tablespoons vegetable oil
1 small onion, chopped
2 stalks celery, thickly sliced
2 cloves garlic, finely chopped
1 can (14.5 ounces) recipe-ready
    diced tomatoes, undrained
1 cup water
2 small carrots, peeled and thickly sliced
2 MAGGI Beef Flavor Bouillon Cubes
1 teaspoon fresh thyme leaves (or
    ¼ teaspoon ground thyme)
1 large potato, peeled and cut into
    1-inch pieces

DIRECTIONS

COMBINE flour, salt, and pepper in medium bowl. Add beef; toss well to coat. Heat oil in large saucepan over medium-high heat. Add beef, onion, celery, and garlic. Cook, stirring frequently, for 6 to 8 minutes or until beef is no longer pink and vegetables are tender. Add tomatoes and juice, water, carrots, bouillon, and thyme. Bring to a boil. Reduce heat to low; cover.

COOK, stirring occasionally, for 25 minutes. Add potato; cover. Cook, stirring occasionally, for an additional 25 to 30 minutes or until beef is tender.

CROCKERY COOKER METHOD:
COOK beef, onion, celery, and garlic as above. Spoon beef mixture into crockery cooker; cover with potato, tomatoes and juice, water, carrots, bouillon, and thyme. Cover; cook on high heat for 5 to 6 hours or on low heat for 10 to 12 hours or until beef is tender.

Estimated Times
Preparation: 20 mins
Cooking: 1 hr

Hearty Corn, Chile, and Potato Soup

This unique combination of flavor creates a soup that is hearty enough to make a meal.

MAKES 8 SERVINGS

INGREDIENTS

2 tablespoons butter

2 stalks celery, sliced

1 medium onion, coarsely chopped

2½ cups water

2 cups diced potatoes

1 can (14.75 ounces) cream-style corn

1 can (11 ounces) whole kernel corn, undrained

1 can (4 ounces) diced green chiles

2 MAGGI Chicken Flavor Bouillon Cubes

1 teaspoon paprika

1 bay leaf

1 can (12 fluid ounces) NESTLÉ CARNATION Evaporated Milk

2 tablespoons all-purpose flour

DIRECTIONS

MELT butter in large saucepan over medium-high heat. Add celery and onion; cook for 1 to 2 minutes or until onion is tender. Add water, potatoes, corn, chiles, bouillon, paprika, and bay leaf. Bring to a boil. Reduce heat to low; cover.

COOK, stirring occasionally, for 15 minutes or until potatoes are tender. Stir small amount of evaporated milk into flour in small bowl to make a smooth paste; gradually stir in remaining evaporated milk. Stir milk mixture into soup. Cook, stirring constantly, until soup comes just to a boil and thickens slightly. Season with salt and ground black pepper.

Estimated Times

Preparation: 15 mins

Cooking: 30 mins

Hearty Corn, Chile, and Potato Soup

Lentil Soup

Lentil Soup

A lip-smackin' vegetarian main dish that boasts high levels of vitamin A and iron.

MAKES 6 SERVINGS

INGREDIENTS
2 tablespoons olive oil
½ cup chopped onion
¼ cup chopped red bell pepper
2 cloves garlic, finely chopped
7 cups water
1 cup dried brown lentils
5 MAGGI Vegetarian Vegetable Flavor
    Bouillon Cubes
1 teaspoon white wine vinegar
1 package (10 ounces) frozen
    spinach, chopped
½ cup quick-cooking brown rice

DIRECTIONS
HEAT oil in large saucepan over medium-high heat. Add onion, bell pepper, and garlic. Cook, stirring occasionally, for 5 to 7 minutes or until vegetables are tender.

ADD water, lentils, bouillon, and vinegar; bring to a boil. Reduce heat to medium; cover. Cook for 18 to 20 minutes or until lentils are tender.

STIR in spinach and rice; cover. Return to boil. Reduce heat to low; uncover. Cook for 15 to 20 minutes or until rice is tender.

Estimated Times
Preparation: 15 mins
Cooking: 50 mins

Mediterranean Chicken and Lemon Soup

This creamy chicken soup is made piquant with a healthy dose of lemon juice and a garnish of fresh basil.

MAKES 4 SERVINGS

INGREDIENTS
2 cans (14.5 fluid ounces each)
    reduced-sodium chicken broth
½ cup long-grain white rice
1 small carrot, sliced
2 cups cooked, cubed chicken
    breast meat
½ cup fresh lemon juice
½ cup thinly sliced red bell pepper strips
1 clove garlic, finely chopped
1 can (12 fluid ounces) NESTLÉ
    CARNATION Evaporated Fat Free
    Milk, divided
1 tablespoon cornstarch
2 tablespoons chopped fresh basil

DIRECTIONS
BOIL broth in medium saucepan. Add rice and carrot; cook until carrot is tender. Stir in chicken, lemon juice, bell pepper, and garlic.

COMBINE 1 tablespoon evaporated milk and cornstarch in small bowl; stir into soup. Gradually stir in remaining evaporated milk. Bring to a boil; reduce heat to low. Cook, stirring occasionally, until soup is slightly thickened. Stir in basil before serving.

Estimated Times
Preparation: 10 mins
Cooking: 15 mins

Mexican Pozole

Pozole is a staple of New Mexican cuisine. This pork and hominy dish, rich in spiciness and flavor, will satisfy the hungriest skiers, sledders, and skaters on the coldest of days.

MAKES 6 SERVINGS

INGREDIENTS

1 tablespoon vegetable oil

2 pounds pork shoulder, trimmed of fat and cut into bite-sized pieces

3 medium onions, chopped

8 large cloves garlic, finely chopped

4 cups water

Evaporated Milk

NESTLÉ CARNATION Evaporated Fat Free Milk has more than twice the nutritional value than regular fat free milk. To every ½ cup of NESTLÉ CARNATION Evaporated Fat Free Milk there's 23 percent more calcium and 11 percent more protein than fat free or skim milk. And because of the special way evaporated milk is made, it adds richness to recipes you cannot get from regular fat free milk.

Mexican Pozole

1 can (29 ounces) Mexican-style hominy, drained

2 cans (10 ounces each) enchilada sauce

1 can (7 ounces) diced green chiles

2 tablespoons MAGGI Instant Chicken Flavor Bouillon

2 teaspoons dried oregano, crushed

½ cup chopped cilantro

8 radishes, finely chopped

DIRECTIONS

HEAT oil in stockpot. Add pork, onions, and garlic. Cook, stirring frequently, for 12 to 14 minutes or until pork is cooked through. Stir in water, hominy, enchilada sauce, chiles, bouillon, and oregano; bring to a boil. Reduce heat to medium. Cook, stirring occasionally, for 40 to 45 minutes or until pork is tender and stew thickens slightly. Top with cilantro and radishes before serving.

Estimated Times

Preparation: 20 mins

Cooking: 1 hr

Pumpkin Pork Stew

Hearty and savory, pumpkin gives this soup a distinctly African essence. The addition of tomatoes, potatoes, and green beans makes this pork dish a complete meal.

MAKES 6 SERVINGS

INGREDIENTS

1 tablespoon olive oil

1 medium onion, finely chopped

1 clove garlic, finely chopped

1 tablespoon crushed dried basil leaves

2 pounds lean pork tenderloin, cut into 1-inch pieces

1 can (28 ounces) diced tomatoes, undrained

Pumpkin Pork Stew

1 can (15 ounces) LIBBY'S 100% Pure Pumpkin

1 can (14.5 fluid ounces) reduced-sodium chicken broth

½ cup rosé or white Zinfandel wine

½ teaspoon salt (optional)

¼ teaspoon ground black pepper

4 medium white rose potatoes, peeled and cubed

½ pound green beans, cut into 1-inch pieces

1 cinnamon stick

DIRECTIONS

HEAT oil in large saucepan over medium-high heat. Add onion, garlic, and basil. Cook for 1 minute or until onion is tender. Add pork; cook for 3 to 4 minutes or until lightly browned. Add tomatoes and juice, pumpkin, broth, wine, salt, and pepper. Bring to a boil. Reduce heat to low; cook, stirring occasionally, for 10 minutes.

ADD potatoes, green beans, and cinnamon stick. Cover; cook over low heat for 1 hour or until potatoes are tender. Remove cinnamon stick before serving.

Estimated Times
Preparation: 25 mins
Cooking: 1 hr, 20 mins

Shrimp Bisque

Shrimp bisque is great for a weekend get-together or to surprise a loved one.

MAKES 6 SERVINGS

INGREDIENTS

½ cup (1 stick) butter or margarine, divided

1 pound raw medium shrimp, peeled and deveined

½ cup chopped onion

½ cup chopped celery

½ cup all-purpose flour

3 cups water

1 tablespoon ketchup

1 MAGGI Chicken Flavor Bouillon Cube

1 bay leaf

1 tablespoon seasoned salt

⅛ teaspoon cayenne pepper (optional)

1 can (12 fluid ounces) NESTLÉ CARNATION Evaporated Milk

2 tablespoons dry white wine or water

DIRECTIONS

MELT 2 tablespoons butter in medium saucepan over medium heat. Add shrimp, onion, and celery. Cook, stirring occasionally, until shrimp turn pink. Remove from saucepan; set aside.

MELT remaining butter in same saucepan over medium heat. Stir in flour. Gradually stir in water, ketchup, bouillon, bay leaf, seasoned salt, and cayenne pepper. Bring to a boil, stirring occasionally; reduce heat to low. Cook, stirring occasionally, for 5 minutes. Add shrimp mixture; cook, stirring occasionally, for 2 minutes. Discard bay leaf. Stir in evaporated milk and wine. Heat through; do not boil.

Estimated Times
Preparation: 10 mins
Cooking: 15 mins

Shrimp Bisque

Pumpkin

LIBBY'S Pumpkin, celebrating over 75 years, is a natural cooking partner because it complements so many different flavors. With pumpkin on the ingredient list, the distinctive orange color, creamy texture, moistness, and mellow taste can enhance any number of dishes. Pumpkin is also a natural flavor carrier. From waffles, pancakes, and pies to breads, dips, and soups, pumpkin easily takes on the essence of sweet spices such as nutmeg, cinnamon, or ginger as well as savory ones like curry, sage, and turmeric. That's why pumpkin pie and other pumpkin desserts carry such seductive spicy aromas. In savory dishes, pumpkin never overpowers flavors; it merely enhances them with its subtle taste.

Spinach and Tortellini en Brodo

Three cheese tortellini and tender baby spinach leaves in broth, or "en brodo," as the Italians say, are a perfect combination for a light lunch or early supper. Served with cooked carrots and broccoli, hot sliced garlic bread, and a refreshing drink, this tortellini soup will satisfy even the pickiest eater.

MAKES 4 SERVINGS

INGREDIENTS

6 cups water
4 MAGGI Chicken Flavor Bouillon Cubes
1 package (9 ounces) BUITONI Refrigerated Three Cheese Tortellini
2 cups packed fresh baby spinach leaves or 1 package (10 ounces) frozen chopped spinach
⅛ to ¼ teaspoon ground black pepper

DIRECTIONS

BOIL water and bouillon in stockpot. Add pasta; reduce heat to medium. Cook, stirring occasionally, for 6 to 7 minutes or until pasta is tender. Stir in spinach and pepper; cook until spinach is wilted.

Estimated Times
Preparation: 5 mins
Cooking: 15 mins

Spinach and Tortellini en Brodo

Thai-Style Pumpkin Soup

Fresh ginger and creamy peanut butter lend a distinct Thai flavor to this soup.

MAKES 4 SERVINGS

INGREDIENTS

2 cups water
1 can (15 ounces) LIBBY'S 100% Pure Pumpkin
1 can (11.5 fluid ounces) mango nectar
3 MAGGI Vegetarian Vegetable Flavor Bouillon Cubes
1 teaspoon peeled, finely chopped fresh ginger (or ¾ teaspoon ground ginger)
2 cloves garlic, finely chopped
¼ to ½ teaspoon crushed red pepper
¼ cup creamy peanut butter
2 tablespoons rice vinegar

2 tablespoons finely chopped
   green onion
¼ cup finely chopped cilantro, divided
½ cup NESTLÉ CARNATION
   Evaporated Milk

DIRECTIONS

PLACE water, pumpkin, nectar, bouillon, ginger, garlic, and crushed red pepper in large saucepan. Bring to a boil, stirring occasionally. Reduce heat to low.

STIR in peanut butter, vinegar, green onion, and 1 tablespoon cilantro. Cook, stirring occasionally, until soup returns to a boil. Stir in evaporated milk. Sprinkle with remaining cilantro before serving.

FOR FREEZE AHEAD:
PREPARE as above; do not sprinkle with remaining cilantro. Cool soup completely. Place in airtight container; freeze for up to 2 months. Thaw overnight in refrigerator.

Thai-Style Pumpkin Soup

HEAT in medium saucepan over medium heat, stirring occasionally, for 15 to 20 minutes or until heated through. Sprinkle with remaining cilantro before serving.

Estimated Times
Preparation: 10 mins
Cooking: 20 mins

Vegetarian Chili

A truly one-pot meal, this hearty vegetarian chili will satisfy the biggest of appetites. Make lots because it's even better the next day.

MAKES 6 SERVINGS

INGREDIENTS
1 small onion, chopped
1 large green bell pepper, chopped
¾ cup chopped celery
¾ cup dry red wine or water
3 cloves garlic, finely chopped
2 cans (14.5 ounces each) recipe-ready
   diced tomatoes, undrained
1½ cups water
¼ cup tomato paste
3 MAGGI Vegetarian Vegetable Flavor
   Bouillon Cubes
1 tablespoon chopped fresh cilantro
1 tablespoon chili powder
½ teaspoon ground cumin

2 cans (15 ounces each) kidney or
   pinto beans, rinsed and drained
1 container (8 ounces) sour cream
   (optional)

DIRECTIONS

PLACE onion, bell pepper, celery, wine, and garlic in large saucepan. Cook over medium-high heat, stirring occasionally, for 6 to 8 minutes or until vegetables are tender.

ADD tomatoes and juice, water, tomato paste, bouillon, cilantro, chili powder, and cumin; stir well. Stir in beans. Bring to a boil; cover. Reduce heat to low; cook, stirring occasionally, for 45 minutes. Serve topped with sour cream.

FOR FREEZE AHEAD:
PREPARE as above; do not top with sour cream. Cool chili completely. Place in airtight container; freeze for up to 2 months. Thaw overnight in refrigerator.

HEAT in large saucepan over medium heat, stirring occasionally, for 30 to 35 minutes or until heated through. Serve topped with sour cream.

Estimated Times
Preparation: 15 mins
Cooking: 1 hr

Hot Apple Pie Sandwiches

Hot Apple Pie Sandwiches

Tender slices of apple seasoned with a sprinkling of cinnamon are enriched with cheddar cheese and encased between toasted bread. Makes a great snack to satisfy and energize your body—or serve with fresh fruit for a tasty lunch.

MAKES 4 SERVINGS

INGREDIENTS

1 package (12 ounces) STOUFFER'S frozen Harvest Apples, defrosted*
½ teaspoon ground cinnamon
4 slices cheddar or American cheese, each cut into 4 strips
8 slices white bread, lightly toasted
2 tablespoons butter or margarine, melted

DIRECTIONS

PREHEAT broiler.

COMBINE harvest apples and cinnamon in small bowl.

PLACE cheese strips on outside perimeter of 4 slices of bread. Spoon apple mixture evenly into centers of each. Top with remaining slices of bread; press down slightly. Brush sandwiches with butter.

BROIL on each side until golden brown and cheese is melted.

*DEFROST harvest apples in microwave on MEDIUM (50%) power for 6 to 7 minutes.

Estimated Times
Preparation: 10 mins
Cooking: 5 mins

Smoked Turkey and Sun-Dried Tomato Wraps

These flavorful, fresh-tasting wraps make a delicious quick lunch or light dinner.

MAKES 2 SERVINGS

INGREDIENTS

¼ cup cream cheese, at room temperature
2 tablespoons BUITONI Refrigerated Pesto with Sun-Dried Tomatoes
2 (10-inch) burrito-size flour tortillas, warmed
4 thin slices smoked turkey breast
2 cups shredded romaine lettuce
1 cup chopped tomatoes
¼ cup thinly sliced red onion or alfalfa sprouts

DIRECTIONS

COMBINE cream cheese and pesto in small bowl; stir well. Spread evenly over each tortilla. Place turkey slices, lettuce, tomatoes, and red onion or alfalfa sprouts over bottom third of tortillas, making sure ingredients don't touch edges.

FOLD the bottom edge of tortilla toward the center and gently roll until tortilla is completely wrapped around the filling.

Wrap tightly in plastic wrap. Refrigerate for 15 minutes. Cut in half and serve.

Estimated Times
Preparation: 15 mins
Refrigerating: 15 mins

Stuffed Sourdough Sandwich

This hot sandwich is pretty to look at and delicious to eat for lunch, dinner, or a snack while watching the big game! Serve with your favorite chips and fresh fruit.

MAKES 6 SERVINGS

1 pound round bread loaf

1 container (7 ounces) BUITONI Refrigerated Pesto with Basil, divided

8 ounces thinly sliced smoked turkey

1 roasted red bell pepper, peeled, seeded, and cut into thin strips

1 medium tomato, thinly sliced

12 slices provolone cheese

DIRECTIONS

PREHEAT oven to 350° F.

CUT off top third of bread; set aside. Remove inside of bread, leaving a ¾-inch wall. Spread half of pesto on inside of loaf. Top with half the turkey, bell pepper, tomato, and cheese. Spread remaining pesto on top of cheese. Repeat layering. Replace top of bread; wrap bread in foil.

BAKE for 40 minutes or until heated through. Let stand for 5 minutes before cutting into wedges.

Estimated Times
Preparation: 20 mins
Cooking: 40 mins
Standing: 5 mins

Pesto

Give your everyday meals a gourmet feel with pesto. Pesto is a combination of fragrant basil leaves, hearty garlic, tangy Parmesan cheese, rich olive oil, and delicate pine nuts or walnuts, puréed to a delectable, thick sauce. Pesto has its origins in Liguria, Italy, where people have been making it for hundreds of years with the brilliant green basil that grows wild on the hillsides. The popularity of pesto has spread like crazy as people across the world have come to love its heady aroma and its bold, satisfying flavor.

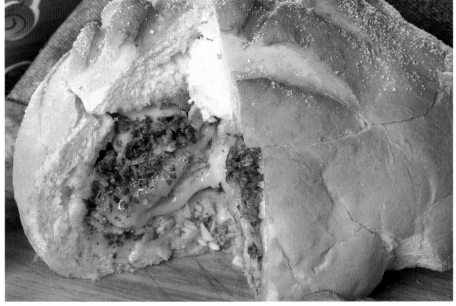

Stuffed Sourdough Sandwich

savory sides

savory sides

With our versatile side dish recipes, meats have met their match. These sides don't have to play second string to the main course. We have gathered our most crowd-pleasing accompaniments, from breads to relishes to potato and vegetable concoctions, and dished up winning serving ideas. You and your family will want to regularly replay these tasty dishes, which complement a variety of entrées featuring beef, pork, poultry, seafood, or meatless menus.

Apple-Filled Sweet Potato Nests

A great new way to serve sweet potatoes at your holiday gatherings! Served with roast turkey, chicken, or pork, these are sure to be the start of a new family tradition.

MAKES 6 SERVINGS

INGREDIENTS

1 package (12 ounces) STOUFFER'S frozen Harvest Apples, defrosted*

1 can (22 ounces) sweet potatoes or yams, drained

2 large eggs

2 tablespoons butter

1 tablespoon granulated sugar

½ teaspoon vanilla extract

¼ teaspoon ground nutmeg

DIRECTIONS

PREHEAT oven to 400° F. Lightly grease baking sheet.

WHIP sweet potatoes until smooth in large mixer bowl. Add eggs, butter, sugar, vanilla extract, and nutmeg. Beat mixture until well combined. Season with salt.

Apple-Filled Sweet Potato Nests

SPOON mixture onto prepared baking sheet, forming 6 mounds, 2 inches apart. Make a depression in each mound using back of a spoon to form a nest. Fill centers of nests with harvest apples.

BAKE for 30 minutes.

*DEFROST harvest apples in microwave on MEDIUM (50%) power for 6 to 7 minutes.

Estimated Times
Preparation: 15 mins
Cooking: 30 mins

Carnation Mashed Potatoes

A side dish everyone will be raving about. The key ingredient is evaporated milk.

MAKES 6 SERVINGS

INGREDIENTS
6 medium potatoes (about 2 pounds total), peeled and cut into 1-inch chunks
1 cup NESTLÉ CARNATION Evaporated Milk
¼ cup (½ stick) butter or margarine

DIRECTIONS
PLACE potatoes in large saucepan. Cover with water; bring to a boil. Cook over medium-high heat for 15 to 20 minutes or until tender; drain.

RETURN potatoes to saucepan. Add evaporated milk and butter. Beat with hand-held mixer until smooth. Season with salt and ground black pepper.

NOTE: Chopped green onions, chopped parsley, or cooked, crumbled bacon may be added to mashed potatoes.

FOR MUSHROOM MASHED POTATOES:
PREPARE potatoes as above. Melt butter in saucepan; add 1 clove finely chopped garlic and 8 ounces finely chopped mushrooms. Cook over medium heat for 4 to 5 minutes or until liquid has evaporated.

ADD potatoes and evaporated milk; beat potatoes with hand-held mixer until smooth and thoroughly mixed with mushrooms. Season with salt and ground black pepper.

Estimated Times
Preparation: 15 mins
Cooking: 20 mins

Evaporated Milk

Have you ever wondered what to do with evaporated milk after you have opened the can? The culinary staff at Nestlé definitely say refrigerate after opening the can and shake can before use. As with any fresh milk, use within a few days. Wipe can top after each use and keep covered or transfer to an airtight glass or plastic container. Unused milk can be frozen, but it's not recommended because it becomes watery when it thaws.

When storing the milk for long periods of time, the milk solids may separate from the water and coagulate. The result is a lumpy, "curdled" appearance or watery product with milk solids settled in the bottom of the can. Separation will also happen more quickly under warm storage conditions.

Cheesy Spoon Bread

Cheesy Spoon Bread

Spoon bread can't be sliced and buttered. This pudding-like casserole made with dry milk and corn meal is so soft and creamy, it has to be eaten with a spoon. Serve as a main dish accompanied by a tossed green salad or as a side dish with pork chops and sliced tomatoes.

MAKES 6 SERVINGS

INGREDIENTS

¾ cup dry NESTLÉ CARNATION Instant Nonfat Dry Milk

½ cup ALBERS Yellow Corn Meal

2 cups water

1¼ cups (5 ounces) shredded cheddar cheese, divided

3 large eggs, separated

2 tablespoons margarine or butter

¼ teaspoon baking powder

DIRECTIONS

PREHEAT oven to 375° F. Grease 1½-quart casserole dish.

COMBINE dry milk and corn meal in large saucepan. Stir in water. Cook, stirring constantly, until mixture comes to a boil and thickens. Remove from heat. Stir in ¾ cup cheese, egg yolks, margarine, and baking powder.

BEAT egg whites in small mixer bowl until stiff peaks form. Fold into corn meal mixture lightly but thoroughly. Pour into prepared dish. Sprinkle with remaining cheese.

BAKE for 30 to 35 minutes or until top is golden and filling is set. Serve warm.

Estimated Times
Preparation: 10 mins
Cooking: 40 mins

Cornbread Stuffing

Green chile peppers give this aromatic cornbread stuffing a little extra kick. Serve it as a side with your favorite poultry.

MAKES 8 SERVINGS

INGREDIENTS

Nonstick cooking spray

¼ cup (½ stick) butter

2 cups chopped onion

1 cup sliced celery

2 cups water

1 can (16 ounces) corn, drained

2 cans (4 ounces each) diced green chiles

3 tablespoons chopped fresh parsley

2 MAGGI Chicken Flavor Bouillon Cubes

½ teaspoon paprika

¼ teaspoon crushed dried oregano

⅛ teaspoon ground black pepper

6 cups crumbled cornbread

½ cup chopped pecans

DIRECTIONS

PREHEAT oven to 350° F. Spray 2½-quart baking dish with nonstick cooking spray.

MELT butter in large skillet over low heat. Cook onion and celery for 5 to 8 minutes or until tender. Add water, corn, chiles, parsley, bouillon, paprika, oregano, and pepper. Mix well. Add cornbread and nuts; mix well. Spoon into prepared baking dish; cover.

BAKE for 30 minutes or until heated through.

Estimated Times
Preparation: 15 mins
Cooking: 35 mins

Creamy Cheesy Mashed Potatoes

Beef up your mashed potatoes with evaporated milk and shredded cheddar cheese! Add green onions and crumbled bacon for an even heartier side dish.

MAKES 6 SERVINGS

Creamy Cheesy Mashed Potatoes

INGREDIENTS

6 medium potatoes (about 2 pounds total), peeled and cut into 1-inch chunks
¾ cup NESTLÉ CARNATION Evaporated Milk
¼ cup (½ stick) butter or margarine
1 cup (4 ounces) shredded cheddar cheese

DIRECTIONS

PLACE potatoes in large saucepan. Cover with water; bring to a boil. Cook over medium-high heat for 15 to 20 minutes or until tender; drain.

RETURN potatoes to saucepan. Add evaporated milk and butter. Beat with hand-held mixer until smooth. Stir in cheese. Season with salt and ground black pepper.

NOTE: Chopped green onions, chopped parsley, or cooked, crumbled bacon may be added to mashed potatoes.

Estimated Times
Preparation: 15 mins
Cooking: 20 mins

Milk

Have you often wondered what the difference is between heavy cream, whipping cream, light creams, half-and-half, and evaporated milk?

The answer lies in how much milk fat they contain. For example, heavy cream and heavy whipping cream have different names but both have 36 percent or more milk fat, and double in volume when whipped. Light whipping cream is between 30 and 36 percent milk fat, and can also be whipped. Light cream, table cream, coffee cream, or single cream are names for cream that are around 18 to 30 percent milk fat and will not whip. Half-and-half is a mixture of cream and milk, and contains about 10½ to 18 percent milk fat and will not whip. Evaporated milk is canned whole milk that contains at least 6½ percent milk fat. Due to how evaporated milk is processed, it will whip for a only a short time.

Crispy Pesto Potatoes

Add a touch of Italian to your potatoes.

MAKES 6 SERVINGS

INGREDIENTS

1½ pounds baby red potatoes, halved, cooked and drained

¼ cup BUITONI Refrigerated Pesto with Basil

DIRECTIONS

PREHEAT broiler. Line baking sheet with heavy-duty foil.

PLACE hot potatoes and pesto in large bowl; toss to coat. Spread potatoes on prepared baking sheet.

BROIL for 4 to 5 minutes or until potatoes are lightly browned.

NOTE: Try substituting BUITONI Refrigerated Reduced-Fat Pesto with Basil.

Estimated Times

Preparation: 20 mins

Cooking: 5 mins

Crispy Pesto Potatoes

Easy Apple Cranberry Relish

This quick relish is a superb choice for special occasions but easy enough to serve at any meal.

MAKES 12 SERVINGS

INGREDIENTS

1 package (12 ounces) STOUFFER'S frozen Harvest Apples, defrosted*

1 can (16 ounces) whole berry cranberry sauce

DIRECTIONS

PLACE harvest apples in food processor or blender; cover. Process until coarsely chopped.

COMBINE harvest apples and cranberry sauce in medium bowl; cover. Refrigerate for at least 1 hour.

*DEFROST harvest apples in microwave on MEDIUM (50%) power for 6 to 7 minutes.

Estimated Times

Preparation: 10 mins

Refrigerating: 1 hr

Pesto Bread

Pesto Bread

A delightful addition to any appetizer line-up or your favorite Italian meal.

MAKES 8 SERVINGS

INGREDIENTS

1 container (7 ounces) BUITONI
  Refrigerated Pesto with Basil
1 baguette, cut in half lengthwise
¼ cup (1 ounce) grated Parmesan cheese

DIRECTIONS

PREHEAT broiler.

SPREAD pesto over bread; sprinkle evenly with cheese. Place on baking sheet.

BROIL for 1 to 2 minutes or until bread is crisp and cheese is melted. Cut into pieces.

Estimated Times
Preparation: 5 mins
Cooking: 2 mins

About Bread

If you're in the mood for a sandwich, then you must start with good, fresh bread. Today there is a rich variety of delicious artisanal breads, focaccia breads and other types found in most bakeries, specialty stores, and supermarkets. Sandwich recipes use a variety of whole-grain or other readily available types of breads. Baguettes are also a great choice, but vary in size and weight, so depending on your recipe and preference, select the bread that has the right texture and balance for your sandwich. And remember, always keep these items on hand in the refrigerator or pantry when making sandwiches: butter, mayonnaise, mustard, lettuce, cheese, sliced meats and poultry, fresh herbs, and tomatoes. You can create your own spur-of-the-moment sandwich or visit us at Meals.com for more tasty choices!

About Albers

Bernhard Albers worked for a wholesale grocer, saving money with the goal of going into business for himself. Convinced of the opportunities in Portland, Oregon, he persuaded his four brothers to join him. In 1895, with $15,000, the brothers and another partner formed a milling company. By 1899, the Albers brothers bought out their business associate and formed the Albers Bros. Milling Company.

In 1914, the Pacific Cereal Association was absorbed by the Albers business. With this came the acquisition of the Carnation Wheat and Carnation Oats products. Due to the acquisition of these two labels, Albers came to the attention of E.A. Stuart, owner of Carnation Milk Products Company.

In 1929, Mr. Stuart believed it was the right time to negotiate for the Albers business and purchased Albers Bros. Milling Company. Nestlé purchased the Carnation Company, along with the Albers brand of products, in 1984.

Polenta Primavera

This cheese-infused polenta makes a great side to chicken and pork dishes or as part of a vegetarian meal.

MAKES 8 SERVINGS

INGREDIENTS

2 cups water
⅔ cup ALBERS Yellow Corn Meal
1 cup (4 ounces) shredded fontina or
   mozzarella cheese
½ cup heavy whipping cream
¼ cup (1 ounce) grated Parmesan cheese
½ teaspoon salt
¼ teaspoon ground black pepper
1 can (14.5 ounces) primavera pasta-
   ready chunky tomatoes, undrained

DIRECTIONS

GREASE 9-inch pie plate.

BRING water to a boil in medium saucepan over medium heat. Slowly add corn meal, stirring constantly, for 2 to 3 minutes or until slightly thickened.

STIR in fontina cheese, cream, Parmesan cheese, salt, and pepper. Cook, stirring constantly, for an additional 2 minutes or until very thick.

SPREAD into prepared pie plate; cool for 1 hour or until firm. Cut into wedges. Heat tomatoes and juice; serve over wedges.

Estimated Times
Preparation: 10 mins
Cooking: 10 mins
Cooling: 1 hr

Potatoes Au Gratin

Who would have thought that potatoes au gratin from scratch would be so easy?

MAKES 4 SERVINGS

INGREDIENTS

1½ cups hot water
1½ cups Original NESTLÉ COFFEE-MATE
   Powdered Coffee Creamer
2 tablespoons butter
2 tablespoons all-purpose flour
1½ pounds new red potatoes, cooked
   and sliced ¼-inch thick
½ cup (2 ounces) shredded
   cheddar cheese
½ cup (2 ounces) shredded Monterey
   Jack cheese

DIRECTIONS

PREHEAT oven to 400° F. Grease 12 x 7-inch baking dish.

WHISK together water and Coffee-mate in small bowl.

MELT butter in medium saucepan over medium heat. Stir in flour; cook for 2 minutes. Whisk in Coffee-mate mixture. Cook, stirring occasionally, for 4 to 6 minutes or until mixture slightly

Potatoes Au Gratin

thickens. Season with salt and ground black pepper. Remove from heat.

SEASON potatoes with salt and ground black pepper. Add to sauce mixture; stir gently to coat. Pour into prepared baking dish. Sprinkle evenly with cheddar and Monterey Jack cheeses.

BAKE for 15 minutes or until golden brown and bubbly.

Estimated Times
Preparation: 20 mins
Cooking: 25 mins

Scalloped Potatoes

Evaporated milk and grated Parmesan cheese combine with fresh boiled potatoes and a dash of ground black pepper to make a rich and aromatic bowl of the old-fashioned favorite, scalloped potatoes.

MAKES 8 SERVINGS

INGREDIENTS

6 medium potatoes (about 2 pounds total), peeled and thinly sliced
3 tablespoons butter or margarine
¼ cup chopped onion
3 tablespoons all-purpose flour
1 teaspoon salt
¼ teaspoon ground black pepper
1 can (12 fluid ounces) NESTLÉ CARNATION Evaporated Milk
1 cup water
⅓ cup grated Parmesan cheese

DIRECTIONS

PREHEAT oven to 350° F. Grease 11 x 7-inch baking dish.

PLACE potatoes in large saucepan. Cover with water; bring to a boil. Cook over medium-high heat for 3 to 4 minutes; drain. Arrange potatoes in prepared baking dish.

HEAT butter in same saucepan over medium heat. Add onion. Cook, stirring occasionally, for 1 to 2 minutes or until onion is tender. Stir in flour, salt, and pepper. Gradually stir in evaporated milk and water. Cook, stirring constantly, until mixture comes to a boil. Pour milk mixture over potatoes. Sprinkle with cheese.

BAKE for 25 to 30 minutes or until potatoes are tender and cheese is light golden brown.

Evaporated Milk

Remember to shake the evaporated milk in the can before opening. As the can sits, milk solids may separate from the fluid milk. This separation in itself is not an indication that the milk is spoiled. It is simply a natural occurrence that can usually be corrected by shaking the can prior to opening or by stirring the contents after the milk has been poured into a container.

If the milk looks discolored the product may be past its normal shelf life or possibly stored improperly. This can happen in a warehouse, grocery store, or one's home. We do not recommend using the product beyond its shelf life, as it may not meet quality standards.

NOTE: For a twist on the traditional, spice up your Scalloped Potatoes with these tips. Add a combination of chopped ham, red bell pepper, and/or diced green chiles to the potatoes prior to baking. Or, add 1 cup (4 ounces) shredded cheddar cheese to the milk mixture after it is removed from the heat and top the dish with additional shredded cheddar cheese in place of Parmesan cheese.

Estimated Times
Preparation: 15 mins
Cooking: 35 mins

Spinach-Stuffed Tomatoes

Serve two tomato halves for a meatless entrée, or pair with roasted chicken from your local grocer.

MAKES 4 SERVINGS

INGREDIENTS

1 package (12 ounces) STOUFFER'S frozen Spinach Soufflé, defrosted*

8 medium tomatoes

½ cup (2 ounces) grated Parmesan, cheddar, or Swiss cheese

DIRECTIONS

PREHEAT oven to 350° F.

CUT ½-inch slice from top of each tomato; scoop out pulp, leaving shell intact. Fill each tomato with spinach soufflé; sprinkle cheese over top. Place in shallow baking dish.

BAKE for 25 minutes.

*DEFROST spinach soufflé in microwave on MEDIUM (50%) power for 6 to 7 minutes.

Estimated Times
Preparation: 15 mins
Cooking: 25 mins

Spinach-Stuffed Tomatoes

Three-Vegetable Bake

An easy-to-prepare vegetable side dish that's bound to get rave reviews.

MAKES 6 SERVINGS

INGREDIENTS

3 cups coarsely chopped red or other waxy potatoes (about 3 medium)

1 cup peeled and coarsely chopped parsnip (1 medium)

3 cups fresh broccoli and/or cauliflower florets

3 tablespoons butter, divided

2 tablespoons all-purpose flour

1 can (12 fluid ounces) NESTLÉ CARNATION Evaporated Fat Free Milk

1 MAGGI Vegetarian Vegetable Flavor Bouillon Cube

⅛ teaspoon ground white pepper

¼ cup seasoned dry bread crumbs

DIRECTIONS

PREHEAT oven to 350° F.

MICROWAVE potatoes and parsnip in covered, medium, microwave-safe casserole dish on HIGH (100%) power for 9 minutes. Drain; return to dish. Top with broccoli.

Three-Vegetable Bake

MELT 2 tablespoons butter in small saucepan over medium heat. Stir in flour; cook, stirring constantly, for 30 seconds. Gradually stir in evaporated milk, bouillon, and pepper. Cook, stirring occasionally, for 3 to 4 minutes or until bouillon is dissolved and sauce is slightly thickened. Pour sauce over vegetables.

MICROWAVE remaining butter in small, microwave-safe bowl on HIGH (100%) power for 10 to 20 seconds or until melted. Stir in bread crumbs until combined. Sprinkle over vegetables; cover.

BAKE for 30 minutes. Uncover; bake for an additional 10 minutes or until top is golden brown.

Estimated Times
Preparation: 15 mins
Cooking: 55 mins

main dishes

main dishes

If you've ever asked or been asked, "What's for dinner tonight?" and we know you have, this group of recipes will bring ready answers to your fingertips. We've compiled dishes, from traditional American fare to Asian-, Mediterranean-, and Mexican-inspired choices that can be proudly featured at an elegant dinner party to kid-friendly selections for the family table. The emphasis is on flavor and ease of preparation, but there are some intriguing twists and surprising marriages of ingredients along the way. Many of our entrées may seem like indulgences but we think you and your family deserve great meals each and every night. And with our serving suggestions, dinner just may be on the table before anyone can ask, "What's for dinner tonight?" And for more great dinner ideas visit us at Meals.com.

Angel Hair Pasta and Chicken with Asian Dressing

Angel Hair Pasta and Chicken with Asian Dressing

The tangy dressing gives this pasta dish a distinctive flair. Serve with a prepared Asian-style salad. For an added touch, garnish with chopped peanuts.

MAKES 4 SERVINGS

INGREDIENTS

1 package (9 ounces) BUITONI Refrigerated Angel Hair Pasta

⅓ cup creamy peanut butter

⅓ cup dark sesame oil

⅓ cup vegetable oil

¼ cup orange juice

3 tablespoons rice vinegar

2 tablespoons soy sauce

1 tablespoon honey mustard

2 teaspoons hot chili oil

1½ cups diced cooked chicken

⅓ cup sliced green onions

DIRECTIONS

PREPARE pasta according to package directions.

COMBINE peanut butter, sesame oil, vegetable oil, orange juice, vinegar, soy sauce, mustard, and chili oil in small bowl. Mix until smooth. Season with salt and ground black pepper.

TOSS pasta, chicken, green onions, and dressing in medium bowl.

Estimated Times

Preparation: 10 mins

Cooking: 5 mins

Angel Hair Pasta and Crab with Alfredo Sauce

The blend of rich crabmeat and creamy Alfredo sauce tossed with delicate angel hair pasta is truly a marriage made in heaven. Add a prepackaged salad and a tall glass of iced tea and spoil your family with this decadent treat.

MAKES 4 SERVINGS

INGREDIENTS

1 package (9 ounces) BUITONI Refrigerated Angel Hair Pasta

1 container (10 ounces) BUITONI Refrigerated Alfredo Sauce

8 ounces fresh lump crabmeat or surimi

½ cup (2 ounces) grated Parmesan cheese

DIRECTIONS

PREPARE pasta according to package directions.

HEAT sauce and crabmeat in large saucepan over medium heat until hot; add pasta. Heat through; top with cheese.

Estimated Times

Preparation: 5 mins

Cooking: 5 mins

Alfredo Sauce

Alfredo makes a great sauce on a pizza. Top a prebaked pizza-style crust with Alfredo sauce, sliced, fresh vegetables of your choosing, and shredded mozzarella cheese. Bake at 400° F for 10 to 15 minutes or until cheese is melted and lightly golden brown.

Try adding two slices of cooked, crumbled bacon to warmed Alfredo sauce for an instant carbonara sauce. Pair this sauce with just-cooked pasta and sprinkle with grated Parmesan cheese.

Add Alfredo sauce to vegetables like peas, carrots, and red or green bell peppers, and make a quick primavera sauce. Toss with just-cooked fettuccine and a light sprinkle of Parmesan cheese, and you'll turn out a dish that can't be beat. Visit Buitoni.com for more great recipe tips.

Angel Hair Pasta and Crab with Alfredo Sauce

Apricot-Glazed Pork Over Fettuccine

Sweet apricot nectar blended with soy sauce, sesame oil, and a hint of cinnamon makes this glazed pork a mouth-watering treat. Serve with honey-drizzled steamed carrots and pumpkin pie from your local grocer's bakery for dessert.

MAKES 4 SERVINGS

INGREDIENTS

1 can (11.5 fluid ounces) apricot nectar

¾ cup chicken broth

2 tablespoons soy sauce

2 tablespoons cornstarch

½ teaspoon lemon juice

½ teaspoon sesame oil

⅛ teaspoon ground cinnamon

1 tablespoon vegetable oil

1 pound pork tenderloin, cut into ¾-inch cubes

¼ cup all-purpose flour

1 package (9 ounces) BUITONI Refrigerated Fettuccine

DIRECTIONS

COMBINE nectar, broth, soy sauce, cornstarch, lemon juice, sesame oil, and cinnamon in small bowl; mix until smooth.

HEAT vegetable oil in medium skillet over medium heat. Dust pork with flour. Cook pork, stirring occasionally, until browned on all sides. Remove from skillet. Add nectar mixture to skillet, stirring to loosen browned bits. Bring to a boil. Reduce heat to low; add pork. Cover; cook for 10 minutes or until pork is thoroughly cooked and sauce is thickened.

PREPARE pasta according to package directions. Serve pork mixture over pasta.

Estimated Times
Preparation: 15 mins
Cooking: 20 mins

Apricot-Glazed Pork Over Fettuccine

Asian Peanut Sauce

Looking for something different? Serve this over pasta or chicken, or as a dipping sauce for apple slices or your favorite vegetables.

MAKES 2½ CUPS

INGREDIENTS

1 can (12 fluid ounces) NESTLÉ CARNATION Evaporated Milk

1 cup creamy peanut butter, divided

Asian Peanut Sauce

2 tablespoons chopped fresh cilantro

2 tablespoons chopped green onion

1 tablespoon lime juice

2 teaspoons granulated sugar

2 teaspoons soy sauce

1 to 3 teaspoons sesame oil

1 teaspoon garlic powder

1 teaspoon ground coriander

¼ teaspoon crushed red pepper or
   ground cayenne pepper (optional)

DIRECTIONS

PLACE evaporated milk, ½ cup peanut butter, cilantro, green onion, lime juice, sugar, soy sauce, oil, garlic powder, coriander, and crushed red pepper in blender; cover. Blend until smooth. Add remaining peanut butter; blend until smooth.

SERVE over pasta or chicken. Sprinkle with sesame seeds, if desired.

Estimated Time
Preparation: 10 mins

Baked Chicken Parmesan

Here's a top-notch trio of golden-crusted chicken, marinara sauce, and linguine!

MAKES 4 SERVINGS

INGREDIENTS

⅓ cup fine dry Italian-seasoned
   bread crumbs

¼ cup (1 ounce) grated Parmesan cheese

4 boneless, skinless chicken breast
   halves (about 1 pound total)

2 large eggs, beaten

2 teaspoons olive oil

½ cup (2 ounces) shredded reduced-fat
   mozzarella cheese

1 package (9 ounces) BUITONI
   Refrigerated Linguine

1 container (23.5 ounces)
   BUITONI Refrigerated Family
   Size Marinara Sauce

Fresh basil sprigs (optional)

DIRECTIONS

PREHEAT oven to 375° F. Lightly grease 8-inch-square baking dish.

COMBINE bread crumbs and Parmesan cheese in shallow dish. Dip chicken in eggs, then cover with bread crumb mixture. Arrange chicken in prepared baking dish. Drizzle with oil.

BAKE for 25 to 30 minutes or until chicken is tender and no longer pink in center. Sprinkle with mozzarella cheese. Bake for an additional 2 minutes or until cheese is melted.

PREPARE pasta according to package directions; drain. Heat sauce according to package directions. Toss pasta with sauce; divide among plates. Top with chicken. Garnish with basil.

Estimated Times
Preparation: 15 mins
Cooking: 30 mins

Marinara Sauce

Frozen meatballs or those purchased at the deli case can be added to marinara sauces. This saves time in the kitchen and tastes great over just-cooked fettuccine or linguine. Meatballs and sauce can also be spooned into toasted hero-style rolls and sprinkled with shredded mozzarella cheese for a meatball sandwich the kids will adore.

Grilled, broiled, or cooked vegetables topped with red sauces and shredded mozzarella cheese make an attractive side dish to any main meal. And, of course, red sauces always provide a great base for a pizza. Keep the pizza simple by just topping the sauce with shredded mozzarella cheese, or go one step further and add some vegetables, fully-cooked sausage, or pepperoni slices. Bake at 400° F for 10 to 15 minutes or until the cheese is melted and lightly golden. For more great ideas visit us at Buitoni.com.

Baked Dijon Chicken

Dijon mustard and Parmesan cheese give this oven-fried chicken a flavorful combination.

MAKES 4 SERVINGS

INGREDIENTS
Nonstick cooking spray
¼ cup Dijon mustard
¼ cup NESTLÉ CARNATION Evaporated Fat Free Milk
¼ cup plain, dry bread crumbs
¼ cup (1 ounce) grated Parmesan cheese
4 boneless, skinless chicken breast halves (about 1 pound total)

DIRECTIONS
PREHEAT oven to 475° F. Spray 13 x 9-inch baking dish with nonstick cooking spray.

COMBINE mustard and evaporated milk in shallow bowl. Combine bread crumbs and cheese in separate shallow bowl. Dip chicken into mustard mixture, coating both sides, then into bread crumb mixture. Place in prepared dish.

BAKE for 15 to 20 minutes or until chicken is golden brown and no longer pink in center.

Estimated Times
Preparation: 10 mins
Cooking: 15 mins

Baked Mini Ravioli 'n' Sauce

Bite-sized and savory, our mini ravioli pair wonderfully with hearty tomato sauce. Baked beneath a delicate mantle of shredded mozzarella, these little pasta pillows form the basis for a rib-sticking meal. Enjoy with warm breadsticks.

Baked Mini Ravioli 'n' Sauce

MAKES 2 SERVINGS

INGREDIENTS

1 container (15 ounces) BUITONI
   Refrigerated Marinara Sauce
1 package (7 ounces) BUITONI
   Refrigerated Three Cheese Mini
   Ravioli, prepared according to
   package directions
½ cup (2 ounces) shredded
   mozzarella cheese

DIRECTIONS

PREHEAT oven to 400° F. Grease
2-quart casserole.

COMBINE sauce and pasta in prepared
casserole; sprinkle with cheese.

BAKE for 12 to 14 minutes or until
cheese is melted.

FOR FREEZE AHEAD:

PREPARE as above; add 1 additional
container (15 ounces) BUITONI
Refrigerated Marinara Sauce. Cover;
freeze for up to 2 months. Thaw
overnight in refrigerator.

PREHEAT oven to 400° F.

BAKE, covered, for 25 to 35 minutes.

Estimated Times
Preparation: 10 mins
Cooking: 12 mins

About Cooking Pasta

Here are some tricks in cooking pasta
perfectly every time. A good rule of
thumb is to use one quart of water
for every four ounces of pasta. Fill a
pot to about three-fourths full with
water and bring to a boil over high
heat on the stovetop. When the
water is rapidly boiling, add the
pasta with about a teaspoon of salt,
if desired. Stir constantly at the
beginning—this is where you find
stickiness if the pasta is not stirred
enough. The water should continue
to boil while cooking the pasta, and
continue to stir from time to time.
You do not need to cover the pasta
with a lid.

The cooking time depends on
the type and package directions.
Dried pasta can take between 8 to
13 minutes, but it's best to test
some noodles during the cooking
time to ensure success. You should
try to cook until al dente, which
means the pasta should be soft
but have a slight bite on your
teeth at the middle. Once, it's done,
pour into a colander to drain. And
then, Mangiamo!

Baked Parmesan Fish with Pasta

Baked Parmesan Fish with Pasta

You don't have to be 'nervous' about serving fish to guests with this 'no-fail' recipe. Fish fillets are baked separately, placed on top of pasta, and covered with a mushroom medley.

MAKES 4 SERVINGS

INGREDIENTS
⅓ cup grated fat free Parmesan cheese
1 teaspoon all-purpose flour
3 thyme sprigs, leaves removed
   and crushed
4 white fish fillets (6 ounces each)
1 package (9 ounces) BUITONI
   Refrigerated Angel Hair Pasta
1 medium onion, chopped

1 cup halved mushroom caps
½ cup finely sliced green onions
2 cloves garlic, crushed

DIRECTIONS
PREHEAT oven to 350° F.

PLACE cheese, flour, and thyme in paper bag. Individually coat fish by gently shaking in bag; discard coating ingredients. Place fish in baking pan with rack.

BAKE for 20 minutes or until fish flakes easily when tested with a fork.

PREPARE pasta according to package directions.

HEAT large, nonstick skillet over medium-high heat. Add onion, mushrooms, green onions, and garlic. Cook, stirring frequently, until onions are tender. Season with salt and ground black pepper.

PLACE pasta on oven-warmed plates. Attractively arrange fish over pasta. Serve with mushroom medley over fish and pasta. Garnish with fresh thyme, if desired.

COOKING TIP
You can easily adapt this unique baked fish recipe to include most firm, white fish fillets, including swordfish, sole, halibut, or red snapper.

Estimated Times
Preparation: 15 mins
Cooking: 25 mins

Baked Pesto Chicken

This is a great dish for entertaining. Not only is it easy, but it's tasty, too.

MAKES 4 SERVINGS

INGREDIENTS

4 boneless, skinless chicken breast
   halves (about 1 pound total)
½ cup BUITONI Refrigerated Pesto
   with Basil
2 plum tomatoes, sliced (optional)
¾ cup (3 ounces) shredded
   mozzarella cheese

DIRECTIONS

PREHEAT oven to 400° F. Line baking
sheet with heavy-duty foil.

PLACE chicken and pesto in medium
bowl; toss to coat. Place chicken
on prepared baking sheet.

BAKE for 20 to 25 minutes or until
chicken is no longer pink in center.
Remove from oven; top with tomatoes
and cheese. Bake for an additional 3 to
5 minutes or until cheese is melted.

Estimated Times
Preparation: 5 mins
Cooking: 25 mins

Baked Pesto Chicken

Pesto Cooking Tip

Try BUITONI Refrigerated Pesto
Sauce on mashed potatoes and
you'll create a whole new look and
flavor. And, if you are in the mood
for a creamy pesto sauce, try adding
a little whipping cream. Toss creamy
pesto with just-cooked pasta and top
with grated Parmesan cheese.

Baked Pork Chops with Corn Stuffing

This dish simmers gently in the oven, allowing you more time to spend with the family.

MAKES 4 SERVINGS

INGREDIENTS

1 package (12 ounces) STOUFFER'S frozen Corn Soufflé, defrosted*
¼ cup water
1 tablespoon margarine or butter
1½ cups plain stuffing mix
4 (about ½-inch-thick) pork loin chops (about 2 pounds total)
1 tablespoon vegetable oil
¼ cup reduced-sodium chicken broth or water

DIRECTIONS

PREHEAT oven to 375° F.

COMBINE water and margarine in medium saucepan; bring to a boil. Remove from heat; stir in stuffing mix and corn soufflé.

SEASON pork with salt and ground black pepper. Heat oil in large skillet over medium-high heat. Add pork; cook on each side for 3 to 4 minutes or until golden brown. Place in 9-inch-square baking dish. Pour broth around pork. Spoon stuffing mixture over each pork chop; cover.

BAKE for 30 minutes. Uncover; bake for an additional 10 to 15 minutes or until stuffing is lightly browned and pork is no longer pink in center.

*DEFROST corn soufflé in microwave on MEDIUM (50%) power for 6 to 7 minutes.

Estimated Times
Preparation: 15 mins
Cooking: 50 mins

Baked Shells with Chicken and Mushrooms

Serve with fresh fruit garnished with mint and NESTLÉ TOLL HOUSE brownies for dessert. Try using bow-tie-shaped farfalle pasta for a more elegant look.

MAKES 8 SERVINGS

INGREDIENTS

1 pound dry medium shell pasta
2 containers (10 ounces each) BUITONI Refrigerated Portabello Mushroom Alfredo Sauce
2 cups cooked diced chicken
1 cup frozen peas, thawed
2 cans (4 ounces each) sliced mushrooms, drained
¼ cup (1 ounce) grated Parmesan cheese
¼ cup dry bread crumbs

Baked Shells with Chicken and Mushrooms

PREHEAT oven to 350° F.

PREPARE pasta according to package directions.

COMBINE pasta, sauce, chicken, peas, and mushrooms in large bowl; spoon into 2-quart baking dish. Combine cheese and bread crumbs in small bowl; sprinkle over pasta mixture.

BAKE for 20 minutes.

Estimated Times
Preparation: 10 mins
Cooking: 30 mins

Baked Ziti with Italian Sausage

A chunky marinara sauce, Italian sausage, and mushrooms make the perfect combination with pasta and fennel seeds. A crisp green salad and garlic bread round out a savory Italian-style dish!

MAKES 4 SERVINGS

INGREDIENTS

8 ounces dry ziti pasta
2 teaspoons olive oil
12 ounces mild Italian sausage links, casings removed
6 ounces sliced mushrooms

Baked Ziti with Italian Sausage

¼ teaspoon fennel seed (optional)
2 containers (15 ounces each) BUITONI Refrigerated Marinara Sauce
1½ cups (6 ounces) shredded mozzarella cheese
2 tablespoons grated Parmesan or Romano cheese

DIRECTIONS

PREHEAT oven to 400° F. Grease 13 x 9-inch baking dish.

PREPARE pasta according to package directions.

HEAT oil in large saucepan over medium-high heat. Add sausage; cook, stirring frequently, until no longer pink. Drain. Add mushrooms and fennel; cook, stirring frequently, until mushrooms are tender. Add sauce; cook, stirring occasionally, until heated through. Remove from heat.

ADD pasta to sauce mixture; toss well to coat. Spoon into prepared baking dish; sprinkle evenly with mozzarella cheese and Parmesan cheese.

BAKE for 15 to 17 minutes or until cheese is bubbly. Cool for 5 minutes before serving.

FOR FREEZE AHEAD:
PREPARE as above; do not bake. Cover; freeze for up to 2 months. Thaw overnight in refrigerator.

PREHEAT oven to 400° F.

BAKE for 25 to 35 minutes or until cheese is bubbly. Cool for 5 minutes before serving.

Estimated Times
Preparation: 10 mins
Cooking: 35 mins
Cooling: 5 mins

Beef and Asparagus Stir-Fry

For those who are busy and health-conscious, stir-frying is the solution! You cook with a minimal amount of fat in a minimal amount of time.

MAKES 4 SERVINGS

INGREDIENTS

½ cup water

2 tablespoons reduced-sodium soy sauce

2 teaspoons MAGGI Instant Beef
  Flavor Bouillon

2 teaspoons cornstarch

1 tablespoon vegetable oil

1 pound fresh asparagus, cut into
  2-inch pieces

12 ounces boneless beef sirloin,
  trimmed and thinly sliced

1 small yellow, red, or green bell
  pepper, chopped

1 small onion, thinly sliced

½ cup carrot strips

2 cups (6 ounces) sliced fresh mushrooms

2 green onions, sliced

Hot cooked rice

DIRECTIONS

COMBINE water, soy sauce, bouillon, and cornstarch in small bowl.

HEAT oil in large skillet over medium-high heat. Add asparagus, beef, bell pepper, onion, and carrot. Cook, stirring frequently, until beef is no longer pink.

ADD mushrooms and green onions; cook until tender. Stir in soy sauce mixture; cook, stirring constantly, until sauce comes to a boil and thickens. Serve over rice. Season with ground black pepper.

Estimated Times
Preparation: 15 mins
Cooking: 15 mins

Beef Penne Pasta Casserole

This casserole with pasta and beef is sure to become a family favorite. It's also easy to prepare ahead and freeze for up to two months. When you're looking for a quick meal, just put it in the oven to bake.

MAKES 6 SERVINGS

INGREDIENTS

1 pound dry penne pasta

8 ounces lean ground beef

1 small onion, chopped

2 cups water

2 cans (6 ounces each) Italian
  tomato paste

⅓ cup red wine or water

1 tablespoon MAGGI Instant Beef
  Flavor Bouillon

2 cups (8 ounces) shredded Monterey
  Jack cheese

DIRECTIONS

PREHEAT oven to 350° F.

PREPARE pasta according to package directions.

COOK beef and onion in large saucepan over medium-high heat, stirring occasionally, until beef is no longer pink. Add water, tomato paste, wine, and bouillon. Cook, stirring occasionally, for 10 to 15 minutes or until flavors are blended.

LAYER ingredients as follows in ungreased 13 x 9-inch baking dish: half pasta, half sauce, and half cheese. Repeat layers; cover.

BAKE for 20 to 25 minutes or until heated through and cheese is melted. Season with salt.

FOR FREEZE AHEAD:
PREPARE as above; do not bake. Cover; freeze for up to 2 months. Thaw overnight in refrigerator.

PREHEAT oven to 350° F.

Beef Penne Pasta Casserole

BAKE for 45 to 55 minutes or until heated through and cheese is melted. Season with salt.

Estimated Times
Preparation: 20 mins
Cooking: 35 mins

Beef Stroganoff

This will easily become one of your family's favorites.

MAKES 4 SERVINGS

INGREDIENTS

1½ pounds beef tenderloin tips or boneless skirt steak, cut into thin strips
1 tablespoon olive oil
2 tablespoons butter
¼ cup finely chopped shallots or red onion
1 package (6 ounces) sliced fresh mushrooms
3 cloves garlic, finely chopped
2 MAGGI Beef Flavor Bouillon Cubes
2 tablespoons cognac
¾ cup sour cream
1 tablespoon Dijon mustard
Hot cooked noodles
1 tablespoon chopped fresh dill (optional)

DIRECTIONS

PAT beef dry with paper towels. Sprinkle with salt and ground black pepper.

HEAT oil in large skillet over high heat. Working in batches, add beef in a single layer and cook until no longer pink. Transfer to bowl. Repeat with remaining beef.

MELT butter in same skillet over medium-high heat. Add shallots; cook, stirring occasionally, for 2 minutes or just until golden. Stir in mushrooms and garlic; cover. Cook, stirring occasionally, for 4 minutes or until mushrooms are tender.

DISSOLVE bouillon in 1½ cups hot water.

STIR in bouillon mixture and cognac. Bring to a boil; reduce heat to medium. Cook for 10 minutes or until liquid is almost reduced by half. Stir in sour cream, mustard and beef; heat through. Serve over noodles; garnish with dill.

Estimated Times
Preparation: 15 mins
Cooking: 25 mins

Beef Tips & Noodles

Grandma would be proud of these. Serve with oven-roasted vegetables. Finish your meal with a freshly baked pumpkin pie.

MAKES 6 SERVINGS

INGREDIENTS

2 teaspoons NESCAFÉ TASTER'S CHOICE 100% Pure Instant Coffee Granules, dissolved in 1 cup hot water
¼ cup olive oil
3 pounds beef tri-tip, cut into bite-sized pieces, seasoned with salt and ground black pepper
¼ cup all-purpose flour
2 cups sliced onions
3 cloves garlic, finely chopped
½ cup red wine
½ cup water
½ teaspoon dried rosemary
½ teaspoon crushed dried oregano
Hot cooked noodles

DIRECTIONS

HEAT oil in large, heavy-duty saucepan over medium-high heat. Toss beef and flour together in large bowl; add to saucepan. Cook, stirring frequently, until beef is no longer pink. Add onions and garlic. Cook for 5 minutes. Add coffee, wine, water, rosemary, and oregano to saucepan. Stir and scrape pan bottom to loosen any browned bits of meat. Bring to a boil. Reduce heat to low; cover.

COOK for 80 to 90 minutes or until meat is tender. Serve over noodles. Season with salt and ground black pepper.

Estimated Times
Preparation: 15 mins
Cooking: 1 hr, 40 mins

About Nescafé

In 1937, Nestlé food scientists perfected a more convenient coffee product that was introduced in 1938 under the brand name Nescafé—the world's first commercially successful instant coffee.

It became so popular during World War II that for one full year the entire output of the Nescafé plant in the United States (more than 1 million cases) was reserved for military use only.

Since then, Nescafé has become one of the world's best-known brands. Visit us at Nescafeusa.com for more coffee recipe ideas.

Broccoli & Pasta

Broccoli & Pasta

Serve this simple pasta with French dinner rolls for a simple and elegant dinner.

MAKES 3 SERVINGS

INGREDIENTS

¼ cup olive oil
2½ cups fresh broccoli florets
3 large cloves garlic, finely chopped
¼ teaspoon crushed red pepper
1 package (9 ounces) BUITONI Refrigerated Fettuccine
⅓ cup grated Romano cheese

DIRECTIONS

HEAT oil in large skillet over medium-high heat. Add broccoli, garlic, and crushed red pepper. Cook, stirring frequently, until broccoli is crisp-tender.

PREPARE pasta according to package directions. Add pasta to broccoli mixture; toss to coat well. Sprinkle with cheese; toss lightly. Serve immediately.

Broccoli Pesto Angel Hair

Serve with tomato slices and warm garlic bread.

MAKES 4 SERVINGS

INGREDIENTS

1 cup hot water
2 MAGGI Chicken Flavor Bouillon Cubes
1 package (16 ounces) frozen chopped broccoli, prepared according to package directions
¼ cup (1 ounce) grated Romano or Parmesan cheese
¼ cup fresh basil leaves
2 tablespoons olive oil
2 large cloves garlic, peeled

Broccoli Pesto Angel Hair

Cheese Ravioli with Pumpkin Sage Sauce

1 package (9 ounces) BUITONI
Refrigerated Angel Hair Pasta

DIRECTIONS

COMBINE water and bouillon
in small bowl; stir to dissolve.

PLACE broccoli, bouillon mixture,
cheese, basil, oil, and garlic in food
processor or blender; cover. Process
until smooth.

PREPARE pasta according to package
directions. Toss broccoli pesto with
pasta. Season with coarsely ground
black pepper.

Estimated Times
Preparation: 15 mins
Cooking: 5 mins

Cheese Ravioli with Pumpkin Sage Sauce

**Alfredo sauce, luscious pumpkin, and
four cheese ravioli make a festive
and savory dish seasoned with white
wine, shallots, and fresh sage. Soft
breadsticks, and a crisp green salad
add contrast and flavor.**

MAKES 4 SERVINGS

INGREDIENTS
½ cup dry white wine
¼ cup chopped shallots
1 container (10 ounces) BUITONI
Refrigerated Alfredo Sauce
½ cup LIBBY'S 100% Pure Pumpkin
1 tablespoon chopped fresh sage (or
1 teaspoon ground sage)

2 packages (9 ounces each) BUITONI
Refrigerated Four Cheese Ravioli
2 tablespoons chopped green onion

DIRECTIONS

COOK wine and shallots in medium
saucepan over medium heat, stirring
occasionally, until reduced to about
1 tablespoon. Stir in sauce, pumpkin,
and sage. Cook, stirring occasionally,
until heated through.

PREPARE pasta according to package
directions; drain, reserving ¼ cup
cooking water. Stir reserved water
into sauce; toss with pasta. Sprinkle
with green onion. Season with
ground black pepper.

Estimated Times
Preparation: 10 mins
Cooking: 15 mins

Fresh sauces taste great on pastas, but why not try sauces on other convenient or homemade items for something a little different?

For something new try combining pizza with burgers by placing fully cooked hamburger patties on hamburger buns and top with marinara sauce and shredded mozzarella cheese.

From your local deli case, pick up some fully cooked, breaded veal patties or chicken cutlets. Top with marinara sauce and shredded mozzarella cheese. Bake at 375° F for 15 to 20 minutes. Your family will ask for this dish again and again. And, for an added bonus to a main meal, try baked potatoes Italian-style with marinara sauce and cheese as toppings.

Cheese-Stuffed Shells in Marinara Sauce

A traditional Italian-style favorite is made easier for you! Combine BUITONI Refrigerated Marinara Sauce with stuffed shells, add a tossed salad and warm bread, and sit down to a satisfying meal!

MAKES 6 SERVINGS

INGREDIENTS

12 dry jumbo pasta shells
1 cup (4 ounces) shredded reduced-fat mozzarella cheese, divided
1 cup fat-free or reduced-fat ricotta cheese
½ cup (2 ounces) grated Parmesan cheese
1 large egg
¼ teaspoon ground black pepper
1 container (15 ounces) BUITONI Refrigerated Marinara Sauce

DIRECTIONS

PREHEAT oven to 350° F.

PREPARE pasta shells according to package directions.

COMBINE ¾ cup mozzarella cheese, ricotta cheese, Parmesan cheese, egg, and pepper in medium bowl. Stuff each shell evenly with cheese mixture; place in ungreased 12 x 7½-inch baking dish. Pour sauce over shells.

BAKE for 25 minutes or until bubbly. Top with remaining mozzarella cheese. Bake for an additional 5 minutes or until cheese is melted.

FOR FREEZE AHEAD:

PREPARE as above; do not bake. Do not top with remaining mozzarella cheese. Cover; freeze for up to 2 months. Thaw overnight in refrigerator.

PREHEAT oven to 350° F.

BAKE for 30 to 40 minutes. Top with remaining mozzarella cheese. Bake for an additional 5 minutes or until cheese is melted.

Estimated Times
Preparation: 20 mins
Cooking: 40 mins

Cheesy Beef and Green Chile Rice

Here's a super-quick skillet meal that's perfect for those evenings when time is at a premium. Serve with a prepackaged salad and a loaf of warm, crusty bread.

MAKES 4 SERVINGS

Cheesy Beef and Green Chile Rice

About Nestlé

Nestlé, with headquarters in Vevey, Switzerland, was founded in 1867 by Henri Nestlé and is today the world's largest food and beverage company. The company employs nearly 247,000 people and has factories or operations in almost every country in the world. The company's main priority is to bring the best and most relevant products to people, wherever they are, whatever their needs, throughout their lives.

INGREDIENTS

1 can (14.5 fluid ounces) beef broth

½ cup chopped onion

2 cups instant rice

1 package (10 ounces) STOUFFER'S
frozen Welsh Rarebit, defrosted*

1 pound ground beef, cooked
and drained

1 can (14.5 ounces) Mexican-style
diced tomatoes

1 can (4 ounces) diced green chiles,
drained

½ cup ketchup

DIRECTIONS

COMBINE broth and onion in medium skillet; bring to a boil. Add rice; cover. Turn off heat. Let stand for 5 minutes.

ADD Welsh rarebit, beef, tomatoes, chiles, and ketchup. Cook over low heat for 5 to 10 minutes or until hot and thickened. Add salt and ground black pepper to taste.

*DEFROST Welsh rarebit in microwave on MEDIUM (50%) power for 5 to 6 minutes.

Estimated Times

Preparation: 15 mins

Cooking: 10 mins

Standing: 5 mins

Cheesy Chicken Florentine

The classic Chicken Florentine is named for the Italian city of Florence. Dishes a la *Fiorentina* feature chicken (or sometimes fish) on a bed of spinach leaves. The dish is dressed in a creamy white sauce mixed with cheese. This casserole will transport your family to this timeless city in Italy.

MAKES 6 SERVINGS

INGREDIENTS

2 packages (12 ounces each) STOUFFER'S frozen Spinach Soufflé, defrosted*

2 tablespoons vegetable oil

6 boneless, skinless chicken breast halves (about 1½ pounds total)

2 cups cooked white rice

1 cup milk

1 cup (4 ounces) shredded Swiss cheese, divided

¼ cup chopped onion

2 teaspoons Dijon mustard

½ teaspoon salt

1 cup coarse fresh bread crumbs

2 tablespoons butter or margarine, melted

DIRECTIONS

PREHEAT oven to 375° F.

HEAT oil in large, nonstick skillet over medium-high heat. Season chicken with salt and ground black pepper. Cook chicken, turning once, until both sides are golden brown.

COMBINE spinach soufflé, rice, milk, ½ cup cheese, onion, mustard, and salt in large bowl; stir well. Spread onto bottom of 13 x 9-inch baking pan; place chicken on top of spinach mixture. Combine bread crumbs, butter, and remaining cheese in small bowl. Sprinkle mixture evenly over casserole. Cover.

BAKE for 25 minutes; uncover. Bake for an additional 35 to 40 minutes or until spinach mixture is set and chicken is no longer pink in center.

*DEFROST spinach soufflé in microwave on MEDIUM (50%) power for 6 to 7 minutes.

Estimated Times

Preparation: 20 mins
Cooking: 1 hr, 5 mins

Cheesy Macaroni and Cheese

Cheesy Macaroni and Cheese

Children and adults alike will love this classic.

**MAKES 6 ENTRÉE SERVINGS OR
8 SIDE DISH SERVINGS**

INGREDIENTS

2 cups dry small elbow macaroni or shells
¼ cup (½ stick) butter or margarine,
    cut into pieces
1 can (12 fluid ounces) NESTLÉ
    CARNATION Evaporated Milk
2 large eggs
1 teaspoon dry mustard
½ teaspoon ground white pepper
2 cups (8 ounces) shredded
    cheddar cheese
1 cup (4 ounces) American cheese,
    cut into pieces

DIRECTIONS

PREHEAT oven to 350° F.

PREPARE pasta according to package directions. Return to saucepan. Add butter; stir until melted.

WHISK together evaporated milk, eggs, mustard, and pepper in medium bowl. Add to pasta mixture; stir. Add cheddar and American cheeses; stir. Cook over low heat, stirring constantly, until cheese begins to melt. Pour into 1½-quart casserole dish.

BAKE for 10 minutes; stir. Bake for an additional 20 to 25 minutes or until bubbly and top is lightly golden. Season with salt.

FOR FREEZE AHEAD:
PREPARE as above; do not bake. Cover; freeze for up to 2 months. Thaw overnight in refrigerator.

PREHEAT oven to 350° F.

BAKE, uncovered, stirring halfway through, for 45 to 50 minutes or until bubbly and top is lightly golden. Season with salt.

Estimated Times
Preparation: 15 mins
Cooking: 45 mins

Cheesy Tuna and Rice Dish

Why get hung up on noodles? This tuna casserole with rice is fabulous!

MAKES 6 SERVINGS

INGREDIENTS

⅓ cup butter
1 small onion, chopped
3 tablespoons all-purpose flour
¼ teaspoon salt
⅛ teaspoon ground black pepper

1 can (12 fluid ounces) NESTLÉ
    CARNATION Evaporated Milk
1½ cups (6 ounces) shredded
    cheddar cheese
2 tablespoons grated Parmesan cheese
1 can (14½ ounces) whole tomatoes,
    drained, and cut in half
1 cup instant rice
1 tablespoon chopped parsley
½ teaspoon paprika
½ teaspoon dried oregano
¼ teaspoon cayenne pepper
2 cans (6 ounces each) tuna packed
    in water, drained

DIRECTIONS

PREHEAT oven to 375° F.

MELT butter in medium saucepan over medium heat. Add onion; cook for 5 minutes. Blend in flour, salt, and black pepper. Stir in evaporated milk. Cook, stirring constantly, until mixture comes just to a boil. Stir in cheddar cheese and Parmesan cheese until melted.

COMBINE tomatoes, rice, parsley, paprika, oregano, and cayenne pepper in 11 x 7-inch baking dish. Top with tuna. Spread cheese sauce over tuna.

BAKE for 20 to 25 minutes or until edges are bubbly.

Estimated Times
Preparation: 15 mins
Cooking: 30 mins

Chicken à la King

Hearty and comforting, Chicken à la King goes equally well over pasta or rice. A healthy alternative to fried chicken.

MAKES 4 SERVINGS

INGREDIENTS

3 tablespoons butter or margarine

1 cup (about 3 ounces) sliced fresh mushrooms

¼ cup chopped green bell pepper

¼ cup chopped onion

2 tablespoons all-purpose flour

½ teaspoon salt

½ teaspoon paprika

2 cans (12 fluid ounces each) NESTLÉ CARNATION Evaporated Milk

3 large egg yolks, beaten

2 cups cooked, chopped chicken breast meat

2 tablespoons diced pimiento (optional)

2 tablespoons dry sherry (optional)

8 refrigerated biscuits, prepared according to package directions

DIRECTIONS

MELT butter in large skillet over medium heat. Add mushrooms, bell pepper, and onion. Cook, stirring occasionally, for 1 to 2 minutes or until tender but not brown. Stir in flour, salt, and paprika. Gradually add evaporated milk. Cook, stirring constantly, until mixture comes to a boil.

WHISK 1 cup thickened sauce into egg yolks; pour into saucepan. Cook, stirring constantly, until mixture comes to a boil. Stir in chicken, pimiento, and sherry. Heat through.

SERVE immediately over hot biscuits.

Chicken à la King

Estimated Times
Preparation: 20 mins
Cooking: 15 mins

Chicken and Rice Casserole with Zesty Cheese

This casserole is the perfect comfort food. It comes together quickly and will satisfy the whole family.

MAKES 4 SERVINGS

INGREDIENTS

2 cups water

3 MAGGI Chicken Flavor Bouillon Cubes

¾ cup long-grain white rice

2 tablespoons butter or margarine

3 cups cooked, chopped chicken breast meat (about 3 boneless, skinless chicken breast halves)

2 cups (8 ounces) shredded Monterey Jack cheese with jalapeños

1 can (12 fluid ounces) NESTLÉ CARNATION Evaporated Milk

½ cup finely chopped red onion

2 large eggs, lightly beaten

3 tablespoons chopped fresh cilantro

DIRECTIONS

PREHEAT oven to 350° F. Lightly grease 2-quart casserole dish.

Chicken and Rice Casserole with Zesty Cheese

BRING water and bouillon to a boil in medium saucepan. Add rice and butter; cover. Reduce heat to low; cook for 15 to 20 minutes or until rice is almost tender and most of liquid is absorbed.

COMBINE prepared rice, chicken, cheese, evaporated milk, onion, eggs, and cilantro in prepared casserole. Stir well.

BAKE for 40 to 45 minutes or until bubbly and edges are golden.

Estimated Times
Preparation: 20 mins
Cooking: 1 hr

Chicken, Fettuccine, and Sun-Dried Tomatoes

BUITONI refrigerated pasta cooks in a flash! Whip up this dish and your family will think you are a magician in the kitchen. A warm and crusty loaf of bread rounds out this quick meal.

MAKES 4 SERVINGS

INGREDIENTS
2 packages (9 ounces each) BUITONI Refrigerated Fettuccine
4 boneless, skinless chicken breast halves (about 1 pound total), cooked and sliced into strips
¾ cup Italian salad dressing, divided
3 cups chopped, cooked vegetables
¾ cup sliced sun-dried tomatoes in olive oil, drained
½ cup (2 ounces) grated Parmesan cheese

DIRECTIONS
PREPARE pasta according to package directions.

HEAT chicken strips and ¼ cup dressing in medium saucepan over medium heat until warm; toss with pasta, remaining dressing, vegetables, tomatoes, and cheese. Season with salt and ground black pepper.

Estimated Times
Preparation: 20 mins
Cooking: 10 mins

Chicken, Fettuccine, and Sun-Dried Tomatoes

Chicken in Creamy Tomato Sauce with Linguine

Need a quick, delicious recipe for dinner? Simply add some fat free half-and-half to BUITONI Refrigerated Marinara Sauce to lighten the flavor of this traditional dish.

MAKES 4 SERVINGS

INGREDIENTS

1 package (9 ounces) BUITONI
  Refrigerated Linguine
1 tablespoon olive or vegetable oil
4 boneless, skinless chicken breast
  halves (about 1 pound total), cut
  into ½-inch strips
2 containers (15 ounces each) BUITONI
  Refrigerated Marinara Sauce
½ cup fat free half-and-half
Shredded Parmesan cheese (optional)
Chopped fresh parsley (optional)

DIRECTIONS

PREPARE pasta according to package directions.

HEAT oil in large, nonstick skillet over medium-high heat. Add chicken; season with salt and ground black pepper. Cook for 4 to 5 minutes or until no longer pink. Remove from skillet.

POUR sauce into same skillet; cook until heated through (do not boil). Add chicken and half-and-half; stir well. Cook, stirring occasionally, for 2 to 3 minutes or until heated through.

TOSS with pasta. Sprinkle with cheese and parsley.

Chicken in Creamy Tomato Sauce with Linguine

Estimated Times
Preparation: 15 mins
Cooking: 10 mins

Chicken in Tarragon-Cheese Sauce

Tarragon evokes the sweetness of Spring with its subtly licorice-scented leaves. Combined with whipped cream cheese and tender bits of chicken breast, this tarragon mixture is perfect served over fresh strands of linguine.

MAKES 4 SERVINGS

INGREDIENTS

2 tablespoons olive oil
4 boneless, skinless chicken breast
  halves (about 1 pound total), cut
  into bite-sized pieces
¼ cup finely chopped shallots
1 can (12 fluid ounces) NESTLÉ
  CARNATION Evaporated Milk
½ cup whipped cream cheese
⅓ cup grated Parmesan cheese
1 tablespoon chopped fresh tarragon
  (or 1 teaspoon dried tarragon)
1½ teaspoons salt
1½ teaspoons coarse ground
  black pepper
1 package (9 ounces) BUITONI
  Refrigerated Linguine

Chicken in Tarragon-Cheese Sauce

DIRECTIONS

HEAT oil in large skillet over medium-high heat. Add chicken; cook, stirring occasionally, until chicken is no longer pink. Remove from skillet; keep warm.

ADD shallots to skillet; stir, scraping up brown bits on bottom. Cook, stirring constantly, until shallots are tender. Whisk in evaporated milk, cream cheese, Parmesan cheese, tarragon, salt, and pepper. Cook, whisking constantly, until sauce thickens slightly. Stir in chicken; cook until heated through.

PREPARE pasta according to package directions. Pour sauce over pasta; serve immediately.

Estimated Times
Preparation: 10 mins
Cooking: 20 mins

Baking Cocoa

Rich in flavor and Nestlé Toll House heritage, baking cocoa is one of Nestlé's tried and true baking ingredients for the perfect addition to any recipe.

Made out of 100 percent cocoa, this baking product provides a smooth, rich chocolate taste in home-baked desserts, frostings, a variety of food dishes, and beverages. The secret of the smooth, rich flavor lies in the special blending of cocoa beans.

For more fun with baking cocoa, try gently sprinkling it over your favorite dessert, or on the rim of a dessert plate. And, to make sure it is always fresh, use it within two years of its purchase date.

Chicken Mole

Legend says that *mole* was created by the nuns of a Mexican convent for a visit by the Spanish Viceroy. Combining New World ingredients such as peanuts and cocoa with European technique, they created the rich and tasty *Mole Poblano*, named for the city of Puebla.

MAKES 8 SERVINGS

INGREDIENTS
2 tablespoons vegetable oil
4 pounds chicken parts
1 small onion, chopped
1 clove garlic, finely chopped
1 jar (24 ounces) chunky salsa
1 cup chicken broth
3 tablespoons chili powder
2 to 3 tablespoons creamy peanut butter
2 tablespoons NESTLÉ TOLL HOUSE Baking Cocoa
8 cups cooked long-grain white rice (optional)
½ cup chopped fresh parsley (optional)

DIRECTIONS
HEAT oil in large skillet over medium-high heat. Add chicken; cook, turning frequently, for 4 to 6 minutes or until browned on all sides. Remove from skillet. Add onion and garlic to skillet. Cook, stirring constantly, for 2 to 3 minutes or until onion is tender.

STIR in salsa, broth, chili powder, peanut butter, and cocoa. Bring to a boil. Reduce heat to medium-low. Add chicken; cook for 20 to 25 minutes or until chicken is no longer pink near bones.

COMBINE rice and parsley in medium bowl. Serve with Chicken Mole.

Estimated Times
Preparation: 20 mins
Cooking: 30 mins

Chicken Paella

This is a complete meal in itself. Perfect for parties. Invite some friends over and have them pitch in!

MAKES 4 SERVINGS

INGREDIENTS
1 tablespoon vegetable oil
4 boneless, skinless chicken breast halves (about 1 pound total)
1 cup (about 3 ounces) sliced fresh mushrooms
¾ cup long-grain white rice
¾ cup chopped onion
1 clove garlic, finely chopped
2 cups water
2 MAGGI Chicken Flavor Bouillon Cubes
½ teaspoon Italian herb seasoning
⅛ teaspoon ground saffron or turmeric
1½ cups loose-pack frozen peas
¼ cup sliced roasted red bell pepper or pimiento

DIRECTIONS

HEAT oil in large skillet over medium-high heat. Add chicken; cook on each side until golden brown and no longer pink in center. Remove from skillet; keep warm. Add mushrooms, rice, onion, and garlic to skillet. Cook, stirring occasionally, until rice is golden brown.

COMBINE water and bouillon in liquid measuring cup. Stir into rice mixture. Add herb seasoning and saffron. Bring to a boil; reduce heat to medium. Cover; cook for 20 to 25 minutes or until rice is tender. Stir in peas and roasted pepper. Spoon rice mixture into 4 individual casserole dishes; top each with a chicken breast. Sprinkle with grated Parmesan cheese, if desired.

FOR FREEZE AHEAD:
PREPARE as above; do not top with Parmesan cheese. Cover; freeze for up to 4 months.

PREHEAT oven to 350° F.

BAKE for 1 hour or until heated through. Or, cover with plastic wrap and microwave on MEDIUM-HIGH (70%) power, rearranging once. Microwave for 8 to 10 minutes for 1 casserole and 13 to 16 minutes for 2 casseroles. Sprinkle with grated Parmesan cheese, if desired.

Estimated Times
Preparation: 15 mins
Cooking: 35 mins

Chicken Piccata

A warm and satisfying meal. Easy to prepare when you're in a rush and everyone is hungry.

MAKES 4 SERVINGS

INGREDIENTS

1 pound chicken cutlets
¼ cup all-purpose flour
¼ cup (½ stick) butter, divided
½ cup dry white wine
2 tablespoons lemon juice
1 clove garlic, finely chopped
1 MAGGI Chicken Flavor Bouillon Cube
1 tablespoon capers
Chopped parsley (optional)

DIRECTIONS

COAT chicken cutlets with flour. Melt 2 tablespoons butter in large skillet over medium-high heat. Add chicken; cook, turning halfway through, for 5 minutes or until lightly browned and tender. Remove to platter; keep warm.

ADD remaining butter to skillet. Stir in wine, lemon juice, garlic, and bouillon. Bring to a boil; cook for 3 to 5 minutes or until sauce is slightly thickened. Stir in capers. Spoon sauce over chicken. Sprinkle with parsley.

Estimated Times
Preparation: 10 mins
Cooking: 15 mins

Nutrition Tip

Parents and kids today are always on the go. Between trips to school, work, and scheduled activities, there seems to be less and less time to prepare nutritious snacks. But a busy lifestyle doesn't mean you have to compromise good nutrition. Parents can promote healthy snacking habits by serving products that are lower in fat and high in nutrition—like NESTLÉ NESQUIK Ready-to-Drink Chocolate Milk, now made with 2% milk.

NESTLÉ NESQUIK Ready-to-Drink Chocolate Milk is lower in fat, but still provides 40 percent of the Recommended Daily Value of calcium per eight fluid-ounce serving. That's great news because, according to the USDA, more than 50 percent of kids don't get enough calcium, an important building block for strong bones.

Garlic and Cheese

Garlic is a staple in any kitchen and promotes health. Try finely chopping and adding to any dish for instant flavor. Rub the salad bowl with garlic before tossing. And, for a great spread on bread, use whole roasted garlic cloves.

Cheese adds great taste to any dish. It originates from milk from cows, goats, sheep, or buffalo. Cheese comes in many forms from crumbly to hard for grating.

Try a cheese sauce with pasta or grated Parmesan with spinach and carrots, or over the top of soups. Use a crumbled feta over scrambled eggs or ricotta cheese with a vegetable gratin. Cheese can be good with almost anything!

Chicken Primavera

This hearty Chicken Primavera comes together quickly for those hectic weeknights.

MAKES 4 SERVINGS

INGREDIENTS
1 tablespoon butter
1½ cups chicken broth
¾ cup Original NESTLÉ COFFEE-MATE Powdered Coffee Creamer
¾ cup water
1 tablespoon cornstarch
3 cloves garlic, finely chopped, divided
¼ cup (1 ounce) grated Parmesan cheese (optional)
1 tablespoon olive oil
1 pound boneless, skinless chicken breast halves, cut into bite-sized strips
1 medium carrot, cut into thin, bite-sized strips
½ cup finely chopped onion
1 medium zucchini, halved lengthwise and thinly sliced
1 package (9 ounces) BUITONI Refrigerated Linguine or Fettuccine

DIRECTIONS
MELT butter in medium saucepan over medium-high heat. Whisk in broth, Coffee-mate, water, cornstarch, and 1 chopped garlic clove. Cook, whisking frequently, until Coffee-mate and cornstarch are dissolved and mixture comes to a gentle boil. Cook for 2 minutes or until thickened and bubbly.

Season with salt and ground black pepper. Stir in cheese until melted. Remove from heat.

HEAT oil in large skillet over medium-high heat. Add chicken and remaining chopped garlic. Cook, stirring occasionally, for 3 to 4 minutes or until chicken is no longer pink. Add carrot and onion. Cook, stirring occasionally, for 5 minutes or until carrot is crisp-tender. Stir in zucchini. Cook, stirring occasionally, for 1 to 2 minutes. Season with salt and ground black pepper. Add sauce to skillet; stir.

PREPARE pasta according to package directions. Toss pasta with sauce.

Estimated Times
Preparation: 20 mins
Cooking: 20 mins

Creamy Chicken and Rice Bake

A quick and hearty meal for your family! Terrific to serve on a frenzied day.

MAKES 8 SERVINGS

Creamy Chicken and Rice Bake

INGREDIENTS

1 can (12 fluid ounces) NESTLÉ
   CARNATION Evaporated Milk

1 package (3 ounces) cream
   cheese, at room temperature

1 can (10¾ fluid ounces) cream
   of chicken soup

½ cup water

½ teaspoon garlic powder

⅛ teaspoon ground black pepper

1 bag (16 ounces) frozen broccoli,
   cauliflower, and carrot medley, thawed

2 cups cubed, cooked chicken

1½ cups instant white rice

½ cup (2 ounces) shredded
   cheddar cheese

DIRECTIONS

PREHEAT oven to 350° F. Grease
13 x 9-inch baking dish.

COMBINE evaporated milk and cream
cheese in baking dish with wire whisk
until smooth. Add soup, water, garlic
powder, and pepper; mix well. Add
vegetables, chicken, and rice. Cover
tightly with foil.

BAKE for 35 minutes. Uncover; top with
cheddar cheese. Bake for an additional
10 to 15 minutes or until cheese is
melted and mixture is bubbly. Let stand
for 5 minutes before serving.

FOR FREEZE AHEAD:

PREPARE as above; do not bake. Do not
top with cheddar cheese. Cover; freeze
for up to 2 months. Thaw overnight
in refrigerator.

PREHEAT oven to 350° F.

BAKE, covered, for 45 to 55 minutes.
Uncover; top with cheddar cheese.
Bake for an additional 10 to 15 minutes
or until cheese is melted and mixture
is bubbly. Let stand for 5 minutes
before serving.

Estimated Times
Preparation: 15 mins
Cooking: 45 mins
Standing: 5 mins

Creamy Poblano Rice with Chicken

Jazz up your chicken and rice with this wonderful combination of flavors. Your guests and family will come back for more!

MAKES 4 SERVINGS

INGREDIENTS

3 tablespoons vegetable oil, divided
1 small onion, finely chopped
1 small poblano chile, finely chopped
2 boneless, skinless chicken breast halves (about 8 ounces total), cut into bite-sized pieces
¼ teaspoon ground black pepper
¼ teaspoon crushed red pepper or paprika (optional)
1 cup medium or short grain rice
3½ cups chicken broth
1 can (12 fluid ounces) NESTLÉ CARNATION Evaporated Milk
1 can (4 ounces) mushroom pieces, drained

DIRECTIONS

HEAT 2 tablespoons oil in large, nonstick saucepan over medium heat. Add onion and chile. Cook, stirring frequently, for 2 minutes. Add chicken, black pepper, and crushed red pepper. Cook, stirring frequently, until chicken is lightly browned and no longer pink. Remove chicken mixture to bowl; set aside.

HEAT remaining oil in same saucepan over medium heat. Add rice; stir to coat well. Microwave broth in 1-quart microwave-safe measuring cup on HIGH (100%) power for 3½ to 4 minutes or until very hot.

ADD hot broth to rice in small amounts at a time, stirring constantly. Allow each addition of broth to be absorbed before adding more. Once broth is gone, add evaporated milk in the same manner, stirring until absorbed. The process will take about 25 to 35 minutes. When the rice is soft, stir in reserved chicken mixture and mushrooms. Rice should be creamy, not soupy.

Estimated Times
Preparation: 15 mins
Cooking: 40 mins

Creamy Poblano Rice with Chicken

Creamy Tuna Noodle Casserole

This homey and comforting tuna casserole is a welcome addition to any weeknight dinner. Round out this quick and easy meal with a tossed green salad.

MAKES 8 SERVINGS

INGREDIENTS

6 cups dry medium egg noodles
6 tablespoons butter or margarine

Creamy Tuna Noodle Casserole

Easy Chicken Cacciatore

Serve plenty of rice to soak up this scrumptious marinara-sauced chicken.

MAKES 4 SERVINGS

4 stalks celery, chopped

½ cup chopped onion

3 cans (6 ounces each) tuna, drained and flaked

2 cans (10 ounces each) condensed cream of mushroom soup

1 can (12 fluid ounces) NESTLÉ CARNATION Evaporated Milk

⅔ cup crushed potato chips

DIRECTIONS

PREHEAT oven to 375° F. Grease 13 x 9-inch baking dish.

PREPARE noodles according to package directions.

MELT butter in large saucepan over medium heat. Add celery and onion. Cook, stirring occasionally, for 1 to 2 minutes or until vegetables are tender. Stir in noodles, tuna, soup, and evaporated milk. Mix well. Pour into prepared casserole dish. Sprinkle with potato chips.

BAKE for 25 to 30 minutes or until chips are golden brown.

Estimated Times
Preparation: 10 mins
Cooking: 35 mins

INGREDIENTS

1 teaspoon olive oil

4 boneless, skinless chicken breast halves (about 1 pound total), cut into 1-inch pieces

1 large green bell pepper, cut into thin strips

1 container (15 ounces) BUITONI Refrigerated Marinara Sauce

½ cup water

2 cups hot cooked rice

DIRECTIONS

HEAT oil in large, nonstick skillet over medium-high heat. Add chicken and bell pepper. Cook, stirring frequently, for 5 minutes or until chicken is lightly browned.

ADD sauce and water to skillet; bring to a boil. Reduce heat to low; cover. Cook for 5 minutes or until chicken is no longer pink. Stir in cooked rice.

Estimated Times
Preparation: 20 mins
Cooking: 15 mins

Olive Oil

Olive oil has been made the same way for thousands of years. The harvest season begins in November and ends in February, depending on geography. Olives destined to become oil are picked by hand when slightly unripe. They are washed, then poured into the press. The traditional stone press, called a frantoio, consists of a circular trough and an upright wheel, driven by a team of oxen, or by a generator, often the only mechanized part of the process.

The olive pulp is scooped into woven sacks, which are stacked atop one another and pressed flat. The resulting watery liquid is siphoned into tanks to separate. The precious oil is then skimmed off the top and bottled.

In Italy, olive oil produced in this way is referred to as "prima spremitura a freddo" (from the first cold pressing) and is considered the best for culinary use. This first pressing is graded according to its oleic acid content, from Extra Virgin (the best) to Virgin. Extra Virgin contains one percent acid; Superfine one and half percent; Fine three percent; and Virgin four percent.

Easy Pasta Casserole

All you need is a handful of ingredients and you can enjoy Italian tonight.

MAKES 5 SERVINGS

INGREDIENTS

2½ cups dry penne pasta

12 ounces lean ground beef

2 containers (15 ounces each) BUITONI Refrigerated Garden Vegetable Sauce (fat-free)

⅓ cup grated Parmesan cheese, divided

¾ cup (3 ounces) shredded reduced-fat mozzarella cheese

DIRECTIONS

PREHEAT oven to 375° F.

PREPARE pasta according to package directions.

COOK beef in large skillet over medium-high heat until no longer pink; drain. Stir in pasta, sauce, and half of Parmesan cheese. Spoon into ungreased 12 x 7½-inch baking dish. Sprinkle with mozzarella cheese and remaining Parmesan cheese; cover.

BAKE for about 20 minutes or until cheese is melted and mixture is bubbly.

FOR FREEZE AHEAD:
PREPARE as above; do not bake. Cover; freeze for up to 2 months. Thaw overnight in refrigerator.

PREHEAT oven to 375° F.

BAKE, covered, for 30 to 40 minutes or until cheese is melted and mixture is bubbly.

Estimated Times
Preparation: 15 mins
Cooking: 35 mins

Fettuccine Alfredo

Add interest and color to Fettuccine Alfredo by including your favorite meat or vegetable combinations. Some popular additions include cooked chicken, shrimp, or crumbled bacon, as well as peas, finely chopped red bell pepper, or broccoli florets.

MAKES 4 SERVINGS

INGREDIENTS

1 package (9 ounces) BUITONI Refrigerated Fettuccine

3 tablespoons butter

2 tablespoons all-purpose flour

1 cup NESTLÉ CARNATION Evaporated Milk

½ cup chicken broth

½ cup (2 ounces) freshly grated Parmesan cheese

½ cup (2 ounces) grated provolone cheese

⅛ teaspoon cayenne pepper

⅛ teaspoon ground black pepper

DIRECTIONS

PREPARE pasta according to package directions.

MELT butter in medium saucepan over medium heat; stir in flour. Gradually add evaporated milk and broth. Cook, stirring constantly, until mixture comes to a boil and thickens. Stir in Parmesan cheese, provolone cheese, cayenne pepper, and black pepper until cheese is melted. Toss with pasta; serve immediately.

Estimated Times
Preparation: 5 mins
Cooking: 15 mins

Fettuccine and Sweet Italian Sausage Alfredo

The irresistible taste of sweet Italian sausage adds an unforgettable flavor to creamy Fettuccine Alfredo. Tender crisp Italian green beans and a cool salad make this meal an instant classic.

MAKES 4 SERVINGS

INGREDIENTS

1 package (9 ounces) BUITONI Refrigerated Fettuccine

1 pound bulk sweet Italian sausage
1 container (10 ounces) BUITONI Refrigerated Alfredo Sauce
⅓ cup grated Parmesan cheese

DIRECTIONS

PREPARE pasta according to package directions.

COOK sausage in large skillet over medium-high heat until no longer pink; drain. Return to skillet. Add pasta and sauce; heat through. Top with cheese.

Estimated Times
Preparation: 5 mins
Cooking: 15 mins

Fettuccine Alfredo

Fettuccine with Creamy Tomato Vodka Sauce

Fettuccine with Creamy Tomato Vodka Sauce

The subtle blending of tomatoes, cream, and vodka make this indulgent fettuccine dish sophisticated enough for unexpected company yet quick and comforting for everyday fare.

MAKES 4 SERVINGS

INGREDIENTS

3 tablespoons olive oil

¼ cup chopped onion

4 cloves garlic, chopped

2 tablespoons crushed dried basil

1 teaspoon crushed dried oregano

1 can (14.5 ounces) recipe-ready diced tomatoes, undrained

4 ounces ham, chopped

⅓ cup vodka

1 cup heavy whipping cream

½ cup (2 ounces) grated Parmesan cheese

1 package (9 ounces) BUITONI Refrigerated Fettuccine

DIRECTIONS

HEAT oil in large skillet over medium-high heat. Add onion, garlic, basil, and oregano. Cook until onion is tender. Add tomatoes and juice and ham; cook for 5 minutes. Add vodka; cook for 5 minutes. Stir in cream and cheese. Cook over low heat, stirring occasionally, until slightly thickened. Season with salt and ground black pepper.

PREPARE pasta according to package directions.

TOSS pasta with cream mixture. Garnish with additional Parmesan cheese, if desired.

Estimated Times

Preparation: 10 mins

Cooking: 20 mins

Fettuccine with Portabellos, Ham, and Asparagus

Portabello mushrooms and tender asparagus make a perfect match for Parmesan cheese and ham in this quick yet elegant pasta dish. Add crispy breadsticks and a Caesar salad for a complete meal.

INGREDIENTS

8 ounces portabello mushrooms, sliced

¼ cup sliced green onions

3 tablespoons olive oil

2 cloves garlic, finely chopped

4 ounces asparagus, cut into ½-inch pieces

1 package (9 ounces) BUITONI Refrigerated Fettuccine

8 ounces cooked ham, cut into thin strips

¼ cup (1 ounce) grated Parmesan cheese

¼ cup chopped fresh parsley

DIRECTIONS

COOK mushrooms, green onions, oil, and garlic in large skillet over medium-high heat until tender. Add asparagus; cook until crisp-tender.

PREPARE pasta according to package directions.

TOSS pasta with mushroom mixture, ham, cheese, and parsley. Season with salt and ground black pepper.

Estimated Times

Preparation: 10 mins

Cooking: 10 mins

Fettuccine with Portabellos, Ham, and Asparagus

About Stouffer's

Back in 1922, Abraham and Mahala Stouffer opened a small coffee shop in Cleveland, Ohio featuring delicious homemade food. The couple's sons later opened a chain of popular restaurants. The customers began asking for take-out versions of their favorite meals and, as demand grew, they began freezing popular items and selling them at a retail outlet nearby.

By 1954, the family had founded the frozen food operation bearing its name. It is this family heritage that you bring home every time you put a Stouffer's meal in your shopping cart. For over 80 years, Stouffer's has been devoted to bringing families together around a table of delicious food. Visit Stouffers.com for more great meals.

Four-Layer Hamburger and Macaroni Casserole

Four-Layer Hamburger and Macaroni Casserole

Frozen macaroni and cheese, ground beef, and taco seasoning mix make a surprise-filled casserole enhanced with sour cream, crushed tortilla chips, and shredded cheddar cheese. Each layer packs lots of zesty flavor.

MAKES 6 SERVINGS

INGREDIENTS

2 packages (12 ounces each)
   STOUFFER'S frozen Macaroni and
   Cheese, defrosted*, divided

8 ounces lean ground beef

2 tablespoons taco seasoning mix

2 tablespoons sour cream

½ cup diced tomato

⅓ cup crushed potato or tortilla chips

½ cup (2 ounces) shredded
   cheddar cheese

DIRECTIONS

PREHEAT oven to 400° F.

COMBINE beef and seasoning mix in large skillet. Cook over medium-high heat, stirring occasionally, for 2 to 3 minutes or until beef is no longer pink.

COMBINE 1 package macaroni and cheese and sour cream in medium bowl; spread over bottom of 8-inch-square baking dish. Top with beef mixture. Spread remaining package macaroni and cheese over beef mixture. Top with tomato, potato chips, and cheese.

BAKE for 20 to 25 minutes or until bubbly around edges.

FOR FREEZE AHEAD:
PREPARE as above; do not top with tomato, potato chips, and cheese. Do not bake. Cover; freeze for up to 2 months. Thaw overnight in refrigerator. Uncover. Top with tomato, potato chips, and cheese.

PREHEAT oven to 400° F.

BAKE for 40 to 45 minutes or until bubbly around edges.

*DEFROST macaroni and cheese in microwave on MEDIUM (50%) power for 5 to 6 minutes.

Estimated Times
Preparation: 15 mins
Cooking: 22 mins

Fusilli with Blue Cheese & Toasted Walnuts

This pasta dish is high in flavor and low in preparation time. Serve with warm crusty rolls and a green salad.

MAKES 4 SERVINGS

INGREDIENTS

1 package (16 ounces) dry fusilli or bow-tie pasta
1 can (12 fluid ounces) NESTLÉ CARNATION Evaporated Milk
1 cup (4 ounces) crumbled blue cheese
1½ cups frozen peas, thawed
¾ cup chopped walnuts, toasted

DIRECTIONS

PREPARE pasta according to package directions.

HEAT evaporated milk in large skillet over medium-high heat, stirring frequently, until hot. Stir in cheese. Cook, stirring occasionally, until cheese is partially melted and sauce is slightly thickened.

ADD pasta and peas. Cook, stirring frequently, until heated through. Sprinkle with nuts before serving.

Estimated Times
Preparation: 10 mins
Cooking: 15 mins

Fusilli with Blue Cheese & Toasted Walnuts

Garden Risotto Bake

Garden Risotto Bake

Tasty and nutritious, this risotto casserole pairs nicely with grilled chicken!

MAKES 4 SERVINGS

INGREDIENTS

2 packages (5.5 ounces each) BUITONI
    Risotto with Garden Vegetables
3 cups fresh broccoli florets
2 cups (8 ounces) grated Fontina
    cheese, divided
⅓ cup plain, dry bread crumbs

DIRECTIONS

PREHEAT oven to 375° F. Lightly grease 2-quart casserole.

PREPARE risotto according to package directions.

MICROWAVE broccoli in covered, medium, microwave-safe bowl on HIGH (100%) power for 5 minutes.

SPREAD 2 cups risotto into prepared casserole. Evenly distribute broccoli over risotto; sprinkle with 1½ cups cheese. Spread remaining risotto over cheese. Sprinkle with remaining cheese and bread crumbs.

BAKE for 20 to 25 minutes or until golden brown.

Estimated Times
Preparation: 10 mins
Cooking: 45 mins

Grilled Apple Curry Chicken

Apple curry chutney and curry powder moistened with apple juice season this tender chicken breast served over pasta. Sprinkles of crisp chopped parsley make an appealing plate.

MAKES 4 SERVINGS

INGREDIENTS

1 jar (8 ounces) apple curry chutney
¼ cup Apple LIBBY'S JUICY JUICE
    Premium 100% Juice
2 cloves garlic, peeled
1 teaspoon curry powder
4 boneless, skinless chicken breast
    halves (about 1 pound total)
1 package (9 ounces) BUITONI
    Refrigerated Linguine
Chopped fresh parsley (optional)

DIRECTIONS

PREHEAT grill or broiler.

PLACE chutney, Juicy Juice, garlic, and curry powder in food processor or blender; cover. Process until smooth. Reserve ⅓ cup.

PREPARE pasta according to package directions; keep warm.

GRILL or broil chicken, brushing frequently with remaining chutney mixture, until chicken is no longer pink in center. Slice chicken; place over pasta. Spoon reserved chutney mixture over chicken; sprinkle with parsley.

Estimated Times
Preparation: 10 mins
Cooking: 15 mins

Grilled Chicken Breasts with Fresh Herbs

Garlic, rosemary, and dry white wine are the perfect ingredients for dressing up tender chicken breasts for the grill.

MAKES 6 SERVINGS

INGREDIENTS

3 large cloves garlic, finely chopped

1 tablespoon chopped fresh rosemary (or 1 teaspoon dried rosemary)

1 tablespoon chopped fresh thyme (or 1 teaspoon dried thyme)

¾ teaspoon MAGGI Instant Chicken Flavor Bouillon

6 boneless, skinless chicken breast halves (about 1½ pounds total)

2 tablespoons olive oil

⅓ cup dry white wine

DIRECTIONS

COMBINE garlic, rosemary, thyme, and bouillon in small bowl.

ARRANGE chicken in 13 x 9-inch baking pan; rub with herb mixture. Drizzle with oil. Pour wine into bottom of pan; cover. Marinate in refrigerator for 2 hours.

PREHEAT grill or broiler.

GRILL or broil chicken on each side until golden brown and no longer pink in center. Season with ground black pepper.

Estimated Times
Preparation: 10 mins
Marinating: 2 hrs
Cooking: 15 mins

Grilled Chicken Breasts with Fresh Herbs

Grilled Chicken with Fiery Jalapeño Sauce

Grilled Chicken with Fiery Jalapeño Sauce

Simple grilled chicken gets a burst of spicy heat from jalapeño, cilantro, and lime juice purée. Serve with steamed potatoes and a green salad.

MAKES 4 SERVINGS

INGREDIENTS

4 boneless, skinless chicken breast halves (about 1 pound total)

⅔ cup packed fresh cilantro leaves

¼ cup diced jalapeños

2 tablespoons MAGGI Liquid Seasoning

2 tablespoons fresh lime juice

2 cloves garlic, peeled

DIRECTIONS

PREHEAT grill or broiler.

GRILL or broil chicken on each side until no longer pink in center.

PLACE cilantro, jalapeños, seasoning, lime juice, and garlic in blender or food processor; cover. Blend until smooth.

SERVE with grilled chicken.

Estimated Times
Preparation: 10 mins
Cooking: 15 mins

Italy

Each region of Italy has its own special dish. So fasten your seatbelts for a whirlwind culinary tour!

The northern province of Lombardy offers rice dishes, such as Risotto allo Safferano, short-grain rice cooked in meat broth with beef marrow, onions, saffron, and white wine.

To the south, coastal Liguria specializes in delicious seafood, such as cioppino, a soup served in two parts, including a rich broth with fish, shrimp, and octopus cooked in it. Fill your bowl with broth, then add pieces of seafood for body.

In Tuscany, food is known for its simplicity. A typical dish might be game birds grilled on a spit with liver, sage, and bay leaf seasonings.

Umbria, in central Italy, is famed for Colombaccio, roasted wood-pigeon, which is an autumn specialty served in a rich sauce of oil, wine, vinegar, and herbs.

Sicily is famous for its desserts: pastries, ice cream, ices, and candied fruits. But be advised, arancini, or "little oranges," are actually fried rice balls filled with ground meat.

Grilled Chicken with Linguine and Pesto

Grilled Chicken with Linguine and Pesto

The toasted walnuts perfectly accent the grilled chicken and pesto in this quick and easy recipe. Serve with a fresh green salad and warm garlic bread.

MAKES 6 SERVINGS

INGREDIENTS

4 boneless, skinless chicken breast halves (about 1 pound total)

1 package (9 ounces) BUITONI Refrigerated Linguine

3 tablespoons olive oil

3 cloves garlic, finely chopped

1 container (7 ounces) BUITONI Refrigerated Pesto with Basil

½ cup chopped walnuts, toasted, divided

¼ cup (1 ounce) grated Parmesan cheese

DIRECTIONS

PREHEAT grill or broiler.

GRILL or broil chicken on each side until

no longer pink in center. Dice chicken.

PREPARE pasta according to package directions.

HEAT oil in large skillet over medium-high heat. Add garlic; cook for 1 minute. Add chicken, pasta, pesto, and ¼ cup nuts. Cook until mixture is heated through. Top with remaining nuts and cheese.

Estimated Times
Preparation: 10 mins
Cooking: 20 mins

Honey Dijon Fettuccine and Chicken

The natural sweetness of honey blended with the distinctive sharpness of Dijon-style mustard makes this dish one to savor. Serve with crunchy dinner rolls and a prepackaged salad of gourmet greens.

MAKES 4 SERVINGS

INGREDIENTS
4 boneless, skinless chicken breast halves (about 1 pound total)
1 package (9 ounces) BUITONI Refrigerated Fettuccine
1 can (14.5 fluid ounces) chicken broth
2 tablespoons Dijon mustard

2 tablespoons honey
2 tablespoons cornstarch
1 cup yellow bell pepper strips
½ cup red bell pepper strips
½ cup red onion strips

DIRECTIONS
COOK chicken until no longer pink in center.

PREPARE pasta according to package directions.

COMBINE broth, mustard, honey, and

cornstarch in small bowl; mix until smooth. Transfer to medium skillet; add chicken, bell peppers, and onion. Bring to a gentle boil over medium heat; reduce heat to low. Cover.

COOK for 10 minutes or until sauce is thickened, vegetables are crisp-tender, and chicken is heated through. Serve over pasta.

Estimated Times
Preparation: 10 mins
Cooking: 30 mins

Honey Dijon Fettuccine and Chicken

Italian-Seasoned Chicken and Fettuccine

Buitoni pasta and Italian-seasoned chicken breasts are sure to delight your family! Round out the meal with your favorite steamed vegetables and a warm loaf of bread.

MAKES 4 SERVINGS

INGREDIENTS

¼ cup olive oil
1½ teaspoons finely chopped garlic
¾ teaspoon Italian seasoning
4 boneless, skinless chicken breast halves (about 1 pound total)
1 package (9 ounces) BUITONI Refrigerated Fettuccine

DIRECTIONS

PREHEAT oven to 350° F. Grease 13 x 9-inch baking dish.

COMBINE oil, garlic, and Italian seasoning in large bowl. Add chicken; turn to coat. Marinate in refrigerator for 15 to 30 minutes. Remove chicken from marinade and place in prepared dish. Discard marinade.

BAKE for 35 to 40 minutes or until chicken is no longer pink in center.

PREPARE pasta according to package directions. Serve chicken over pasta.

Italian-Seasoned Chicken and Fettuccine

Estimated Times
Preparation: 10 mins
Marinating: 15 mins
Cooking: 40 mins

Kid's Cheeseburger Pie

Satisfy those cravings for a cheeseburger without breaking out the grill.

MAKES 6 SERVINGS

INGREDIENTS

1 unbaked 9-inch (4-cup volume) deep-dish pie shell
1 pound lean ground beef
¼ teaspoon garlic powder
¼ cup all-purpose flour
⅓ to ½ cup chopped dill pickles
⅓ cup dill pickle juice
⅓ cup NESTLÉ CARNATION Evaporated Milk
8 ounces American cheese, cut into pieces, divided
Mustard (optional)
Ketchup (optional)

DIRECTIONS

PREHEAT oven to 425° F.

COOK beef and garlic powder in large skillet over medium-high heat, stirring frequently, until beef is no longer pink. Sprinkle with flour; stir. Stir in pickles, pickle juice, evaporated milk, and half

Kid's Cheeseburger Pie

the cheese. Spoon mixture into pie shell.

BAKE for 20 minutes; top with remaining cheese. Bake for an additional 5 minutes or until cheese is melted. Cool on wire rack for 5 minutes. Serve with mustard and ketchup.

Estimated Times
Preparation: 10 mins
Cooking: 35 mins
Cooling: 5 mins

Lasagna Cucina

Cook once. Eat twice. One recipe of this Italian favorite makes two (eight- or nine-inch) panfuls to freeze, so dinner's ready when you need it.

MAKES 8 SERVINGS

INGREDIENTS

1 package (8 ounces) lasagna noodles
8 ounces mild Italian sausage
1 can (14.5 ounces) recipe-ready
    diced tomatoes, undrained
2 cans (6 ounces each) Italian
    tomato paste
1 cup water
2 MAGGI Beef Flavor Bouillon Cubes
½ teaspoon crushed dried basil
1 container (15 ounces) ricotta cheese
¼ cup (1 ounce) grated Romano cheese
1 large egg
3 cups (12 ounces) shredded mozzarella
    cheese, divided

DIRECTIONS

PREHEAT oven to 350° F.

PREPARE noodles according to package directions.

CRUMBLE sausage in large skillet. Cook over medium-high heat, stirring occasionally, until no longer pink; drain. Stir in tomatoes and juice, tomato paste, water, bouillon, and basil; bring to a boil. Reduce heat to low; cook for 10 to 15 minutes. Combine ricotta cheese, Romano cheese, and egg in small bowl.

LAYER in one 13 x 9-inch or two 8- or 9-inch-square baking dishes as follows: ⅓ lasagna noodles, ½ meat sauce, ⅓ lasagna noodles, all ricotta cheese mixture, ½ mozzarella cheese, remaining noodles, remaining meat sauce, and remaining mozzarella cheese; cover.

BAKE for 40 minutes. Uncover; bake for an additional 15 minutes or until bubbly and cheese is melted.

FOR FREEZE AHEAD:
PREPARE and assemble lasagna as above; do not bake. Cover; freeze for up to 2 months. Thaw overnight in refrigerator.

PREHEAT oven to 350° F.

BAKE for 40 minutes. Uncover; bake for 15 minutes or until bubbly and cheese is melted.

Estimated Times
Preparation: 20 mins
Cooking: 1 hr, 20 mins

Lemon Risotto with Sautéed Shrimp

The creamy consistency of this Mediterranean-inspired risotto will certainly prompt requests for repeat performances. Add a prepackaged herb salad mix with balsamic vinaigrette for a standing ovation.

MAKES 4 SERVINGS

INGREDIENTS

¼ cup (½ stick) butter, divided

¼ cup finely chopped onion

2 tablespoons olive oil

1 tablespoon freshly grated lemon peel

1½ cups Arborio rice or other short-grain white rice

4 cups warm water

2 tablespoons dry white wine

1 tablespoon lemon juice

3 MAGGI Vegetarian Vegetable Flavor Bouillon Cubes

¼ teaspoon ground black pepper

2 tablespoons freshly grated Parmesan cheese

8 ounces raw medium shrimp, peeled and deveined

Gremolata (recipe follows)

DIRECTIONS

MELT 2 tablespoons butter in medium saucepan over medium-low heat. Add onion, oil, and lemon peel. Cook for 2 to 3 minutes or until tender. Stir in rice and cook for 1 minute. Stir in water, wine, lemon juice, bouillon, and pepper. Cover; cook for 30 to 35 minutes. Stir in cheese.

MELT remaining butter in medium skillet over medium-high heat. Cook shrimp for 3 to 4 minutes or until pink. Serve shrimp over risotto; sprinkle with gremolata.

FOR GREMOLATA:

COMBINE 1 teaspoon finely chopped garlic, 1 teaspoon finely chopped fresh parsley, and 1 teaspoon grated lemon peel in small bowl.

Estimated Times
Preparation: 15 mins
Cooking: 40 mins

Light Pesto Mushroom Pizza

Light Pesto Mushroom Pizza

Quicker than waiting for the pizza man to deliver. Prepare this flavorful pesto pizza in a jiffy by buying a premade pizza crust.

MAKES 4 SERVINGS

INGREDIENTS

1 premade (12-inch) pizza crust

½ cup BUITONI Refrigerated Pesto with Basil

8 ounces white mushrooms, trimmed and thinly sliced

2 cups (8 ounces) shredded mozzarella cheese

DIRECTIONS

PREHEAT oven to 350° F.

PLACE pizza crust on baking sheet; spread with pesto. Top with mushrooms and cheese.

BAKE for 15 minutes or until cheese is melted and bubbly.

Estimated Times
Preparation: 10 mins
Cooking: 15 mins

Meatloaf

This meatloaf is practically "no fail!" Give it a try!

MAKES 12 SERVINGS

INGREDIENTS

1 large onion, chopped
1 small green bell pepper, chopped
1 ¼ cups plain dry bread crumbs
¾ cup dry NESTLÉ CARNATION Instant
  Nonfat Dry Milk
⅔ cup water
½ cup ketchup, divided
2 large eggs, lightly beaten
1 tablespoon dried parsley
1 tablespoon garlic salt
1 teaspoon ground black pepper
3 pounds ground beef

DIRECTIONS

PREHEAT oven to 375° F.

COMBINE onion, bell pepper, bread crumbs, dry milk, water, 2 tablespoons ketchup, eggs, parsley, garlic salt, and black pepper in large bowl. Add ground beef; mix lightly but thoroughly. Divide mixture in half and shape into 2 loaves. Place in ungreased 13 x 9-inch baking dish. Flatten loaves on top. Cover with remaining ketchup.

BAKE for 55 to 60 minutes or until no longer pink in center. Let stand for 10 to 15 minutes before serving.

Estimated Times
Preparation: 15 mins
Cooking: 55 mins
Standing: 10 mins

Meatloaf

Pesto Sauce

When you are looking for the convenience of ready-made pesto that compares to the flavors of homemade with fresh basil, Parmesan, and garlic, BUITONI Refrigerated Pesto with Basil has the delicious taste you're looking for in a pesto sauce. You won't need any added seasonings or cheese, and it freezes well, too, making it a fast sauce to use with your favorite pasta dish anytime.

Pesto is also great with potatoes, used as a spread in sandwiches, with grilled eggplant, or as dip with fresh mixed cheese.

Mediterranean Shrimp Pasta

Shrimp, garlic, white wine, and pasta make an unbeatable combination served with crumbled feta and capers.

MAKES 4 SERVINGS

INGREDIENTS
2 tablespoons olive oil

1 medium red or green bell pepper, cut into strips
1 clove garlic, finely chopped
8 ounces raw small shrimp
¼ cup dry white wine
¼ cup sliced ripe olives
1 package (9 ounces) BUITONI Refrigerated Linguine
1 container (7 ounces) BUITONI Refrigerated Pesto with Sun-Dried Tomatoes
¼ cup (1 ounce) crumbled feta cheese
1 tablespoon capers

Mediterranean Shrimp Pasta

HEAT oil in large skillet over medium-high heat. Add bell pepper and garlic; cook for 2 minutes. Add shrimp and wine; cook until shrimp are pink. Stir in olives.

PREPARE pasta according to package directions. Lightly warm pesto; toss pasta with pesto in medium bowl. Serve topped with shrimp mixture. Sprinkle with cheese and capers.

Estimated Times
Preparation: 10 mins
Cooking: 10 mins

Mexicali Macaroni and Cheese

Try this recipe for a south-of-the border accent to this classic American dish. Add warm rolls and a prepackaged salad for a quick and complete meal that will please the whole family.

MAKES 6 SERVINGS

INGREDIENTS
2 packages (12 ounces each) STOUFFER'S frozen Macaroni and Cheese, defrosted*
½ cup (2 ounces) shredded cheddar cheese

Mexicali Macaroni and Cheese

½ cup frozen corn
⅓ cup mild salsa
¾ cup crushed tortilla chips

DIRECTIONS
PREHEAT oven to 400° F.

COMBINE macaroni and cheese, cheese, corn, and salsa in medium bowl. Spoon into 8-inch-square baking pan. Top with chips.

BAKE for 25 to 30 minutes or until bubbly around edges.

*DEFROST macaroni and cheese in microwave on MEDIUM (50%) power for 5 to 6 minutes.

Estimated Times
Preparation: 10 mins
Cooking: 25 mins

Mexican Linguine

Salsa, corn, and taco seasoning team up together to create a spicy and satisfying sauce served over linguine, for a dish rich in the flavors of Mexican cuisine.

MAKES 4 SERVINGS

INGREDIENTS

12 ounces lean ground beef or turkey

1 small onion, chopped

1 jar (16 ounces) salsa

1 cup frozen whole-kernel corn

¾ cup water

1 package (1.25 ounces) taco seasoning mix

1 package (9 ounces) BUITONI Refrigerated Linguine

½ cup (2 ounces) shredded Monterey Jack cheese (optional)

DIRECTIONS

COOK beef and onion in large, nonstick skillet over medium-high heat, stirring frequently, until beef is no longer pink. Drain. Stir in salsa, corn, water, and seasoning mix. Cook, stirring occasionally, until thickened and bubbly.

PREPARE pasta according to package directions. Toss warm pasta with sauce. Sprinkle with cheese.

Estimated Times
Preparation: 5 mins
Cooking: 15 mins

One-Pot Pasta with Tomatoes, White Beans, and Pesto

This rustic Italian meal with wonderful flavor requires the use of only one pot. Serve with warm, crusty bread.

MAKES 4 SERVINGS

INGREDIENTS

3¼ cups dry bow-tie pasta

3 cups water

2 MAGGI Chicken or Vegetarian Vegetable Flavor Bouillon Cubes

1 container (7 ounces) BUITONI Refrigerated Pesto with Basil

2 medium tomatoes, chopped

1 can (15 ounces) cannellini beans or small white beans, rinsed and drained

⅓ cup grated Parmesan cheese

DIRECTIONS

COMBINE pasta, water, and bouillon in large saucepan. Bring to a boil. Cook, stirring frequently, for 8 to 10 minutes or until pasta is tender and broth

One-Pot Pasta with Tomatoes, White Beans, and Pesto

has reduced to about ½ cup. Do not drain. Reduce heat to low; add pesto.

COOK, stirring frequently, until sauce has reduced slightly. Stir in tomatoes and beans. Cook, stirring occasionally, until heated through. Sprinkle with cheese before serving. Season with ground black pepper.

Estimated Times
Preparation: 5 mins
Cooking: 15 mins

Pasta with Chicken and Roasted Red Pepper Cream Sauce

Roasting concentrates and enhances the flavor of bell peppers.

MAKES 4 SERVINGS

INGREDIENTS

1 package (9 ounces) BUITONI Refrigerated Fettuccine
1 jar (7.25 ounces) roasted red peppers, drained
1 container (10 ounces) BUITONI Refrigerated Alfredo Sauce
1 package (6 ounces) fully-cooked, ready-to-eat chicken breast strips
Grated Parmesan cheese (optional)
Chopped fresh parsley (optional)

Pasta with Chicken and Roasted Red Pepper Cream Sauce

DIRECTIONS

PREPARE pasta according to package directions.

PLACE peppers in food processor or blender; cover. Pulse until peppers are ⅛- to ¼-inch in size.

COOK sauce, peppers, and chicken in large, nonstick skillet over medium-low heat, stirring occasionally, until heated through (do not boil). Add pasta; toss well.

SERVE with cheese and chopped fresh parsley.

Estimated Times
Preparation: 5 mins
Cooking: 10 mins

Cooking Tip

A true Italian meal would not be complete without certain Italian flavorings. To ensure your sauces and dishes are flavorful every time, try these Italian herbs.

One bay leaf is pungent enough to give flavor to sauces and should be removed after cooking. Bay leaf is almost always used dry. Basil should always be used fresh to flavor tomato sauces and salads. Marjoram can be used fresh or dry in soups and braised meat dishes. Oregano is usually used dry and sprinkled in tomato sauces and on fish.

Always use fresh Italian parsley (the kind with the flat leaves). The other types of parsley are used mainly as decoration. Rosemary can be used fresh or dried in roasted chicken and meat dishes. Sage leaves are best when used fresh, most frequently with veal. With these herbs on hand, you'll be on your way to cooking Italian-style!

Poached Salmon with Alfredo Sauce

Simple yet elegant, poached salmon is a dish that may be prepared for any sophisticated occasion. Complete the meal with steamed zucchini, yellow squash, and asparagus.

MAKES 2 SERVINGS

INGREDIENTS

½ cup water

¼ cup dry white wine or chicken broth

2 salmon fillets or steaks (about
   6 ounces each)

1 package (9 ounces) BUITONI
   Refrigerated Linguine

2 tablespoons finely grated
   carrot (optional)

1 tablespoon chopped fresh
   parsley (optional)

1 container (10 ounces) BUITONI
   Refrigerated Alfredo Sauce

Fresh dill sprigs (optional)

DIRECTIONS

BOIL water and wine in large skillet; add salmon. Reduce heat to low; cover. Cook for 8 to 10 minutes or until thickest part of salmon flakes easily when tested with a fork.

PREPARE pasta according to package directions. Toss pasta with carrot and parsley; divide among plates. Top with salmon. Warm sauce; spoon over each serving. Garnish with dill. Season with salt and ground black pepper.

Estimated Times
Preparation: 10 mins
Cooking: 15 mins

Pork Tenderloin with Creamy Mustard Sauce

Pork and creamy mustard sauce pair well together for a dish that is sure to be a crowd pleaser.

MAKES 4 SERVINGS

INGREDIENTS

½ cup Original NESTLÉ COFFEE-MATE
   Powdered Coffee Creamer

½ cup hot water

1 pound pork tenderloin

1 teaspoon vegetable oil

2 tablespoons Dijon mustard

3 green onions, sliced

DIRECTIONS

WHISK together Coffee-mate and water in small bowl until smooth. Set aside.

CUT pork into 1-inch-thick slices. Place pork between 2 pieces of plastic wrap. Flatten to ½-inch-thickness using meat mallet or rolling pin. Season pork with salt and ground black pepper.

HEAT oil in large skillet over medium-high heat. Add pork; cook on each side for 3 minutes or until browned and cooked through. Remove from skillet; set aside and keep warm.

REDUCE heat to medium; add Coffee-mate mixture to skillet, stirring constantly. Stir in mustard. Cook for 2 minutes or until sauce has thickened slightly. Stir in green onions. Return pork to skillet. Cook for 2 minutes, turning to coat with sauce.

Estimated Times
Preparation: 20 mins
Cooking: 10 mins

Pork Tenderloin with Creamy Mustard Sauce

Ravioli Lasagna

This is a real twist on a classic. You and your family will be delighted by this fun combination that is both easy and tasty! This meal also performs double-duty—make one for now and one to freeze and enjoy later.

MAKES 4 SERVINGS

INGREDIENTS

1 package (20 ounces) BUITONI Refrigerated Family Size Four Cheese Ravioli

1 container (15 ounces) lowfat ricotta cheese

1 package (10 ounces) frozen chopped spinach, thawed and squeezed dry

2 large eggs, lightly beaten

⅓ cup fat free milk

1 container (23.5 ounces) BUITONI Refrigerated Family Size Marinara Sauce

¼ cup (1 ounce) grated Parmesan cheese

DIRECTIONS

PREHEAT oven to 350° F. Grease two 8 x 4-inch loaf dishes.

PREPARE pasta according to package directions.

COMBINE ricotta cheese, spinach, eggs, and milk in medium bowl. Place one-fourth pasta in each prepared baking dish. Add one-fourth sauce and half ricotta mixture to each baking dish. Top each with half of the remaining pasta and half of the remaining sauce. Sprinkle both baking dishes with Parmesan cheese. Cover one baking dish with plastic wrap, then overwrap with foil. Freeze for up to 2 months.

COVER remaining baking dish with foil. Bake for 40 to 45 minutes or until heated through. Let stand for 10 minutes before serving.

FOR FREEZE AHEAD:
PLACE baking dish in refrigerator overnight.

PREHEAT oven to 375° F. Remove plastic wrap and recover with foil.

BAKE for 1 hour or until heated through. Let stand for 10 minutes before serving.

Estimated Times
Preparation: 30 mins
Cooking: 50 mins
Standing: 10 mins

Cooking Tip

Poaching requires handling the cooking very gently. This is especially true for fish, which cooks best just covered by liquid in a flat pot like a skillet—which makes it easier to determine when the fish is done cooking. When cooking larger chunks of fish, use a flat, oval fish poacher for ideal cooking.

When testing doneness, it's a good idea to use a fork to see if it flakes easily, and when removing the fish from the pot, use a ladle, skimmer, or lifter with holes so that everything stays in one piece.

About Albers

The Albers line of corn meal and grits has been used for generations. ALBERS Yellow and White Corn Meal are essential ingredients to prepare everything from sweet corn bread and corn muffins to fried fish and chicken. ALBERS Grits are used to create tasty satisfying side dishes and main meals at breakfast, lunch, and dinner. The ALBERS brand represents a heritage of providing rich, natural flavor from premium corn.

Still recognizable on the Albers orange and blue corn meal package is the fresh ear of corn. The ALBERS Grits package remains familiar with its red and blue colors and traditional breakfast plate of grits, eggs, and bacon.

ALBERS Yellow Corn Meal, White Corn Meal, and Grits are available in 20- and 40-ounce packages.

Rich and Zesty Tamale Pie

Rich and Zesty Tamale Pie

Tamale pie is a delicious dish to serve and enjoy family-style when you want the taste of tamales but prefer the ease of a casserole. Made with yellow corn meal, sliced ripe olives, and diced green chiles, tamale pie is a Southwestern favorite.

MAKES 6 SERVINGS

INGREDIENTS

FILLING

1½ pounds ground beef

1 small onion, chopped

2 cloves garlic, finely chopped

2 cans (10 ounces each) enchilada sauce

1 cup whole kernel corn

1 can (2.25 ounces) sliced ripe olives, drained

1 teaspoon salt

CRUST

2¼ cups ALBERS Yellow Corn Meal

2 cups water

1 can (12 fluid ounces) NESTLÉ CARNATION Evaporated Milk

1 teaspoon salt

1 can (4 ounces) diced green chiles

½ cup (2 ounces) shredded cheddar cheese

Pickled jalapeños (optional)

DIRECTIONS

PREHEAT oven to 425° F. Grease 12 x 7½-inch baking dish.

FOR FILLING:

COOK beef, onion, and garlic in large skillet over medium-high heat until beef is no longer pink. Drain. Stir in enchilada sauce, corn, olives, and salt.

FOR CRUST:

COMBINE corn meal, water, evaporated milk, and salt in medium saucepan. Cook over medium-high heat, stirring frequently, for 5 to 7 minutes or until thick. Stir in chiles. Reserve 2 cups corn meal mixture; cover with plastic wrap. Spread remaining corn meal mixture on bottom and up sides of prepared baking dish.

BAKE for 10 minutes. Cool on wire rack.

SPOON meat filling into corn meal crust. Spread reserved corn meal mixture over meat filling.

BAKE for 15 to 20 minutes; sprinkle with cheese.

BAKE for an additional 5 to 10 minutes or until cheese is melted. Garnish with pickled jalapeños.

Estimated Times
Preparation: 20 mins
Cooking: 50 mins

Rosemary-Garlic Pork Chops with Shallots and Artichokes

Pork loin chops slowly simmered in white balsamic vinegar, sliced shallots, and crushed red pepper are zesty and flavorful. Artichoke hearts and fresh rosemary round out the flavors in perfect balance.

MAKES 4 SERVINGS

INGREDIENTS

2 tablespoons olive oil, divided
2 large shallots, sliced
3 large cloves garlic, finely chopped
½ teaspoon MAGGI Instant Chicken Flavor Bouillon
¼ teaspoon crushed red pepper

1 package (8 ounces) frozen artichoke hearts, thawed
4 pork loin chops (about ½-inch-thick)
2 tablespoons white balsamic vinegar
1 tablespoon chopped fresh rosemary

DIRECTIONS

HEAT 1 tablespoon oil in large skillet over medium heat. Add shallots, garlic, bouillon, and crushed red pepper. Cook, stirring occasionally, until shallots are tender. Stir in artichoke hearts. Cook, stirring constantly, until artichokes are cooked through. Transfer to medium bowl.

HEAT remaining oil in same skillet over medium-high heat. Add pork; cook on one side until brown. Turn pork over; reduce heat to medium. Add artichoke mixture; sprinkle with vinegar and rosemary. Cover.

COOK for 18 to 20 minutes or until pork is no longer pink in center. Season with salt and ground black pepper.

Estimated Times
Preparation: 10 mins
Cooking: 40 mins

Rosemary-Garlic Pork Chops with Shallots and Artichokes

Quick Salsa Chicken and Rice

In many Mexican households, rice flavored with broth, tomatoes, and chiles constitutes a full meal. This dish, featuring flavorful rice and chicken with salsa, is a speedy version of the classic.

MAKES 4 SERVINGS

INGREDIENTS

1 tablespoon vegetable oil

4 boneless, skinless chicken breast halves (about 1 pound total), cut into cubes

1 teaspoon garlic powder

2 cups instant white or brown rice

1 jar (16 ounces) mild salsa

1¼ cups water

1 MAGGI Chicken Flavor Bouillon Cube

Chopped green onions (green parts only)

DIRECTIONS

HEAT oil in stockpot over medium heat. Add chicken and garlic powder. Cook, stirring occasionally, until chicken is no longer pink.

ADD rice, salsa, water, and bouillon. Bring to a boil. Cover; reduce heat to low. Cook, stirring occasionally, for 10 to 12 minutes or until rice is tender and liquid is absorbed. Sprinkle with green onions.

Estimated Times

Preparation: 10 mins

Cooking: 20 mins

Sensible Alfredo Sauce

Sensible Alfredo Sauce

This classic sauce continues to be a favorite and can be prepared in a snap.

MAKES 6 SERVINGS

INGREDIENTS

1¾ cups water

¼ cup all-purpose flour

2 cloves garlic, finely chopped

1½ teaspoons MAGGI Instant Chicken Flavor Bouillon

¼ teaspoon ground black pepper

⅛ teaspoon ground nutmeg

6 tablespoons freshly grated Parmesan or Romano cheese

⅓ cup plain yogurt

Hot cooked pasta

Chopped fresh parsley (optional)

DIRECTIONS

COMBINE water, flour, garlic, bouillon, pepper, and nutmeg in large skillet. Stir

Quick Salsa Chicken and Rice

until smooth. Cook over medium heat, stirring constantly, for 8 to 10 minutes or until mixture boils and thickens. Remove from heat; stir in cheese and yogurt.

SERVE over pasta. Sprinkle with parsley.

Estimated Times
Preparation: 10 mins
Cooking: 10 mins

Shrimp and Pasta in Lemon Cream Sauce

Simple yet elegant, this shrimp dish may be prepared for any sophisticated occasion. It will be sure to impress your family and friends.

MAKES 4 SERVINGS

INGREDIENTS

1 package (9 ounces) BUITONI Refrigerated Four Cheese Ravioli
12 ounces cooked medium shrimp
1 container (10 ounces) BUITONI Refrigerated Alfredo Sauce
1 tablespoon lemon juice
1 teaspoon grated lemon peel
Chopped fresh parsley (optional)

DIRECTIONS

PREPARE pasta according to package directions.

COMBINE shrimp, sauce, lemon juice, and lemon peel in small saucepan. Heat over medium-low heat, stirring occasionally, until heated through (do not boil).

SERVE over pasta. Sprinkle with parsley.

Estimated Times
Preparation: 5 mins
Cooking: 15 mins

Cheese

An Italian meal would not be complete without fresh cheese. Make sure you keep cheeses available in your kitchen as you never know when you'll need them. Try Parmesan or Romano, both hard cow's-milk cheeses, they add a pungent flavor to pasta dishes with meat and vegetables.

Gorgonzola is excellent alone on bread or crackers, or as a creamy pasta sauce. Try mozzarella combined with tomatoes, basil, and balsamic vinegar and create *Insalata Caprese*, a classic Italian dish. Ricotta is a must in baked lasagna and sweetened, in desserts such as cannoli.

Cheeses are also great additions to salads, vegetable gratins, oven-grilled breads, fresh vegetables, soups, fried or scrambled eggs, and fresh fruit.

Shrimp and Pasta in Lemon Cream Sauce

Shrimp with Garlic Cream Sauce over Linguine

The decadent garlic cream sauce with shrimp is elegant enough to serve at your next intimate dinner party.

MAKES 4 SERVINGS

INGREDIENTS

1 cup hot water
1 cup Original NESTLÉ COFFEE-MATE Powdered Coffee Creamer
8 large cloves garlic, unpeeled
16 raw large shrimp, peeled and deveined
2 tablespoons olive oil
1 teaspoon cornstarch
¾ cup (3 ounces) freshly grated Parmesan cheese
3 tablespoons finely chopped parsley
Salt and ground black pepper
1 package (9 ounces) BUITONI Refrigerated Linguine

DIRECTIONS

WHISK together water and Coffee-mate until smooth.

BRING 6 cups water to a boil in medium saucepan. Add garlic; cook for 2 minutes. Add shrimp; cook for 2 minutes or until shrimp turn pink. Drain. Peel and chop garlic.

HEAT oil in large skillet over medium-high heat. Add garlic; cook, stirring frequently, for 1 minute.

WHISK in Coffee-mate mixture and cornstarch. Whisk until cornstarch is dissolved. Cook, whisking occasionally, for 3 to 4 minutes or until sauce begins to thicken. Stir in shrimp, cheese, and parsley. Season with salt and pepper.

PREPARE pasta according to package directions. Pour sauce over pasta; toss to coat.

Estimated Times
Preparation: 10 mins
Cooking: 20 mins

Skewered Sesame Chicken

Skewered Sesame Chicken

**Really quick and easy.
Great with rice and a salad.**

MAKES 4 SERVINGS

INGREDIENTS

½ cup MAGGI Seasoning Sauce
½ cup saké (rice wine)
⅓ cup granulated sugar
2 large cloves garlic, finely chopped
1 teaspoon peeled, finely chopped fresh ginger

Shrimp with Garlic Cream Sauce over Linguine

½ teaspoon MAGGI Instant Chicken Flavor Bouillon

½ teaspoon sesame oil

4 boneless, skinless chicken breast halves (about 1 pound total), cut into 1½-inch pieces

12 (6-inch) skewers

1 tablespoon toasted sesame seeds

2 tablespoons finely chopped cilantro (optional)

DIRECTIONS

COMBINE seasoning sauce, saké, sugar, garlic, ginger, bouillon, and oil in medium bowl. Reserve ⅓ cup marinade. Add chicken to remaining marinade; toss to coat. Marinate in refrigerator for 1 to 2 hours.

THREAD chicken onto skewers. Discard marinade.

PREHEAT grill or broiler.

GRILL or broil chicken, turning and basting with reserved marinade, for 10 to 15 minutes or until no longer pink. Sprinkle with sesame seeds and cilantro.

NOTE: If using wooden skewers, soak in water for 30 minutes before threading.

Estimated Times
Preparation: 30 mins
Marinating: 1 hr
Cooking: 10 mins

Spinach and Cheese Strata

This strata is perfect for a Sunday brunch or a holiday breakfast.

MAKES 6 SERVINGS

INGREDIENTS

3 tablespoons butter

1 large onion, finely chopped

3 large cloves garlic, finely chopped

1 teaspoon salt, divided

½ teaspoon ground black pepper, divided

1 package (10 ounces) frozen chopped spinach, thawed and squeezed dry

8 cups French bread cubes (about 1-inch), divided

2 cups (8 ounces) shredded Gruyère or Monterey Jack cheese, divided

1 cup (4 ounces) grated Parmesan cheese, divided

1½ cups hot water

1 cup Original NESTLÉ COFFEE-MATE Powdered Coffee Creamer

9 large eggs

2 tablespoons Dijon mustard

DIRECTIONS

GREASE 3-quart casserole dish or 13 x 9-inch baking dish.

MELT butter in large saucepan over medium-high heat. Add onion and garlic. Cook, stirring frequently, for 4 to 5 minutes or until onion is soft. Add

½ teaspoon salt and ¼ teaspoon pepper. Stir in spinach; remove from heat.

PLACE 4 cups bread cubes in prepared dish. Top evenly with half of spinach mixture. Sprinkle with 1 cup Gruyère cheese and ½ cup Parmesan cheese. Repeat layering, ending with cheese.

WHISK together water and Coffee-mate in medium bowl until smooth. Whisk in eggs, mustard, remaining salt, and remaining pepper. Pour evenly over strata. Cover with plastic wrap; refrigerate for 8 hours or overnight. Let strata stand at room temperature for 30 minutes prior to baking.

PREHEAT oven to 350° F.

BAKE, uncovered, for 45 to 50 minutes or until puffed and golden brown.

Estimated Times
Preparation: 20 mins
Refrigerating: 8 hrs
Standing: 30 mins
Cooking: 50 mins

Spinach and Cheese Strata

Tex-Mex Pasta Bake

This layered casserole is sure to become one of your family's favorites. Ground turkey or chicken can be substituted for the ground beef. Serve with steamed broccoli.

MAKES 8 SERVINGS

INGREDIENTS

1 package (9 ounces) STOUFFER'S frozen Creamed Spinach, defrosted*

1 package (16 ounces) dry penne pasta

1 pound ground beef

1 package (8 ounces) cream cheese, at room temperature

1 jar (16 ounces) salsa

1 can (14.5 ounces) tomato sauce

1 tablespoon chili powder

1 cup (4 ounces) shredded cheddar or Monterey Jack cheese

DIRECTIONS

PREHEAT oven to 400° F.

PREPARE pasta according to package directions.

COOK beef in large skillet over medium-high heat until no longer pink; drain.

COMBINE creamed spinach and cream cheese in medium bowl. Combine pasta, salsa, beef, tomato sauce, and chili powder in large bowl. Spoon half of pasta mixture into 13 x 9-inch baking pan. Top with spinach mixture. Top with remaining pasta; cover.

BAKE for 30 minutes; uncover. Sprinkle with cheddar cheese; bake for an additional 10 minutes or until bubbly.

FOR FREEZE AHEAD:

PREPARE as above; do not bake. Do not sprinkle with cheddar cheese. Cover; freeze for up to 2 months. Thaw overnight in refrigerator.

PREHEAT oven to 400° F.

BAKE, uncovered, for 45 to 55 minutes; uncover. Sprinkle with cheddar cheese; bake for an additional 10 minutes or until bubbly.

*DEFROST creamed spinach in microwave on MEDIUM (50%) power for 5 to 6 minutes.

Estimated Times
Preparation: 10 mins
Cooking: 55 mins

Tex-Mex Pasta Bake

Tortellini with Pesto and Sun-Dried Tomatoes

Garlicky pesto and rich sun-dried tomatoes make this tortellini irresistible. This is an easy dish for a picnic or potluck. A salad and loaf of bread will complete this meal.

Tortellini with Pesto and Sun-Dried Tomatoes

Cooking Tip

Most people would agree that nothing goes better with Italian food than a nice glass of wine. Try red wine with rich poultry and game dishes as well as with risottos, rich pasta dishes, and vegetable soups. The well-known Chianti is thought by some to be the ultimate Italian red. Chianti comes from Tuscany. It goes well with robust meat dishes, such as osso buco and bistecca alla Fiorentina, creamy pastas such as Fettuccini Alfredo and Spaghetti Carbonara, and mild cheeses. If you want to try some Italian whites, pour a glass of Pinot Grigio. It is a terrific white wine that goes with all types of seafood, poultry, and vegetable dishes. Italy has some sparkling versions of Champagne and pair well with light pastas, egg dishes, and of course, dessert!

MAKES 4 SERVINGS

INGREDIENTS

2 packages (9 ounces each) BUITONI Refrigerated Three Cheese Tortellini

½ cup BUITONI Refrigerated Pesto with Basil

½ cup (2 ounces) grated Parmesan cheese

¼ cup sun-dried tomatoes, drained and chopped

½ bunch basil, chopped

DIRECTIONS

PREPARE pasta according to package directions. Drain pasta. Toss with pesto, cheese, tomatoes, and basil. Serve hot or at room temperature.

Estimated Times
Preparation: 10 mins
Cooking: 10 mins

Turkey Scaloppine

Turkey cutlets are crosswise cuts from the turkey breast that are one-fourth- to one-half-inch thick. Look for them in your supermarket's poultry section.

MAKES 4 SERVINGS

INGREDIENTS

1 pound turkey breast cutlets or slices
3 tablespoons all-purpose flour
3 teaspoons olive oil, divided
¼ cup water
¼ cup chicken broth or dry white wine
1 tablespoon butter
2 cloves garlic, finely chopped
½ teaspoon crushed dried sage
½ teaspoon MAGGI Instant Chicken
   Flavor Bouillon

DIRECTIONS

COAT turkey with flour; sprinkle with salt and ground black pepper.

HEAT 1½ teaspoons oil in large, nonstick skillet over medium-high heat. Add half the turkey; cook on each side for 1 to 2 minutes or until no longer pink in center. Remove from skillet; keep warm. Repeat with remaining oil and turkey.

ADD water, broth, butter, garlic, sage, and bouillon to skillet. Bring to a boil; cook for 1 to 2 minutes. Add turkey to skillet; reduce heat to low. Cook, stirring and turning turkey over to coat, for 1 to 2 minutes.

Estimated Times
Preparation: 10 mins
Cooking: 15 mins

Turkey Scaloppine

Turkey Tetrazzini

This is an easy meal to make with limited time yet without sacrificing great taste.

MAKES 8 SERVINGS

INGREDIENTS

8 ounces dry spaghetti
¼ cup dry bread crumbs
3 tablespoons butter or
   margarine, divided
¾ cup (3 ounces) grated Parmesan
   cheese, divided

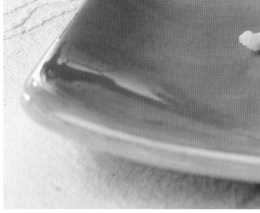

Turkey Tetrazzini

½ cup chopped onion
¼ cup all-purpose flour
¼ teaspoon salt
⅛ teaspoon ground white pepper
1 can (14.5 fluid ounces) chicken broth
1 can (12 fluid ounces) NESTLÉ
   CARNATION Evaporated Milk
2 cups cooked, chopped turkey
   breast meat
2 cans (4 ounces each) sliced
   mushrooms, drained
1 cup frozen peas, thawed
2 tablespoons dry sherry

DIRECTIONS

PREHEAT oven to 350° F. Lightly grease 13 x 9-inch baking dish.

PREPARE pasta according to package directions; keep warm.

COMBINE bread crumbs and 2 tablespoons butter in small bowl. Stir in ¼ cup cheese.

MELT remaining butter in medium saucepan over medium heat. Add onion.

Cook, stirring occasionally, for 1 to 2 minutes or until tender. Stir in flour, salt, and pepper. Cook, stirring constantly, for 1 minute. Remove from heat; gradually stir in broth. Return to heat; bring to boil over medium heat, stirring constantly. Stir in evaporated milk and remaining cheese. Cook over low heat until cheese melts. Remove from heat. Stir in turkey, mushrooms, peas, and sherry.

COMBINE pasta and turkey mixture in large bowl. Pour into prepared baking dish. Sprinkle with bread crumb topping.

BAKE for 20 to 25 minutes or until topping is lightly browned. Serve immediately while hot.

Estimated Times
Preparation: 15 mins
Cooking: 30 mins

favorite refreshments

favorite refreshments

We've pulled together some of our favorite coffee house, tea shop, and smoothie bar recipes and put them within easy reach, right in your own kitchen. Some are soothing, while others are a bit adventurous—tropical even! But these beverages are not only delicious, they're hard-working, just like you. They're cooling on a hot day, warming on a cold one. They provide liquid replenishment and important nutrients to your family and friends. Yet these tasty concoctions are simple to make, courtesy of a few key flavor combinations. So blend, brew, stir, shake, pour, sip, slurp, or gulp. And enjoy a tall glass—or a hearty mug—of refreshment in good health.

Arctic Java

Arctic Java

A frozen coffee is just what you need on a hot day.

MAKES 2 SERVINGS

INGREDIENTS

¾ cup brewed double-strength coffee,
    at room temperature
½ cup Original NESTLÉ COFFEE-MATE
    Half & Half
3 tablespoons granulated sugar
3 cups ice cubes

DIRECTIONS

PLACE coffee, Half & Half, sugar, and ice
in blender; cover. Blend until smooth.

Estimated Time
Preparation: 5 mins

Berry Smoothie

A berry, berry yummy drink for smoothie lovers!

MAKES 2 SERVINGS

INGREDIENTS

1 cup strawberry nectar
1 packet Strawberry Sensation Flavor
    NESTLÉ CARNATION INSTANT
    BREAKFAST Complete Nutritional Drink
½ to 1 cup frozen berries (e.g.,
    strawberries, raspberries, blueberries)
½ cup ice cubes

DIRECTIONS

PLACE nectar, Carnation Instant
Breakfast, berries, and ice in blender;
cover. Blend until smooth.

Estimated Time
Preparation: 5 mins

Berry Smoothie

Blue Monkey Smoothie

Blue Monkey Smoothie

The name makes this healthy smoothie a hit with the kids.

MAKES 2 SERVINGS

INGREDIENTS

1 cup fat free milk

1 container (8 ounces) blueberry fat free yogurt

1 packet No Sugar Added Classic French Vanilla Flavor NESTLÉ CARNATION INSTANT BREAKFAST Complete Nutritional Drink

½ cup frozen unsweetened blueberries

½ banana

DIRECTIONS

PLACE milk, yogurt, Carnation Instant Breakfast, blueberries, and banana in blender; cover. Blend until smooth.

NOTE: For added variety, blend in any flavor of fat free yogurt or unsweetened berries. For a frostier drink, omit yogurt and blend in 1 cup (about 2 large scoops) of your favorite fat free frozen yogurt.

Estimated Time

Preparation: 5 mins

Caramel Latte Cooler

Now you can enjoy a delicious and refreshing blended iced coffee with NESCAFÉ ICE JAVA iced coffee syrup, sweet caramel, and creamy ice cream at home. This recipe is sure to save you both time and money at the coffee house.

MAKES 1 SERVING

INGREDIENTS

1 pint vanilla ice cream

½ cup milk

3 tablespoons Cappuccino Flavor NESCAFÉ ICE JAVA Iced Coffee Syrup

2 tablespoons caramel syrup or ice cream topping

DIRECTIONS

PLACE ice cream, milk, Nescafé syrup, and caramel syrup in blender; cover. Blend until smooth. Serve immediately.

Estimated Time

Preparation: 5 mins

Caramel Latte Cooler

Champurrado: Mexican Hot Chocolate Beverage

Try this sweet and nutritious Mexican beverage: Champurrado! With its combination of chocolate and cinnamon, it is a delicious way to warm you up on a cold day.

MAKES 12 SERVINGS

INGREDIENTS

12 cups water, divided

3 cinnamon sticks

1½ cups masa harina (Mexican corn masa mix)

1½ cups packed brown sugar (or 2 large piloncillo cones-Mexican brown sugar; about 6 ounces each)

1 ounce NESTLÉ TOLL HOUSE Unsweetened Chocolate Baking Bar (half of 2-ounce bar)

2 teaspoons vanilla extract

DIRECTIONS

COMBINE 8 cups water and cinnamon in large saucepan. Bring to a boil.

PLACE remaining water and masa harina in blender; cover. Blend until smooth. Pour mixture through fine mesh sieve into cinnamon-water mixture. Bring to a boil. Reduce heat to low; cook, stirring constantly with wire whisk, for 6 to 7 minutes or until mixture is thickened.

Champurrado: Mexican Hot Chocolate Beverage

Chocolate Caramel Cappuccino

Chocolate Caramel Cappuccino

With a great blend of flavors, this cappuccino drink is a sure way to start your morning off right.

MAKES 2 SERVINGS

INGREDIENTS

1 cup hot water

¾ cup milk

3 tablespoons caramel syrup or ice cream topping

2 tablespoons Chocolate Flavor NESTLÉ NESQUIK Calcium Fortified Syrup

1 tablespoon NESCAFÉ TASTER'S CHOICE 100% Pure Instant Coffee Granules

DIRECTIONS

PLACE water, milk, caramel syrup, Nesquik, and coffee granules in microwave-safe pitcher. Microwave on HIGH (100%) power for 2 to 3 minutes or until hot; stir. Serve immediately.

NOTE: Try substituting Gourmet Roast NESCAFÉ TASTER'S CHOICE 100% Pure Instant Coffee Granules or Decaffeinated NESCAFÉ TASTER'S CHOICE 100% Pure Instant Coffee Granules.

Estimated Times
Preparation: 5 mins
Cooking: 2 mins

STIR in sugar, chocolate, and vanilla extract. Cook, stirring frequently, for 4 to 5 minutes or until chocolate is melted and flavors are blended.

Estimated Times
Preparation: 5 mins
Cooking: 15 mins

Chocolate Bunnana Blaster

Go bananas with this easy to make, delicious drink.

MAKES 4 SERVINGS

INGREDIENTS

2½ cups milk

1 cup vanilla ice cream

½ banana

½ cup Chocolate Flavor NESTLÉ NESQUIK Calcium Fortified Powder

DIRECTIONS

PLACE milk, ice cream, banana, and Nesquik in blender; cover. Blend until smooth.

NOTE: 2½ cups NESTLÉ NESQUIK Refrigerated Ready-to-Drink Chocolate Milk may be used in place of milk and Nesquik powder.

Estimated Time
Preparation: 5 mins

Chocolate Milk Shake

This Chocolate Milk Shake tastes just like the ones you had as a kid.

MAKES 1 SERVING

INGREDIENTS

1 cup vanilla fat free frozen yogurt
1 packet Rich Milk Chocolate
   Flavor NESTLÉ CARNATION
   INSTANT BREAKFAST Complete
   Nutritional Drink
½ cup fat free milk

DIRECTIONS

PLACE frozen yogurt, Carnation Instant Breakfast, and milk in blender; cover. Blend until smooth.

Estimated Time
Preparation: 5 mins

Chocolate Polar Bears

This awesome treat will satisfy your kids' roar and their need for calcium. Chocolate Polar Bears are also an excellent source of calcium.

MAKES 2 SERVINGS

INGREDIENTS

1 cup fat free milk
½ cup ice cubes
¼ cup Chocolate Flavor NESTLÉ
   NESQUIK Calcium Fortified Powder
¼ cup chocolate or vanilla fat free
   frozen yogurt
2 tablespoons whipped cream

DIRECTIONS

PLACE milk, ice, Nesquik, and frozen yogurt in blender; cover. Blend until smooth. Pour into 2 glasses; top with whipped cream. Serve immediately.

TWIST IT UP!
Make Pink Polar Bears by substituting Strawberry Flavor NESTLÉ NESQUIK Calcium Fortified Powder and vanilla fat free frozen yogurt.

Estimated Time
Preparation: 5 mins

Cocoa Cola Float

A nice chocolate twist on the old-fashioned cola floats.

MAKES 4 SERVINGS

Chocolate Milk Shake

Cocoa Cola Float

INGREDIENTS

2 tablespoons (1 envelope) Rich
    Chocolate Flavor NESTLÉ Hot
    Cocoa Mix

1 cup hot milk

2 cups carbonated cola beverage, chilled

4 cups vanilla ice cream, divided

DIRECTIONS

PLACE cocoa mix in medium, heat-proof
container. Stir in milk until cocoa mix is
dissolved. Let cool slightly. Stir in cola.
Place 1 cup ice cream in each of 4 tall
glasses; top with cola mixture.

NOTE: For a fat free version of this recipe,
substitute Fat Free Rich Chocolate Flavor
NESTLÉ Hot Cocoa Mix, fat free milk, diet
cola, and fat free vanilla frozen yogurt.

Estimated Time
Preparation: 10 mins

Cocoa Shiver

**This recipe can be made in a fat free
version by substituting fat free milk,
fat free frozen yogurt, and using
Fat Free NESTLÉ Hot Cocoa Mix.**

MAKES 2 SERVINGS

INGREDIENTS

2 cups vanilla ice cream or frozen yogurt

2 cups milk

6 tablespoons (3 envelopes) Rich
    Chocolate or Milk Chocolate Flavor
    NESTLÉ Hot Cocoa Mix

DIRECTIONS

PLACE ice cream, milk, and cocoa mix
in blender; cover. Blend until smooth.
Serve immediately.

Estimated Time
Preparation: 5 mins

NESQUIK Nutrition Tip

In addition to its delicious taste,
NESTLÉ NESQUIK provides the
added nutrition adults and kids
need. NESQUIK Powder, Syrup, and
Ready-To-Drink products make milk
into a delicious treat that kids of all
ages will drink. NESQUIK Powder
also has been specially fortified with
added calcium, vitamin C, and other
essential vitamins and minerals to
help build strong bones.

A glass of NESQUIK milk contains
33% more calcium than milk alone.
It also contains nutrients that help
build strong bones, including
calcium, a major part of bone
mass; vitamin C helps to build the
connective tissue that holds bone
mass together; vitamin D (from milk)
facilitates the absorption of calcium
into the body to create bone tissue
and the connective tissues and helps
in the conversion of calcium into
bone; vitamin B6 plays a key factor
in building of the connective tissue
that holds bone mass together; zinc,
an essential for the conversion of
calcium into bone; and manganese
helps maintain connective tissue that
holds bone mass together and helps
in cartilage formation.

Dreamy Creamy Chocolate Chai

Dreamy Creamy Chocolate Chai

No need to get out a lot of spices for this easy recipe! Warm up with a creamy, chocolate version of a chai beverage that is a snap to make.

MAKES 1 SERVING

INGREDIENTS

2 tablespoons (1 envelope) Rich
    Chocolate Flavor NESTLÉ Hot
    Cocoa Mix
1 cup hot milk
⅛ teaspoon vanilla extract
1 chai-flavored tea bag or
    ¼ teaspoon pumpkin pie spice
Whipped cream
Dried or fresh orange rind (optional)

DIRECTIONS

PLACE cocoa mix in large mug. Stir in milk and vanilla extract until combined. Place tea bag or pumpkin pie spice in

cocoa; let stand for at least 1 minute. Garnish with whipped cream and orange rind. Serve immediately.

Estimated Time
Preparation: 5 mins

Festive Hot Tea Punch

This tea is especially good on a cool day.

MAKES 8 SERVINGS

INGREDIENTS

6 cups water
¾ cup granulated sugar
⅓ cup NESTEA Unsweetened Instant
    100% Tea
8 whole cloves
2 cinnamon sticks
2½ cups Punch Flavor LIBBY'S JUICY
    JUICE Premium 100% Juice
¼ cup fresh lemon juice

DIRECTIONS

COMBINE water, sugar, Nestea, cloves, and cinnamon sticks in large saucepan. Bring to a boil over high heat, stirring occasionally. Boil for 2 to 4 minutes. Remove whole spices, if desired. Stir in Juicy Juice and lemon juice. Serve hot.

Estimated Times
Preparation: 5 mins
Cooking: 10 mins

Fiesta Tea Spritzer

This iced tea with bubbles will please all your party-goers. Served in margarita glasses, this cool beverage seems a little more special than regular iced tea. Serve it at your next get-together.

MAKES 6 SERVINGS

INGREDIENTS

4 cups PERRIER Sparkling Natural
    Mineral Water
2 cups water
1 cup Lemon Flavor NESTEA
    Sweetened Iced Tea Concentrate
3 tablespoons honey
Lemon juice
Granulated sugar
Crushed ice cubes
Lemon and lime slices

DIRECTIONS

PLACE sparkling water, water, Nestea, and honey in large pitcher. Stir until combined.

MOISTEN rims of margarita glasses with lemon juice. Put enough sugar on a small plate to coat rims. Dip rims into sugar.

FILL glasses with ice. Top with Nestea mixture. Garnish with lemon and lime slices.

Estimated Time
Preparation: 10 mins

Fiesta Tea Spritzer

About Tea

Tea is nearly 5,000 years old, and as legend has it, was discovered quite by accident by the Chinese Emperor Shen Nung in 2737 B.C. Tea has since played a major role in American history, through the well-known protest to English taxation on Tea in 1767. The men of Boston, dressed as Indians, threw hundreds of pounds of tea into Boston Harbor. In retaliation to this uprising, the port of Boston was closed and the city was occupied by royal troops. The colonial leaders met and revolution was declared, beginning what is known as The Boston Tea Party.

The first use of iced tea was invented by an American tea plantation owner, Richard Blechynden, at the 1904 World's Fair in St. Louis. Because of a heat wave no one wanted to sample his hot tea, so he dumped a load of ice into it and served the first iced tea. It was the hit of the fair!

Today much of the world's tea is grown in mountainous areas usually 3,000 to 7,000 feet above sea level, situated between the Tropic of Cancer and the Tropic of Capricorn. Nestlé is a leading maker of tea, producing 50 percent of the world's processed tea.

French Vanilla Mocha

Treat yourself to this rich delight!

MAKES 1 SERVING

INGREDIENTS
¾ cup hot water
1 tablespoon NESCAFÉ TASTER'S
   CHOICE 100% Pure Instant
   Coffee Granules
¼ cup French Vanilla Flavor NESTLÉ
   COFFEE-MATE Liquid Coffee Creamer
1 tablespoon Chocolate Flavor NESTLÉ
   NESQUIK Calcium Fortified Syrup
Whipped cream (optional)

DIRECTIONS
COMBINE water and coffee granules in
large mug; stir until coffee is dissolved.
Stir in Coffee-mate and Nesquik. Top
with whipped cream.

Estimated Time
Preparation: 5 mins

French Vanilla Mocha

Frothy Cappuccino Punch

**Serve this holiday beverage when
you have family and friends over
for a holiday brunch.**

MAKES 50 SERVINGS

INGREDIENTS
1 gallon freshly brewed, double-strength
   coffee*, chilled
3 cans (about 12 fluid ounces each)
   NESTLÉ CARNATION Evaporated Milk,
   chilled, divided
1 cup granulated sugar, divided
1 teaspoon vanilla extract
1 quart chocolate ice cream
NESTLÉ TOLL HOUSE Semi-Sweet
   Chocolate Baking Bars, made
   into curls
Ground cinnamon (optional)

DIRECTIONS
POUR coffee into large punch bowl.
Combine 2¼ cups evaporated milk,
½ cup sugar, and vanilla extract in
blender; blend until frothy. Add milk
mixture to coffee. Repeat with remaining
evaporated milk and remaining sugar.
Add scoops of ice cream to punch and
top with chocolate curls.

LADLE punch into cups; sprinkle
with cinnamon.

*Measure 2 rounded tablespoons of ground coffee to every 6 ounces of water. Vary measurements to suit your individual taste.

NOTE: To make chocolate curls, carefully draw a vegetable peeler across a bar of NESTLÉ TOLL HOUSE Semi-Sweet Chocolate. Vary the width of your curls by using different sides of the chocolate bar.

Estimated Times
Preparation: 30 mins

Frozen Mocha Café

A perfect frozen coffee drink when you really need to cool down.

MAKES 1 SERVING

INGREDIENTS

1 cup strong brewed coffee, chilled
1 large scoop coffee ice cream or
    frozen yogurt
¼ cup Creamy Chocolate Flavor
    NESTLÉ COFFEE-MATE Powdered
    Coffee Creamer

DIRECTIONS

PLACE coffee, ice cream, and Coffee-mate in blender; cover. Blend until smooth.

Estimated Time
Preparation: 5 mins

Frozen Mocha Café

Nutrition Tip

Vitamins are essential for normal metabolism, growth, and maintenance of body tissues. But on its own, the body cannot synthesize them in sufficient amounts to meet its needs—most vitamins must be consumed in food.

Vitamins are classified into two distinct groups based on their solubility: Fat-soluble vitamins are vitamins A, D, E, and K. Water-soluble vitamins are vitamin C, and those of the so-called B complex. Unlike the fat-soluble vitamins, the water-soluble ones are not stored in the body and any excess usually is eliminated.

Vitamins are essential nutrients that must be consumed in the diet, with three notable exceptions. The three exceptions are vitamin D, which can be synthesized from a cholesterol metabolite by the action of sunlight on the skin; niacin, for which the requirement can be met in part by its synthesis in the body from the amino acid, tryptophan; and vitamin K, which can be produced by bacteria in the large intestine.

Frozen Sunset

Frozen Sunset

This wonderful orange smoothie is perfect on a hot summer morning.

MAKES 2 SERVINGS

INGREDIENTS
1 cup orange juice
¼ cup Vanilla Flavor NESTLÉ
    COFFEE-MATE Half & Half
2 cups ice cubes

DIRECTIONS
PLACE orange juice, Half & Half, and ice in blender; cover. Blend until smooth.

Estimated Time
Preparation: 5 mins

Fuzzy Navel

A refreshing non-alcoholic alternative.

MAKES 2 SERVINGS

INGREDIENTS
1 cup orange juice
½ cup fresh or frozen sliced peaches
½ medium banana
¼ cup plain fat free yogurt

1 packet No Sugar Added Classic French Vanilla Flavor NESTLÉ CARNATION INSTANT BREAKFAST Complete Nutritional Drink

DIRECTIONS

PLACE orange juice, peaches, banana, yogurt, and Carnation Instant Breakfast in blender; cover. Blend until smooth.

Estimated Time
Preparation: 5 mins

Heavenly Hazelnut Hot Chocolate Liqueur

Hot chocolate with coffee and hazelnut liqueurs will warm your soul on a cold night.

MAKES 4 SERVINGS

INGREDIENTS

3 tablespoons NESTLÉ TOLL HOUSE Baking Cocoa
2 tablespoons granulated sugar
1¼ cups water, divided
1 cup Vanilla Flavor NESTLÉ COFFEE-MATE Half & Half
¼ cup coffee liqueur
¼ cup hazelnut liqueur
Whipped cream (optional)

Heavenly Hazelnut Hot Chocolate Liqueur

DIRECTIONS

COMBINE baking cocoa and sugar in small saucepan. Gradually whisk in ¼ cup water. Heat over medium-low heat, whisking frequently, until mixture comes to a gentle boil. Stir in remaining water and Half & Half. Heat through.

DIVIDE hot chocolate between 4 mugs; top each with 1 tablespoon coffee liqueur and 1 tablespoon hazelnut liqueur. Top with whipped cream.

Estimated Times
Preparation: 5 mins
Cooking: 5 mins

Hot Cocoa Mix in a Jar

This makes a great gift at the holidays as well as a tasty cup of cocoa during a cool day.

MAKES 12 SERVINGS

INGREDIENTS

6 cups dry NESTLÉ CARNATION Instant Nonfat Dry Milk
1½ cups granulated sugar
1½ cups miniature marshmallows (optional)
1 cup, plus 2 tablespoons NESTLÉ TOLL HOUSE Baking Cocoa

DIRECTIONS

COMBINE dry milk, sugar, marshmallows, and cocoa in large bowl. Pour into 2-quart jar or tall container. Seal with lid and decorate with fabric and ribbon.

RECIPE TO ATTACH:

Measure ½ cup cocoa mix into mug. Stir in 1 cup hot water or milk. Makes 12 servings.

VARIATION USING PINT JAR (SERVES 4):

1½ cups dry NESTLÉ CARNATION Instant Nonfat Dry Milk
⅓ cup granulated sugar
½ cup miniature marshmallows (optional)
¼ cup, plus 2 tablespoons NESTLÉ TOLL HOUSE Baking Cocoa

RECIPE TO ATTACH:

Measure ½ cup cocoa mix into mug. Stir in 1 cup hot water or milk. Makes 4 servings.

Estimated Time
Preparation: 10 mins

Hot Raspberry Cocoa

Hot Raspberry Cocoa

Raspberry-flavored hot cocoa! A delicious break from ordinary cocoa!

MAKES 2 SERVINGS

INGREDIENTS

4 tablespoons (2 envelopes) Rich Chocolate Flavor NESTLÉ Hot Cocoa Mix

3 teaspoons raspberry jam

2 cups hot milk

DIRECTIONS

PLACE cocoa mix and jam in small, heat-proof container. Stir in milk; mix until jam is dissolved. Strain, if desired. Serve immediately.

Estimated Time
Preparation: 5 mins

Iced Café Mocha

Coffee lovers who enjoy café mocha hot will also find it cool served this way.

MAKES 2 SERVINGS

INGREDIENTS

¾ cup milk

2 teaspoons NESCAFÉ TASTER'S CHOICE 100% Pure Instant Coffee Granules

1 cup ice cubes

½ cup chocolate ice cream or frozen yogurt

1 tablespoon granulated sugar

DIRECTIONS

PLACE milk and coffee granules in blender; cover. Blend until coffee is dissolved. Add ice, ice cream, and sugar; blend until smooth. Serve immediately.

Estimated Time
Preparation: 5 mins

Iced Horchata

Horchatas are popular drinks in Spain and Mexico.

MAKES 6 SERVINGS

INGREDIENTS

4 cups hot water

1 cup white rice, rinsed and drained

2 cinnamon sticks (about 3 inches each)

¾ cup granulated sugar

1 cup Original NESTLÉ COFFEE-MATE Half & Half

Ice cubes

Ground cinnamon

DIRECTIONS

COMBINE water, rice, and cinnamon sticks in large bowl; cool. Cover; refrigerate for 2 hours or overnight.

REMOVE cinnamon sticks. Spoon rice into food processor or blender (reserve soaking liquid); cover. Process on high for 3 to 4 minutes. Add reserved soaking liquid and sugar; process for 2 minutes. Strain mixture through a cheesecloth or fine sieve into a pitcher, pressing the rice solids until only a dry paste remains; discard paste. Stir Half & Half into mixture.

SERVE over ice. Sprinkle with cinnamon.

Estimated Times

Preparation: 10 mins

Refrigerating: 2 hrs

Nutrition Tip

If you are wondering about the amount of caffeine in NESTEA products, here are some answers. Our Sweetened with Lemon and Lemonade Tea varieties contain 20 to 30 milligrams of caffeine per 8-fluid-ounce serving. Our unsweetened 100 percent regular teas contain 20 to 30 milligrams per 8-fluid-ounce serving. Our unsweetened decaffeinated tea contains less than 1 milligram of caffeine per 8-fluid-ounce serving.

If the weather turns cooler, NESTEA can also be used for hot tea. The only caution is that our sugar free mixes must be consumed within 15 minutes of preparation for maximum flavor enjoyment.

NESTEA products are good for 24 months for freshness and quality. And for more cool drink ideas visit us at Nestea.com. Enjoy!

Iced Horchata

All LIBBY'S JUICY JUICE products are made from 100 percent real fruit juice and contain no added sugars, sweeteners, preservatives, or artificial flavors. They are made with only 100 percent premium natural fruit juice from concentrate. LIBBY'S JUICY JUICE is an excellent source of vitamin C and provides 100 percent of the US RDA of vitamin C (40 mg) for children in each serving. Like other juices, LIBBY'S JUICY JUICE does not contain any caffeine, gluten, or lactose. For more information on products check out JuicyJuice.com.

Iced Strawberry Tea

Iced Strawberry Tea

Good after school or on warm days.

MAKES 2 SERVINGS

INGREDIENTS

2½ cups hot water

5 tablespoons NESTEA Iced Tea Mix Sweetened with Sugar and Lemon

¼ cup strawberry preserves

Ice cubes

Lemon slices (optional)

DIRECTIONS

COMBINE water, Nestea, and preserves in 1-quart pitcher. Refrigerate for at least 2 hours. Strain before serving, if desired.

SERVE over ice; garnish with lemon slices.

Estimated Times

Preparation: 5 mins

Refrigerating: 2 hrs

Juicy Beetle Punch

Kids won't mind these "beetles" in their punch.

MAKES 10 SERVINGS

INGREDIENTS

4 cups Punch Flavor LIBBY'S JUICY JUICE Premium 100% Juice, chilled

4 cups ginger ale, chilled

1 jar (16 ounces) maraschino cherries, undrained

Juicy Beetle Punch

DIRECTIONS

COMBINE Juicy Juice, ginger ale, and maraschino cherry juice in large punch bowl; stir to combine. Cut cherries in half; add to punch.

Estimated Time
Preparation: 15 mins

Jungle Smoothie

A quick pick-me-up after school or anytime!

MAKES 1 SERVING

INGREDIENTS
½ cup fat free milk
½ cup pineapple or other
   tropical-flavored juice
½ cup cubed frozen tropical fruit (e.g.,
   mango, papaya, and/or pineapple)
¼ banana
1 packet No Sugar Added Classic French
   Vanilla Flavor NESTLÉ CARNATION
   INSTANT BREAKFAST Complete
   Nutritional Drink
½ cup ice cubes

DIRECTIONS

PLACE milk, juice, fruit, banana, Carnation Instant Breakfast, and ice in blender; cover. Blend until smooth.

Estimated Time
Preparation: 5 mins

Jungle Smoothie

Mocha Blast!

Here's a smoothie for coffee lovers everywhere.

MAKES 2 SERVINGS

INGREDIENTS
1 cup fat free milk
1 cup chocolate fat free frozen yogurt
1 packet Rich Milk Chocolate
   Flavor NESTLÉ CARNATION
   INSTANT BREAKFAST Complete
   Nutritional Drink
1½ teaspoons NESCAFÉ TASTER'S
   CHOICE 100% Pure Instant
   Coffee Granules

DIRECTIONS

PLACE milk, frozen yogurt, Carnation Instant Breakfast, and coffee granules in blender; cover. Blend until smooth.

Estimated Time
Preparation: 5 mins

Mocha Chiller

PB and Chocolate Smoothie

The peanut butter in this cold beverage adds a nice homey, comforting taste.

MAKES 1 SERVING

INGREDIENTS

1 cup vanilla or plain soy milk
1 packet Rich Milk Chocolate
    Flavor NESTLÉ CARNATION
    INSTANT BREAKFAST Complete
    Nutritional Drink
⅓ cup ice cubes
1 tablespoon creamy peanut butter

DIRECTIONS

PLACE soy milk, Carnation Instant Breakfast, ice, and peanut butter in blender; cover. Blend until smooth.

Mocha Chiller

Mocha-flavored iced coffee is the perfect summer morning treat.

MAKES 2 SERVINGS

INGREDIENTS

1 cup brewed double-strength coffee,
    at room temperature
1 cup Original NESTLÉ COFFEE-MATE
    Half & Half

½ cup Chocolate Flavor NESTLÉ
    NESQUIK Calcium Fortified Syrup
Ice cubes
Whipped cream (optional)

DIRECTIONS

COMBINE coffee, Half & Half, and Nesquik in pitcher. Stir well to combine. Serve over ice. Top with whipped cream.

Estimated Time
Preparation: 5 mins

PB and Chocolate Smoothie

Peanut Butter S'Mores Cocoa

Estimated Time
Preparation: 5 mins

Peanut Butter S'Mores Cocoa

This peanut buttery cocoa is a twist on a traditional s'mores recipe. For an extra-special treat, sprinkle chocolate graham cracker crumbs over the top just before serving.

MAKES 2 SERVINGS

INGREDIENTS
4 tablespoons (2 envelopes) Rich
  Chocolate Flavor NESTLÉ Hot
  Cocoa Mix

2 tablespoons creamy peanut butter

2 cups hot milk

6 tablespoons marshmallow creme or
  marshmallow fluff, divided

4 chocolate graham crackers (optional)

DIRECTIONS
PLACE cocoa mix and peanut butter in small, heat-proof container. Stir in milk until peanut butter is dissolved. Divide between 2 mugs; top each with 3 tablespoons marshmallow creme. Serve immediately with chocolate graham crackers.

NOTE: Try substituting Milk Chocolate Flavor NESTLÉ Hot Cocoa Mix.

Estimated Time
Preparation: 5 mins

Nutrition Tip

Kids are just plain hungry when they come home from school. Nutrition experts have found that if kids are making poor food choices, they're more likely to do so between the end of school and dinnertime.

Here are some tips to ensure that your kids are eating healthier snacks. Introduce your kids to banana and carrot breads. They taste like cake, but if you spread a little cream cheese on them, they'll deliver calcium and satisfy hunger. Teach your children the joy of dipping. If they learn to love the taste of hummus, salsas, and lowfat ranch or honey-mustard dips, they're less likely to object to baby carrots, celery sticks, and any other veggies you set out for dipping. Encourage adolescents and teens in growth spurts to eat small meals throughout the day rather than grazing for hours at a time.

Raspberry-Mango Nestea Slush

This delicious summer drink will be a hit with the kids.

MAKES 4 SERVINGS

INGREDIENTS

5 cups ice cubes

1 cup water

¾ cup mango nectar, chilled

½ cup Raspberry Flavor NESTEA Sweetened Iced Tea Concentrate

⅓ cup powdered sugar

Fresh raspberries (optional)

DIRECTIONS

PLACE ice, water, nectar, Nestea, and sugar in blender; cover. Blend until smooth. Pour into glasses. Garnish with raspberries.

Estimated Time

Preparation: 5 mins

Raspberry Tea Sparkler

This sparkling tea with raspberry and apple flavors is sure to be a hit at your next outdoor party.

MAKES 4 SERVINGS

INGREDIENTS

2 cups Apple LIBBY'S JUICY JUICE Premium 100% Juice

2 cups PERRIER Sparkling Natural Mineral Water

½ cup Raspberry Flavor NESTEA Sweetened Iced Tea Concentrate

Ice cubes

Fresh mint leaves (optional)

DIRECTIONS

PLACE Juicy Juice, sparkling water, and Nestea in large pitcher. Stir until combined. Serve over ice. Garnish with mint.

Estimated Time

Preparation: 5 mins

Sensational Strawberry-Mint Smoothie

Sensational Strawberry-Mint Smoothie

Boost your morning energy with this seasonally fresh recipe for Sensational Strawberry-Mint Smoothie.

MAKE 2 SERVINGS

INGREDIENTS

2 cups fresh strawberries, plus more for garnish

1 cup ice cubes

¼ to ½ cup plain yogurt

¼ cup orange juice

1 tablespoon honey (optional)

1 packet Classic French Vanilla Flavor NESTLÉ CARNATION INSTANT BREAKFAST Complete Nutritional Drink

1 mint sprig, plus more for garnish

Raspberry-Mango Nestea Slush

DIRECTIONS

PLACE strawberries, ice, yogurt, orange juice, honey, Carnation Instant Breakfast, and mint in blender; cover. Blend until smooth. Garnish with strawberry slice and mint leaf.

Estimated Time
Preparation: 5 mins

Simplicity Mint Tea

This mint tea is so simple to make and is a great ending to a summer meal.

MAKES 1 SERVING

INGREDIENTS

1 cup hot water
¼ cup fresh mint leaves
2 tablespoons Unsweetened
    NESTEA Iced Tea Concentrate
Ice cubes

DIRECTIONS

COMBINE water and mint leaves; let steep for 5 minutes. Strain out mint leaves. Add Nestea concentrate. Serve over ice.

Simplicity Mint Tea

Estimated Times
Preparation: 5 mins
Steeping: 5 mins

Spiced Thai Nestea

Those Thai iced teas they serve in Thai restaurants are so delicious but seem difficult to make. Nothing could be further from the truth once you try this easy recipe. And they taste just like the real thing.

MAKES 2 SERVINGS

INGREDIENTS

2 cups water
6 tablespoons Unsweetened NESTEA
    Iced Tea Concentrate
¼ cup NESTLÉ CARNATION Sweetened
    Condensed Milk
⅛ to ¼ teaspoon ground cardamom
    and/or ground cinnamon
Ice cubes
2 tablespoons heavy cream, divided

DIRECTIONS

COMBINE water, Nestea, sweetened condensed milk, and cardamom and/or cinnamon in small pitcher. Fill 2 glasses with ice; divide mixture between glasses. Top each with 1 tablespoon cream.

Estimated Time
Preparation: 5 mins

Strawberry Dream Smoothie

If you are a strawberry lover, this smoothie will satisfy your craving for those delicious and antioxidant-rich red berries.

MAKES 1 SERVING

INGREDIENTS

1 container (8 ounces) strawberry
    fat free yogurt
1 packet Strawberry Sensation
    Flavor NESTLÉ CARNATION
    INSTANT BREAKFAST Complete
    Nutritional Drink
½ cup frozen strawberries (optional)
½ cup fat free milk
½ cup ice cubes

DIRECTIONS

PLACE yogurt, Carnation Instant Breakfast, strawberries, milk, and ice in blender; cover. Blend until smooth.

Estimated Time
Preparation: 5 mins

Strawberry Dream Smoothie

Toll House Chocolate Chip Cookie Milk Shake

Serve this milk shake for a special treat, after school, or in place of dessert. Kids of all ages will love it in tall glasses with a cherry on top!

MAKES 4 SERVINGS

INGREDIENTS

1 quart vanilla ice cream

2 cups freshly baked and crumbled NESTLÉ TOLL HOUSE Refrigerated Chocolate Chip Cookies (about 8 cookies)

1 can (12 fluid ounces) NESTLÉ CARNATION Evaporated Milk, chilled (or 1¼ cups milk)

DIRECTIONS

PLACE ice cream, cookies, and evaporated milk in blender; cover. Blend until smooth.

Estimated Time

Preparation: 5 mins

Tropical Island Tea

Tropical Island Tea

This tropical beverage will make you feel like booking a trip to an island paradise.

MAKES 6 SERVINGS

INGREDIENTS
NECTAR CUBES
1 can (11.5 fluid ounces) guava nectar

TEA MIXTURE
4 cups water
2 cups PERRIER Sparkling Natural Mineral Water
¾ cup Lemon Flavor NESTEA Sweetened Iced Tea Concentrate
¼ cup honey
6 kiwifruit or pineapple slices (optional)

DIRECTIONS
FOR NECTAR CUBES:
POUR nectar into 1 ice cube tray. Freeze until cubes are set.

FOR TEA MIXTURE:
PLACE water, sparkling water, Nestea, and honey in large pitcher. Stir until combined. Serve over nectar cubes. Garnish with kiwifruit or pineapple slices.

Estimated Times
Preparation: 5 mins
Freezing: 2 hrs

Vanilla, Vanilla, Vanilla Milk Shake

This milk shake has three kinds of vanilla and is for serious vanilla fans only!

MAKES 4 SERVINGS

INGREDIENTS
4 cups vanilla fat free frozen yogurt
2 cups fat free milk
⅔ cup Very Vanilla Flavor NESTLÉ NESQUIK Calcium Fortified Powder
⅛ teaspoon vanilla extract

DIRECTIONS
PLACE frozen yogurt, milk, Nesquik, and vanilla extract in blender; cover. Blend until smooth.

TWIST IT UP!
Vanilla, Vanilla, Vanilla Milk Shake— Nice with Spice
To spice up your Vanilla, Vanilla, Vanilla Milk Shake, add 1 teaspoon ground cinnamon and ¼ teaspoon ground nutmeg before blending. Divide among glasses; dust each with a sprinkle of ground cinnamon or ground nutmeg as garnish.

Vanilla, Vanilla, Vanilla Milk Shake

Vanilla, Vanilla, Vanilla Milk Shake with a Twist
Substitute orange juice for half or all of the milk before blending. Serve each milk shake with an orange wedge as garnish.

Vanilla, Vanilla, Vanilla Float
Divide frozen yogurt among 4 tall glasses. Combine milk, Nesquik, and vanilla extract in small pitcher; divide among glasses. Top each with ⅓ to ½ cup chilled club soda.

Add some color to your Vanilla, Vanilla, Vanilla Milk Shake—dress it up with a skewer of fresh berries and orange wedges.

Estimated Time
Preparation: 5 mins

desserts, sweets, and more

desserts, sweets, and more

Sometimes dinner is just another evening meal without a grand finale. Occasionally, lunch boxes need a little something special to help growing kids get through hectic school days. And every now and then, we all need to treat ourselves to a little somethin'-somethin.' That's where our extensive repertoire of triple-tested recipes comes in.

Whether you like it chewy, moist, crunchy, chocolatey, fruity, hot out of the oven, frosty from the freezer, or combinations thereof, we've got a cake, cookie, pie, cobbler, tart, truffle, brownie, bar, pudding, flan, mousse, nibble, quiver, or twinkle just for you. And for even more great dessert recipes visit Meals.com.

All-American Baby Ruth Pie

Perfect for a hot summer day, this frozen pie features a chocolate cookie crust filled with a delightful combination of chocolate ice cream, miniature marshmallows, and nutty, chewy pieces of BABY RUTH candy bars.

MAKES 8 SERVINGS

INGREDIENTS

1½ cups crushed creme-filled chocolate cookies (about 18 cookies)

3 tablespoons butter or margarine, melted

2 pints chocolate ice cream, softened

3 (2.1 ounces each) NESTLÉ BABY RUTH Candy Bars, finely chopped

1 cup miniature marshmallows

Chocolate Flavor NESTLÉ NESQUIK Calcium Fortified Syrup

DIRECTIONS

COMBINE crushed cookies and butter in small bowl. Press onto bottom of 9-inch pie plate. Freeze for 5 minutes.

COMBINE ice cream, chopped Baby Ruth and marshmallows in large bowl; spoon into prepared crust. Freeze for about 1 hour or until firm. Drizzle with Nesquik before serving.

About Baby Ruth

If you're ever wondering how the BABY RUTH candy bar got its name, here's the answer to your mystery. BABY RUTH was introduced in the early 1920s by the Curtiss Candy Company. The rumor that the BABY RUTH candy bar was named for Babe Ruth, the homerun king, is false. The name honors President and Mrs. Grover Cleveland's daughter, endearingly referred to as 'Baby Ruth.' For more tidbits on your favorite candy bar visit BabyRuth.com.

Estimated Times

Preparation: 15 mins

Freezing: 1 hr, 5 mins

Apple Cinnamon Empanadas

Serve these warm with vanilla ice cream and caramel sauce for a great finale to a Mexican meal. Paired with steaming mugs of hot cocoa, these make a wonderful breakfast as well!

MAKES 36 EMPANADAS

All-American Baby Ruth Pie

Apple Cinnamon Empanadas

INGREDIENTS

2 packages (12 ounces each) STOUFFER'S frozen Harvest Apples, prepared according to package directions, chilled

1 package (8 ounces) cream cheese, at room temperature

¾ cup granulated sugar, divided

1 teaspoon vanilla extract

1 teaspoon ground cinnamon

1 package (36 count) frozen roll dough, defrosted

¼ cup milk

⅓ cup butter, melted

DIRECTIONS

PREHEAT oven to 375° F. Lightly grease 2 baking sheets.

COMBINE cream cheese, ¼ cup sugar, and vanilla extract in medium bowl; mix until smooth. Combine remaining sugar and cinnamon in small bowl.

PLACE dough for 1 roll on lightly floured surface; roll into 4-inch circle. Spoon about 1 tablespoon cream cheese mixture and 1 tablespoon harvest apples onto lower half; brush edges with milk. Fold dough in half; crimp edges with fork. Repeat with remaining dough. Place on prepared baking sheets.

BRUSH each empanada with butter; sprinkle with cinnamon-sugar.

BAKE for 15 minutes or until golden brown; serve warm.

Estimated Times
Preparation: 1 hr
Cooking: 15 mins

Baby Ruth Crater Bars

If you're a BABY RUTH fan (or even if you're not), you'll love these peanut buttery bars with the candy melted on top. They're a cinch to make and the kids will love them!

MAKES 36 BARS

INGREDIENTS

2¼ cups all-purpose flour

1 teaspoon baking soda

½ teaspoon salt

¾ cup packed brown sugar

¾ cup granulated sugar

½ cup (1 stick) butter or
  margarine, softened

½ cup creamy or chunky peanut butter

2 large eggs

1 teaspoon vanilla extract

6 (2.1 ounces each) NESTLÉ BABY RUTH
  Candy Bars, coarsely chopped

Baby Ruth Crater Bars

DIRECTIONS

PREHEAT oven to 375° F. Grease 15 x 10-inch jelly-roll pan.

COMBINE flour, baking soda, and salt in small bowl. Beat brown sugar, granulated sugar, butter, and peanut butter in large mixer bowl until creamy. Beat in eggs and vanilla extract. Gradually beat in flour mixture.

SPREAD dough evenly into prepared pan. Sprinkle chopped Baby Ruth over top; press in lightly.

BAKE for 18 to 20 minutes or until golden brown. Cool completely in pan on wire rack. Cut into bars.

Estimated Times
Preparation: 15 mins
Cooking: 18 mins
Cooling: 20 mins

Birthday Cake Cones

This birthday cake looks like an ice cream cone, but tastes like candy! Try this at your next party—it's sure to be a big hit with your guests.

MAKES 30 CONES

INGREDIENTS

1 package (18.25 ounces) chocolate
  or yellow cake mix

Birthday Cake Cones

30 flat-bottomed ice cream cones
  (buy extra in case some are broken)

1 cup prepared frosting

1 (2.1 ounces) NESTLÉ BUTTERFINGER
  Candy Bar, chopped, divided

DIRECTIONS

PREHEAT oven to 400° F.

PREPARE cake mix batter according to package directions. Stir in half of chopped Butterfinger. Spoon 2 tablespoons cake batter into each cone. Place cones in the cups of muffin pans or on a baking sheet.

BAKE for 15 to 20 minutes or until wooden pick inserted in cake comes out clean. Cool completely.

DECORATE with frosting. Sprinkle with remaining chopped Butterfinger. The cones are best served the same day they are prepared.

Black Bottom Irish Cream Pie

The perfect dessert for the Irish cream lover. And it requires very little effort.

MAKES 10 SERVINGS

INGREDIENTS

1 package (18 ounces) NESTLÉ
TOLL HOUSE Refrigerated
Brownie Bar Dough

2 packages (2.8 ounces each) Milk
Chocolate Irish Cream NESTLÉ
EUROPEAN STYLE Mousse Mix

3 (6 ounces total) NESTLÉ TOLL HOUSE
Semi-Sweet Chocolate Baking Bars,
made into curls (optional)

DIRECTIONS

PREHEAT oven according to brownie
bar dough package directions. Grease
9-inch, deep-dish pie plate.

PRESS brownie bar dough into prepared
pie plate. Bake according to package
directions. Let cool completely.

PREPARE mousse mix according to
steps 1 and 2 of package directions;
spread over brownie. Sprinkle with
chocolate curls. Refrigerate for 4 hours
or until set.

TO MAKE CHOCOLATE CURLS:
MICROWAVE baking bar on LOW (10%)
power for 10 seconds. Hold bar over a
sheet of foil or wax paper. Pull vegetable
peeler along chocolate surface. As
curls form, let them drop onto foil or
gently lift from peeler. Transfer curls to
refrigerator for 5 minutes to firm. Try
making curls with NESTLÉ TOLL HOUSE
Premier White Baking Bars, too.

Estimated Times

Preparation: 15 mins

Cooking: 25 mins

Cooling: 20 mins

Refrigerating: 4 hrs

About Butterfinger

BUTTERFINGER was introduced in
1928 by the Curtiss Candy Company
and got its name through a contest.
"Butterfinger" was a popular term
in the day to describe jocks that
couldn't hang onto the ball. And
the peanut buttery aspects along
with the fact that you hold it in your
hand made the name a natural.
('Butterfoot' was submitted by a
contortionist, but did not sound very
appealing to the folks at Curtiss.)

If you're wondering what exactly
is a BUTTERFINGER, first, to be
clear—there are no fingers! But there
is a creamy blend of crispety sugar
candy and peanut buttery taste.
This unique substance is kneaded,
rolled, cut, and finished with a
chocolatey topping. (OK, so it
happens on a big machine!)
Together they make for that
unique one-of-a-kind taste that
people have been enjoying
for over 70 years. Visit us at
Butterfinger.com to find out
what's new.

Black Bottom Irish Cream Pie

Blonde Brownies

Blonde Brownies

Golden brownies with pure brown sugar, butter, and vanilla for a caramelesque, butterscotchy flavor. A super treat to tuck into lunch bags.

MAKES 36 BROWNIES

INGREDIENTS

2¼ cups all-purpose flour

2½ teaspoons baking powder

½ teaspoon salt

1¾ cups packed brown sugar

¾ cup (1½ sticks) butter or margarine, softened

3 large eggs

1 teaspoon vanilla extract

2 cups (12-ounce package) NESTLÉ TOLL HOUSE Semi-Sweet Chocolate Morsels

DIRECTIONS

PREHEAT oven to 350° F. Grease 15 x 10-inch jelly-roll pan.

COMBINE flour, baking powder, and salt in small bowl. Beat sugar and butter in large mixer bowl until creamy. Beat in eggs and vanilla extract; gradually beat in flour mixture. Stir in morsels. Spread into prepared pan.

BAKE for 20 to 25 minutes or until top is golden brown. Cool completely in pan on wire rack. Cut into bars.

Estimated Times

Preparation: 10 mins

Cooking: 20 mins

Cooling: 20 mins

Butterfinger Caramel Apples

Just a few ingredients mixed together make this an "easy" after-school snack.

MAKES 6 SERVINGS

INGREDIENTS

6 wooden craft sticks (found in cake decorating or hobby shops)

6 tart apples, washed, dried, and stems removed

1 package (14 ounces) caramels

2 tablespoons water

2 (2.1 ounces each) NESTLÉ BUTTERFINGER Candy Bars, chopped

DIRECTIONS

LINE tray or baking sheet with wax paper. Insert 1 wooden craft stick into stem end of each apple.

MICROWAVE caramels and water in large, microwave-safe bowl on HIGH (100%) power for 2 minutes; stir. Microwave at additional 10- to 20-second intervals, stirring until smooth.

DIP each apple in melted caramel; scrape excess caramel from bottoms. Quickly roll bottom half of apples in chopped Butterfinger, then place on prepared tray. Refrigerate for 45 minutes or until set. Store apples in refrigerator in an airtight container. Apples are best if they are served the same day as they are prepared.

NOTE: If caramel becomes firm, microwave for 20 to 30 seconds or until dipping consistency is reached. Two (1.5 ounces each) NESTLÉ CRUNCH Candy Bars may be used in place of NESTLÉ BUTTERFINGER Candy Bars.

Butterfinger Caramel Apples

Butterfinger Cookies

A great cookie for those BUTTERFINGER candy lovers in your family!

MAKES ABOUT 2½ DOZEN COOKIES

INGREDIENTS

1¾ cups all-purpose flour
¾ teaspoon baking soda
¼ teaspoon salt
¾ cup granulated sugar
½ cup (1 stick) butter or
    margarine, softened
1 large egg
3 (2.1 ounces each) NESTLÉ
    BUTTERFINGER Candy Bars,
    coarsely chopped

DIRECTIONS

PREHEAT oven to 375° F.

COMBINE flour, baking soda, and salt in small bowl. Beat sugar and butter in large mixer bowl until creamy. Beat in egg; gradually beat in flour mixture. Stir in chopped Butterfinger pieces. Drop by slightly rounded tablespoon onto ungreased baking sheets.

BAKE for 10 to 12 minutes or until lightly browned. Cool on baking sheets for 2 minutes; remove to wire racks to cool completely.

Estimated Times
Preparation: 15 mins
Cooking: 2 mins
Refrigerating: 45 mins

Butterfinger Crème Brûlée

BUTTERFINGER pieces are the surprise ingredient at the bottom of these fun brûlées.

MAKES 4 SERVINGS

INGREDIENTS

¼ cup chopped NESTLÉ BUTTERFINGER
    Candy Bar, divided
2 cups heavy whipping cream
10 tablespoons granulated sugar, divided
⅛ teaspoon salt
4 large egg yolks
1 teaspoon vanilla extract

DIRECTIONS

PREHEAT oven to 300° F. Place 1 tablespoon chopped Butterfinger into each of four 6-ounce custard cups or ramekins.

PLACE cream, 7 tablespoons sugar, and salt in medium saucepan. Cook over medium heat, stirring occasionally, for 5 to 6 minutes or until sugar is dissolved.

Butterfinger Crème Brûlée

BEAT egg yolks in medium bowl; gradually whisk cream mixture into egg yolks. Stir in vanilla extract.

POUR cream mixture through a fine sieve into prepared custard cups. Place cups in 9-inch-square baking pan; fill pan with hot water to 1-inch depth. Loosely cover with foil.

BAKE for about 1 hour, 30 minutes or until knife inserted in centers comes out clean. Remove to wire rack to cool slightly. Refrigerate for several hours or overnight.

SPRINKLE each crème brûlée evenly with remaining sugar. Broil until sugar is melted and caramelized. Refrigerate for 10 to 15 minutes or until caramel has hardened.

Estimated Times
Preparation: 20 mins
Cooking: 1 hr, 35 mins
Refrigerating: 3 hrs, 10 mins

About Cream

Many elegant baked goods contain cream. Cream is usually beaten until stiff. Whipped cream is given a very special place next to strawberry shortcake or pumpkin pie, among a few favorites.

Whipped cream also provides baked goods with that special finishing touch. It's both airy and heavy, providing a fruit tart with just the right base, lightening the richness of a sweet chocolate torte or tiramisu, or offering the traditional topping over fresh fruit pies. The tastes and flavors of most cakes, pastries, and other baked goods are best served with cream, thanks to its high percentage of fat and air. When beaten, cream transforms to a foamy consistency of small bubbles that expand as more air is beaten into them.

Most of the dessert recipes in this book call for "heavy whipping cream," which contains about 40 percent butterfat and provides that richer, thicker consistency and great flavor. There are other choices like regular "whipping cream" or lighter versions, if you'd like to cut down on fat, but be prepared for a difference.

Butterfinger Popcorn Balls

This recipe's "hands-on" preparation is a thrill for kids and results in a sweet and chewy combination of chopped BUTTERFINGER, crunchy popcorn, and miniature marshmallows.

MAKES 6 SERVINGS

INGREDIENTS

6 cups popped popcorn
3 (2.1 ounces each) NESTLÉ
    BUTTERFINGER Candy Bars, chopped
¼ cup (½ stick) butter or margarine
3½ cups miniature marshmallows
Nonstick cooking spray

DIRECTIONS

COMBINE popcorn and chopped Butterfinger in large bowl.

MELT butter in medium saucepan over low heat. Stir in marshmallows. Heat, stirring constantly, until marshmallows are melted and mixture is smooth.

Butterfinger Popcorn Balls

POUR over popcorn mixture; quickly toss to coat well. Spray hands with nonstick cooking spray. Form popcorn mixture into six 3-inch balls. Place on wax paper to cool. Store in an airtight container.

NOTE: Try substituting 9 NESTLÉ BUTTERFINGER Fun Size Candy Bars (21 grams each).

Estimated Times
Preparation: 15 mins
Cooking: 5 mins
Cooling: 15 mins

Butterscotch Apple Crisp

Bring the fun of caramel apples into your kitchen. Chopped nuts and oats make for a chewy and delicious baked dessert perfect for crisp Fall nights.

MAKES 12 SERVINGS

INGREDIENTS
APPLE LAYER
2½ pounds tart apples, peeled and
    thinly sliced
1⅔ cups (11-ounce package)
    NESTLÉ TOLL HOUSE Butterscotch
    Flavored Morsels
¼ cup packed brown sugar
¼ cup all-purpose flour
½ teaspoon ground cinnamon

Butterscotch Gingerbread Cookies

TOPPING

½ cup all-purpose flour

¼ cup packed brown sugar

¼ cup (½ stick) butter or margarine

1 cup chopped nuts

¾ cup quick or old-fashioned oats

DIRECTIONS

PREHEAT oven to 375° F.

FOR APPLE LAYER:

ARRANGE apples in 13 x 9-inch baking pan. Combine morsels, sugar, flour, and cinnamon in small bowl. Sprinkle over apples.

BAKE for 20 minutes.

FOR TOPPING:

COMBINE flour and sugar in medium bowl. Cut in butter with pastry blender or two knives until crumbly. Stir in nuts and oats; sprinkle over apple layer.

BAKE for an additional 30 to 40 minutes or until apples are tender and topping is lightly browned. Cool slightly. Serve warm with ice cream, if desired.

Estimated Times

Preparation: 25 mins

Cooking: 50 mins

Cooling: 10 mins

Butterscotch Gingerbread Cookies

Butterscotch morsels add their sweet creaminess to this classic gingerbread cookie. The ultimate treat, warm from the oven with a glass of cold milk.

MAKES ABOUT 3½ DOZEN COOKIES

INGREDIENTS

3 cups all-purpose flour

2 teaspoons baking soda

1½ teaspoons ground cinnamon

1½ teaspoons ground ginger

¾ teaspoon ground cloves

½ teaspoon salt

1½ cups packed brown sugar

1 cup (2 sticks) butter or
    margarine, softened

⅓ cup light molasses

1 large egg

1⅔ cups (11-ounce package)
    NESTLÉ TOLL HOUSE
    Butterscotch Flavored Morsels

DIRECTIONS

PREHEAT oven to 350° F.

COMBINE flour, baking soda, cinnamon, ginger, cloves, and salt in small bowl.

BEAT sugar, butter, molasses, and egg in large mixer bowl until creamy. Gradually beat in flour mixture until well blended. Stir in morsels. Drop by rounded tablespoon onto ungreased baking sheets.

BAKE for 9 to 11 minutes or until cookies are lightly browned. Cool on baking sheets for 2 minutes; remove to wire racks to cool completely.

Estimated Times

Preparation: 15 mins

Cooking: 9 mins

Cooling: 15 mins

desserts, sweets, and more **185**

Butterscotch Haystacks

Butterscotch Haystacks

Tasty enough for any occasion, these haystacks are mounded with a mixture of peanut butter, butterscotch morsels, marshmallows, and chow mein noodles. To enjoy in a snap, make them the microwave way.

MAKES ABOUT 4 DOZEN HAYSTACKS

INGREDIENTS

1⅔ cups (11-ounce package)
   NESTLÉ TOLL HOUSE Butterscotch
   Flavored Morsels
¾ cup creamy peanut butter
1 can (8.5 ounces) or 2 cans (5 ounces
   each) chow mein noodles
3½ cups miniature marshmallows

DIRECTIONS

LINE trays with wax paper.

MICROWAVE morsels in large, uncovered, microwave-safe bowl on

MEDIUM-HIGH (70%) power for 1 minute; STIR. The morsels may retain some of their original shape. If necessary, microwave at additional 10- to 15-second intervals, stirring just until morsels are melted.

STIR in peanut butter until well blended. Add chow mein noodles and marshmallows; toss until all ingredients are coated. Drop by rounded tablespoon onto prepared trays. Refrigerate until ready to serve.

DOUBLE BOILER METHOD:
PLACE morsels in top of double boiler over hot (not boiling) water. Do not cover. When most of the morsels are shiny, stir just until melted. (Prevent water from coming in contact with morsels.) Remove from heat; stir in peanut butter. Transfer to large bowl. Add chow mein noodles and marshmallows; proceed as above.

Estimated Times
Preparation: 10 mins
Cooking: 2 mins
Refrigerating: 30 mins

"Cakey" Chocolate Jingle Bars

These bars are the perfect addition to any holiday bake sale. And with chocolate in every bite, they are sure to become a holiday favorite.

MAKES 16 BARS

INGREDIENTS

2 cups all-purpose flour
⅔ cup NESTLÉ TOLL HOUSE
   Baking Cocoa
1 teaspoon baking soda
¼ teaspoon salt
¾ cup granulated sugar
⅔ cup packed light brown sugar
½ cup (1 stick) butter or
   margarine, softened
1 teaspoon vanilla extract
2 large eggs
30 NESTLÉ BUTTERFINGER or NESTLÉ
   CRUNCH Jingles, unwrapped
Powdered sugar (optional)

DIRECTIONS

PREHEAT oven to 375° F.

COMBINE flour, cocoa, baking soda, and salt in large bowl.

BEAT granulated sugar, brown sugar, butter, and vanilla extract in large mixer bowl until combined. Beat in eggs. Gradually beat in flour mixture. Stir in Nestlé Jingles. Press into ungreased 9-inch-square baking pan.

BAKE for 18 to 20 minutes or until wooden pick inserted near center comes out clean. Cool completely in pan on wire rack. Cut into bars. Dust with powdered sugar before serving.

NOTE: Try substituting NESTLÉ Hearts or NESTLÉ NestEggs.

Estimated Times

Preparation: 10 mins

Cooking: 18 mins

Cooling: 30 mins

Candy Shop Pizza

Kids and adults will delight as they bite into this chewy chocolate chip cookie topped with creamy chocolate morsels, chunky peanut butter, and an assortment of chopped candy. This delicious treat also provides the perfect way to use up those trick-or-treating leftovers!

MAKES 12 SERVINGS

INGREDIENTS

1 package (18 ounces) NESTLÉ TOLL HOUSE Refrigerated Chocolate Chip Cookie Bar Dough

1 cup (6 ounces) NESTLÉ TOLL HOUSE Semi-Sweet Chocolate Morsels

Candy Shop Pizza

½ cup creamy or chunky peanut butter

1 cup coarsely chopped NESTLÉ CRUNCH, BUTTERFINGER, BABY RUTH, GOOBERS, and/or RAISINETS

DIRECTIONS

PREHEAT oven to 325° F. Grease baking sheet or pizza pan.

PLACE whole bar of dough scored-side-down onto prepared baking sheet or pizza pan.

BAKE for 30 to 35 minutes or until golden brown. Immediately sprinkle morsels over hot crust; drop peanut butter by spoonfuls onto morsels. Let stand for 5 minutes or until morsels are shiny. Gently spread chocolate and peanut butter evenly over cookie crust.

SPRINKLE candy in single layer over pizza. Cut into wedges; serve warm or at room temperature.

NOTE: Try substituting 1 package (18 ounces) NESTLÉ TOLL HOUSE Refrigerated Sugar Cookie Bar Dough. Press cookie dough onto greased, large baking sheet or pizza pan to measure an 8-inch circle. Bake at 325° F for 16 to 18 minutes or until lightly golden.

Estimated Times

Preparation: 15 mins

Cooking: 30 mins

Standing: 5 mins

Baking Tip

Nothing beats a batch of freshly baked cookies or brownies! To keep your cookies and brownies tasting like you just made them, remember these tips. Unopened dough can be stored in the refrigerator until the "use or freeze by" date. To keep cookies and brownies from sticking together, make sure they are completely cool before storing. Make sure you store crisp and soft cookies in separate containers. Cooled cookies can be stored in tightly sealed containers or resealable plastic bags. Bar or big cookies can be stored either in a tightly sealed container or in their own baking pan, sheet, or dish covered tightly with plastic wrap or foil.

Cappuccino Cheesecake

A most elegant dessert sure to please family and friends!

MAKES 12 SERVINGS

INGREDIENTS

1¾ cups crushed chocolate cookies
  (about 18 cookies)

½ cup granulated sugar, divided

⅓ cup butter, melted

3 packages (8 ounces each) cream
  cheese, at room temperature

1 cup French Vanilla Flavor NESTLÉ
  COFFEE-MATE Liquid Coffee Creamer

4 large eggs

6 teaspoons NESCAFÉ TASTER'S CHOICE
  100% Pure Instant Coffee Granules

¼ cup all-purpose flour

¾ cup NESTLÉ TOLL HOUSE Premier
  White Morsels

1 container (16 ounces) sour cream,
  at room temperature

DIRECTIONS

PREHEAT oven to 350° F.

COMBINE cookie crumbs and ¼ cup sugar in small bowl; stir in butter. Press onto bottom and 1 inch up side of ungreased 9-inch springform pan.

BAKE for 5 minutes.

BEAT cream cheese and Coffee-mate in large mixer bowl until creamy. Combine eggs and coffee granules in medium bowl; stir until coffee is dissolved. Add egg mixture, flour, and remaining sugar to cream cheese mixture. Beat until combined. Pour into crust.

BAKE for 45 to 50 minutes or until edges are set but center still moves slightly.

MICROWAVE morsels in medium, uncovered, microwave-safe bowl on MEDIUM-HIGH (70%) power for 1 minute; STIR. The morsels may retain some of their original shape. If necessary, microwave at additional 10- to 15-second intervals, stirring just until morsels are melted. Stir in sour cream. Spread over top of cheesecake.

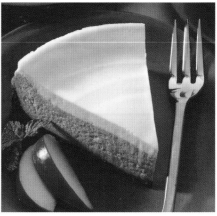

Cappuccino Cheesecake

BAKE for 10 minutes. Cool completely in pan on wire rack. Refrigerate for several hours or overnight.

Estimated Times

Preparation: 20 mins

Cooking: 1 hr

Cooling: 1 hr

Refrigerating: 3 hrs

Baking Tip

Here are some useful tips when using morsels in your baking. Always use a dry measuring cup, and fill the cup with morsels to the top only, not a heaping amount.

Caramel Apple Quesadillas

Serve these as a finale to your favorite Mexican meal.

MAKES 10 QUESADILLAS

INGREDIENTS

2 packages (12 ounces each)
  STOUFFER'S frozen Harvest Apples,
  prepared according to package
  directions, kept hot

¼ cup granulated sugar

¼ teaspoon ground cinnamon

¼ cup (½ stick) butter

10 (6-inch) fajita-size flour tortillas

Caramel syrup or ice cream topping

Whipped cream (optional)

Chopped almonds (optional)

DIRECTIONS

COMBINE sugar and cinnamon in small bowl. Melt butter in large skillet over medium-low heat. Heat each tortilla on one side for 3 minutes or until golden. Sprinkle heated side of tortillas with cinnamon-sugar mixture; keep warm.

PLACE tortillas uncooked-side-up on cutting board; top with harvest apples. Fold over; cut in half. Place on serving plates. Drizzle with caramel syrup; top with whipped cream and nuts.

Estimated Times

Preparation: 15 mins

Cooking: 10 mins

Caramel Sauce

Cooking sugar is an art, but an art worth developing when the result is as good as this sauce. Drizzle this luscious concoction over baked apples, waffles, cake, or vanilla ice cream.

MAKES 3 CUPS

INGREDIENTS

2 cups granulated sugar

½ cup water

1 can (14 ounces) NESTLÉ CARNATION Sweetened Condensed Milk

½ cup (1 stick) butter, softened, divided

2 teaspoons vanilla extract

DIRECTIONS

COMBINE sugar and water in medium, heavy-duty saucepan. Cook over medium-high heat, stirring occasionally, until mixture comes to a boil. Continue to boil, without stirring, for 10 to 14 minutes, tilting pan occasionally to keep color even until mixture turns a deep caramel color. Remove from heat.

STIR in sweetened condensed milk (mixture will foam up); do not scrape sides of pan. Add ¼ cup (½ stick) butter, one tablespoon at a time, stirring well after each addition. Stir in remaining butter and vanilla extract until smooth.

Estimated Times

Preparation: 10 mins

Cooking: 15 mins

Caramel Apple Quesadillas

Carnation Famous Fudge

This famous fudge will make you a star. Don't skip the nuts with their crunchy touch.

MAKES 49 PIECES

INGREDIENTS

1½ cups granulated sugar

⅔ cup (5 fluid-ounce can) NESTLÉ CARNATION Evaporated Milk

2 tablespoons butter or margarine

¼ teaspoon salt

2 cups miniature marshmallows

Milk

Have you ever wondered what the difference is between evaporated milk and sweetened condensed milk? The answer lies in the sugar and water ratios. Evaporated milk has been processed to remove half the water. There is no sugar added to this product. Sweetened Condensed Milk is milk that has half the water removed and then sugar added to it. These products should not be used as direct substitutes for one another.

Carnation Famous Fudge

1½ cups (9 ounces) NESTLÉ TOLL HOUSE Semi-Sweet Chocolate Morsels

½ cup chopped pecans or walnuts (optional)

1 teaspoon vanilla extract

DIRECTIONS

LINE 8-inch-square baking pan with foil.

COMBINE sugar, evaporated milk, butter, and salt in medium, heavy-duty saucepan. Bring to a full rolling boil over medium heat, stirring constantly. Boil, stirring constantly, for 4 to 5 minutes. Remove from heat.

STIR in marshmallows, morsels, nuts, and vanilla extract. Stir vigorously for 1 minute or until marshmallows are melted. Pour into prepared baking pan; refrigerate for 2 hours or until firm. Lift from pan; remove foil. Cut into pieces.

FOR MILK CHOCOLATE FUDGE:
SUBSTITUTE 1¾ cups (11.5-ounce package) NESTLÉ TOLL HOUSE Milk Chocolate Morsels for Semi-Sweet Chocolate Morsels.

FOR BUTTERSCOTCH FUDGE:
SUBSTITUTE 1⅔ cups (11-ounce package) NESTLÉ TOLL HOUSE Butterscotch Flavored Morsels for Semi-Sweet Chocolate Morsels.

FOR PEANUTTY CHOCOLATE FUDGE:
SUBSTITUTE 1⅔ cups (11-ounce package) NESTLÉ TOLL HOUSE Peanut Butter & Milk Chocolate Morsels for Semi-Sweet Chocolate Morsels and ½ cup chopped peanuts for pecans or walnuts.

Estimated Times
Preparation: 10 mins
Cooking: 6 mins
Refrigerating: 2 hrs

Carnation Key Lime Pie

This no-fail recipe makes the best key lime pie you'll ever taste. Keep a few cans of NESTLÉ CARNATION Sweetened Condensed Milk on hand for quick baking projects.

MAKES 8 SERVINGS

INGREDIENTS

1 prepared 9-inch (6 ounces) graham
   cracker crust

1 can (14 ounces) NESTLÉ CARNATION
   Sweetened Condensed Milk

½ cup fresh lime juice (about
   3 medium limes)

1 teaspoon grated lime peel

2 cups frozen whipped topping, thawed

8 thin lime slices (optional)

DIRECTIONS

BEAT sweetened condensed milk
and lime juice in small mixer bowl
until combined. Stir in lime peel.

POUR into crust; spread with whipped
topping. Refrigerate for 2 hours or until
set. Garnish with lime slices.

Estimated Times
Preparation: 5 mins
Refrigerating: 2 hrs

Cheesecake Cookie Cups

Cheesecake Cookie Cups

**These individually-sized dessert cups
are handy for entertaining.**

MAKES 12 SERVINGS

INGREDIENTS

12 pieces NESTLÉ TOLL HOUSE
   Refrigerated Chocolate Chip Cookie
   Bar Dough

1 package (8 ounces) cream cheese,
   at room temperature

½ cup NESTLÉ CARNATION Sweetened
   Condensed Milk

1 large egg

1 teaspoon vanilla extract

1 can (21 ounces) cherry pie filling

DIRECTIONS

PREHEAT oven to 325° F. Paper-line
12 muffin cups.

PLACE 1 piece of cookie dough in
each prepared muffin cup.

BAKE for 10 to 12 minutes or until
cookie has spread to edge of cup.

BEAT cream cheese, sweetened
condensed milk, egg, and vanilla
extract in medium bowl until smooth.
Pour about 3 tablespoons cream cheese
mixture over each cookie in cup.

BAKE for an additional 15 to 18 minutes
or until set. Cool completely in pan on
wire rack. Top with pie filling. Refrigerate
for 1 hour.

Estimated Times
Preparation: 15 mins
Cooking: 25 mins
Cooling: 15 mins
Refrigerating: 1 hr

Carnation Key Lime Pie

Chewy Brownie Mix in a Jar

What a lovely hostess gift! Your friends will remember your visit as they smell wonderful brownies baking.

MAKES 24 BROWNIES

Chewy Brownie Mix in a Jar

INGREDIENTS

1⅔ cups granulated sugar
¾ cup NESTLÉ TOLL HOUSE Baking Cocoa
1⅓ cups all-purpose flour
½ teaspoon baking powder
¼ teaspoon salt
¾ cup NESTLÉ TOLL HOUSE Semi-Sweet Chocolate Morsels or chopped nuts

DIRECTIONS

LAYER ingredients in order listed above in 1-quart jar, pressing firmly after adding each ingredient. (After adding cocoa, wipe out inside of jar with paper towel.) Seal with lid and decorate with fabric and ribbon.

RECIPE TO ATTACH:

PREHEAT oven to 350° F. Grease 13 x 9-inch baking pan. Pour brownie mix into large mixer bowl; stir. Add ¾ cup (1½ sticks) melted butter or margarine, 2 large eggs, 2 tablespoons water, and 2 teaspoons vanilla extract; stir well. Spread into prepared baking pan. Bake for 18 to 25 minutes or until wooden pick inserted in center comes out slightly sticky. Cool completely in pan on wire rack. Dust with powdered sugar. Makes 24 brownies.

Estimated Time
Preparation: 10 mins

Choco-Holic Cake

Chocolate, chocolate, chocolate is what this cake is made of! Sour cream and pudding mix enrich and make this cake moist and delicious.

MAKES 16 SERVINGS

INGREDIENTS

1 package (18.25 ounces) chocolate cake mix
1 package (about 3.4 ounces) chocolate instant pudding and pie filling mix
1 cup milk
½ cup sour cream
4 large eggs
2 cups (12-ounce package) NESTLÉ TOLL HOUSE Semi-Sweet Chocolate Morsels
1 cup chopped walnuts
Powdered sugar (optional)
Fresh raspberries (optional)

DIRECTIONS

PREHEAT oven to 350° F. Grease and flour 12-inch Bundt pan or other tube pan.

COMBINE cake mix, pudding mix, milk, sour cream, and eggs in large mixer bowl. Beat on low speed just until blended. Beat on high speed for 2 minutes. Stir in morsels and nuts. Pour into prepared baking pan.

BAKE for 55 to 65 minutes or until wooden pick inserted in cake comes out clean.

COOL in pan on wire rack for 20 minutes. Invert onto wire rack to cool completely. Sprinkle with powdered sugar; garnish with raspberries.

Estimated Times
Preparation: 15 mins
Cooking: 55 mins
Cooling: 40 mins

Chocolate Amaretto Bars

A layer of chocolate fudge with a hint of amaretto rests upon a buttery crust. Top it all off with a drizzling of chocolate and you've got dessert.

MAKES 30 BARS

INGREDIENTS
CRUST
2 cups all-purpose flour
¾ cup (1½ sticks) butter or margarine, cut into pieces, softened
⅓ cup packed brown sugar

FILLING
4 large eggs
¾ cup light corn syrup
¾ cup granulated sugar
¼ cup amaretto liqueur (or ½ teaspoon almond extract)
2 tablespoons butter or margarine, melted
1 tablespoon cornstarch

2 cups sliced almonds
2 cups (12-ounce package) NESTLÉ TOLL HOUSE Semi-Sweet Chocolate Morsels, divided
Chocolate Drizzle (recipe follows)

DIRECTIONS
PREHEAT oven to 350° F. Grease 13 x 9-inch baking pan.

FOR CRUST:
BEAT flour, butter, and sugar in large mixer bowl until crumbly. Press into prepared baking pan.

BAKE for 12 to 15 minutes or until golden brown.

FOR FILLING:
BEAT eggs, corn syrup, sugar, liqueur, butter, and cornstarch in medium bowl with wire whisk. Stir in nuts and

1⅔ cups morsels. Pour over hot crust; spread evenly.

BAKE for 25 to 30 minutes or until center is set. Cool completely in pan on wire rack. Top with chocolate drizzle.

FOR CHOCOLATE DRIZZLE:
PLACE remaining morsels in heavy-duty plastic bag. Microwave on HIGH (100%) power for 30 to 45 seconds; knead. Microwave at additional 10- to 15-second intervals, kneading until smooth. Cut tiny corner from bag; squeeze bag to drizzle chocolate over bars. Refrigerate for a few minutes to firm chocolate before cutting into bars.

Estimated Times
Preparation: 15 mins
Cooking: 38 mins
Cooling: 30 mins

Chocolate Amaretto Bars

Chocolate Banana Cream Pie

Banana cream pie made easy! A chocolate chip cookie dough crust makes this dessert.

MAKES 8 SERVINGS

INGREDIENTS

1 package (18 ounces) NESTLÉ TOLL HOUSE Refrigerated Chocolate Chip Cookie Bar Dough, softened

1 can (12 fluid ounces) NESTLÉ CARNATION Evaporated Milk or 1½ cups milk

1 package (about 3.4 ounces) banana cream or vanilla instant pudding and pie filling mix

2 medium bananas, peeled and sliced

1½ cups frozen whipped topping, thawed

3 tablespoons Chocolate Flavor NESTLÉ NESQUIK Calcium Fortified Syrup

3 tablespoons NESTLÉ TOLL HOUSE Semi-Sweet Chocolate Mini Morsels

DIRECTIONS

PREHEAT oven to 350° F. Grease 9-inch pie plate.

PRESS three-fourths package cookie dough* onto bottom and up side of prepared pie plate.

BAKE for 18 to 24 minutes or until golden brown; flatten down with back of spoon to form pie shell. Cool completely on wire rack.

BEAT evaporated milk and pudding mix according to package directions in medium bowl; refrigerate for 5 minutes. Spread 1 cup pudding over cookie crust (use remaining pudding as you wish). Top pudding with bananas; spread with whipped topping. Refrigerate for at least 1 hour or until set. Drizzle with Nesquik; top with morsels.

*Bake extra for even more treats the kids (and grown-ups) will love!

Estimated Times
Preparation: 20 mins
Cooking: 18 mins
Cooling: 20 mins
Refrigerating: 1 hr

Chocolate Butterfinger-Caramel Cake

The smiles will keep coming when you serve this cake for the birthday boy or birthday girl's next party.

MAKES 15 SERVINGS

INGREDIENTS

1 package (18.25 ounces) chocolate cake mix

1 can (14 ounces) NESTLÉ CARNATION Sweetened Condensed Milk

3 (2.1 ounces each) NESTLÉ BUTTERFINGER Candy Bars, chopped, divided

1 jar (12.25 ounces) caramel syrup or ice cream topping

1 pint whipping cream, whipped

DIRECTIONS

PREPARE cake according to package directions using a 13 x 9-inch baking pan. Cool completely in pan on wire rack.

POKE holes in cake about 1-inch apart and 1-inch deep using handle of wooden spoon. Pour sweetened condensed milk over cake. Sprinkle with half of chopped Butterfinger. Pour caramel syrup over Butterfinger.

SPREAD whipped cream over cake; sprinkle with remaining chopped Butterfinger. Store in refrigerator until ready to serve. Refrigerate any uneaten cake—for a delicious late night snack!

Chocolate Butterfinger-Caramel Cake

Chocolate Caramel Brownies

Chocolate cake mix, evaporated milk, and caramels make these the most moist and tender brownies this side of paradise. Add chocolate morsels and chopped nuts, and you'll think you've already arrived!

MAKES 24 BROWNIES

INGREDIENTS

1 package (18.25 ounces) chocolate
   cake mix
1 cup chopped nuts
1 cup NESTLÉ CARNATION Evaporated
   Milk, divided
½ cup (1 stick) butter or
   margarine, melted
35 (10-ounce package)
   caramels, unwrapped
2 cups (12-ounce package) NESTLÉ
   TOLL HOUSE Semi-Sweet
   Chocolate Morsels

DIRECTIONS

PREHEAT oven to 350° F.

COMBINE cake mix and nuts in large bowl. Stir in ⅔ cup evaporated milk and

Chocolate Caramel Brownies

butter (batter will be thick). Spread half of batter into ungreased 13 x 9-inch baking pan.

BAKE for 15 minutes.

HEAT caramels and remaining evaporated milk in small saucepan over low heat, stirring constantly, until caramels are melted. Sprinkle morsels over brownie; drizzle with caramel mixture.

DROP remaining batter by heaping teaspoon over caramel mixture.

BAKE for 25 to 30 minutes or until center is set. Cool completely in pan on wire rack. Cut into bars.

Estimated Times
Preparation: 15 mins
Cooking: 45 mins
Cooling: 30 mins

Baking Tip

Are you looking for products that do not contain nuts? How do you know which Nestlé products are nut free? It is Nestlé's policy to put a full ingredients list on all their confectionary products, and if nuts are used it must always be declared. Nestlé Consumer Services can provide additional information and answer any questions on all our products and are willing to help consumers with all their baking needs. They can reply to inquiries about nutritional data, Halal, or Kosher status as well as the presence or absence of any allergy-causing ingredients (including nuts, milk, Soya, or eggs). Look on Nestlé product packages for the toll free numbers.

Cooking Tips

Here are some tips for different types of pans and what and how to use them for your every baking need.

Plastic pans should not be used in the oven because they can not withstand cooking temperatures. Surfaces of all plastic utensils, bowls, funnels, and other instruments retain grease. This makes it impossible to successfully beat egg whites with plastic utensils or in a plastic bowl, as they will not become stiff.

Porcelain enamel pans are poor heat conductors that also scratch and chip quite easily. Unless they are made of the best quality and specially treated, the glaze of enamelware is quickly affected by foods with acids. Use wooden or plastic utensils with this type of pan.

Shiny metal pans produce more even browning. Stainless steel pans are the easiest to keep clean and are one of the best choices for surface-cooking utensils. Buy better-quality stainless steel with an inner core of aluminum or copper, which increases heat diffusion. Poor quality stainless steel pans may have hot spots that can cause food to burn easily. Tempered glass pans are poor heat conductors.

Chocolate Chews

Chocolate cookies are always welcomed as an afternoon snack. Serve with a cold glass of milk.

MAKES ABOUT 2 DOZEN COOKIES

INGREDIENTS

1¼ cups all-purpose flour
½ teaspoon baking powder
½ teaspoon baking soda
½ cup (1 stick) butter or margarine, softened
½ cup granulated sugar
½ cup packed brown sugar
1 large egg
4 packets (1 ounce each) NESTLÉ TOLL HOUSE CHOCO BAKE Unsweetened Chocolate Flavor
½ cup chopped nuts or shredded coconut

DIRECTIONS

PREHEAT oven to 350° F.

COMBINE flour, baking powder, and baking soda in small bowl. Beat butter, granulated sugar, brown sugar, and egg in large mixer bowl until creamy. Beat in Choco Bake. Gradually beat in flour mixture. Stir in nuts. Drop by rounded tablespoon onto ungreased baking sheets.

BAKE for 10 to 12 minutes or until edges are set but centers are still soft. Cool on baking sheets for 3 minutes; remove to wire racks to cool completely.

Chocolate Chews

Estimated Times
Preparation: 15 mins
Cooking: 10 mins
Cooling: 15 mins

Chocolate Chip Cheesecake

Chocolate morsels dot this creamy, luscious cheesecake. It's a winning dessert that will please the eyes as well as the tastebuds.

MAKES 14 SERVINGS

INGREDIENTS

1½ cups crushed chocolate sandwich cookies (about 15 cookies)

2 tablespoons butter or
  margarine, melted

2 cups (12-ounce package)
  NESTLÉ TOLL HOUSE Semi-Sweet
  Chocolate Morsels, divided

2 packages (8 ounces each) cream
  cheese, at room temperature

½ cup granulated sugar

1 tablespoon vanilla extract

2 large eggs

2 tablespoons all-purpose flour

¾ cup NESTLÉ CARNATION
  Evaporated Milk

½ cup sour cream

DIRECTIONS

PREHEAT oven to 300° F.

COMBINE cookie crumbs with butter
in medium bowl until moistened; press
onto bottom of ungreased 9-inch springform pan. Sprinkle with 1 cup morsels.

BEAT cream cheese, sugar, and vanilla
extract in large mixer bowl until smooth.
Beat in eggs and flour. Gradually beat in

Chocolate Chip Cheesecake

evaporated milk and sour cream. Pour
over crust. Sprinkle with remaining
morsels.

BAKE for 25 minutes. Cover loosely
with foil.

BAKE for an additional 30 to 40 minutes
or until edge is set but center still moves
slightly. Place in refrigerator immediately;
refrigerate for 2 hours or until firm.
Remove side of springform pan.

NOTE: Cheesecake may be baked in
13 x 9-inch baking pan. Prepare as above.
Bake in preheated oven at 300° F for
20 minutes. Cover loosely with foil.
Bake for an additional 20 to 30 minutes.

Estimated Times

Preparation: 20 mins

Cooking: 55 mins

Refrigerating: 2 hrs

Chocolate Chip Cookie Brittle

**A cross between cookies and brittle,
this adds variety to your holiday
cookie repertoire.**

MAKES ABOUT 50 PIECES

INGREDIENTS

1 cup (2 sticks) butter or margarine,
  softened

1 cup granulated sugar

1½ teaspoons vanilla extract

1 teaspoon salt

2 cups all-purpose flour

2 cups (12-ounce package) NESTLÉ
  TOLL HOUSE Semi-Sweet
  Chocolate Morsels, divided

1 cup chopped nuts

DIRECTIONS

PREHEAT oven to 375° F.

BEAT butter, sugar, vanilla extract, and
salt in large mixer bowl. Gradually beat
in flour. Stir in 1½ cups morsels and
nuts. Press into ungreased 15 x 10-inch
jelly-roll pan.

BAKE for 20 to 25 minutes or until
golden brown and set. Cool in pan
until just slightly warm.

MICROWAVE remaining morsels in
small, heavy-duty plastic bag on HIGH
(100%) power for 30 to 45 seconds;
knead. Microwave at additional 10-
to 15-second intervals, kneading until
smooth. Cut tiny corner from bag;
squeeze bag to drizzle chocolate over
cookie. Allow chocolate to cool and set;
break into irregular pieces.

NOTE: Omitting nuts could cause cookie
to become dry.

Estimated Times

Preparation: 10 mins

Cooking: 22 mins

Cooling: 20 mins

Chocolate Chip Cookie Mix in a Jar

A gift of love from your own kitchen.

MAKES ABOUT 2 DOZEN COOKIES

INGREDIENTS

1¾ cups all-purpose flour

¾ teaspoon baking soda

¾ teaspoon salt

1½ cups (9 ounces) NESTLÉ TOLL
  HOUSE Semi-Sweet Chocolate Morsels

¾ cup packed brown sugar

½ cup granulated sugar

Chocolate Chip Cookie Mix in a Jar

DIRECTIONS

COMBINE flour, baking soda, and salt in small bowl. Place flour mixture in 1-quart jar. Layer remaining ingredients in order listed above, pressing firmly after each layer. Seal with lid and decorate with fabric and ribbon.

RECIPE TO ATTACH:

PREHEAT oven to 375° F. Beat ¾ cup (1½ sticks) softened butter or margarine, 1 large egg, and ¾ teaspoon vanilla extract in large mixer bowl until blended. Add cookie mix and ½ cup chopped nuts (optional); mix well, breaking up any clumps. Drop by rounded tablespoon onto ungreased baking sheets. Bake for 9 to 11 minutes or until golden brown. Cool on baking sheets for 2 minutes; remove to wire racks to cool completely. Makes about 2 dozen cookies.

Estimated Time
Preparation: 15 mins

Chocolate Chip Mexican Wedding Cakes

These Mexican dessert "cakes" are actually cookies, much loved for their delicate texture and flavor. Here, they're drizzled with chocolate for extra pizzazz.

MAKES ABOUT 4½ DOZEN COOKIES

INGREDIENTS

1 cup (2 sticks) butter, softened

½ cup sifted powdered sugar

1 teaspoon vanilla extract

2 cups all-purpose flour

⅔ cup finely chopped nuts

2 to 2½ teaspoons ground cinnamon

2 cups (12-ounce package) NESTLÉ
  TOLL HOUSE Semi-Sweet
  Chocolate Morsels, divided

DIRECTIONS

PREHEAT oven to 350° F.

BEAT butter and sugar in large mixer bowl until creamy. Beat in vanilla extract. Gradually beat in flour, nuts, and cinnamon. Stir in 1½ cups morsels. Roll dough into 1-inch balls; place on ungreased baking sheets.

BAKE for 10 to 12 minutes or until set and light golden brown on bottom. Cool on baking sheets for 2 minutes; remove to wire racks to cool completely.

MICROWAVE remaining morsels in heavy-duty plastic bag on HIGH (100%) power for 30 seconds; knead. Microwave at additional 10- to 15-second intervals, kneading until smooth. Cut a tiny corner from bag; squeeze bag to drizzle chocolate over cookies. Refrigerate cookies for about 5 minutes or until chocolate is set. Store at room temperature in airtight container.

Estimated Times

Preparation: 20 mins

Cooking: 10 mins

Cooling: 15 mins

Refrigerating: 5 mins

Chocolate Chip Strawberry Shortcakes

Introduce chocolate morsels to your shortcakes and you have a delicious variation on this summertime favorite.

MAKES 16 SHORTCAKES

INGREDIENTS

3½ cups all-purpose flour

⅓ cup granulated sugar

4 teaspoons baking powder

1 teaspoon baking soda

½ teaspoon salt

¾ cup (1½ sticks) cold butter or
    margarine, cut into pieces

2 cups (12-ounce package) NESTLÉ
    TOLL HOUSE Semi-Sweet
    Chocolate Morsels

1½ cups buttermilk

1 container (12 ounces) frozen
    whipped topping, thawed

4 cups sliced strawberries

DIRECTIONS

PREHEAT oven to 400° F. Grease baking sheets.

COMBINE flour, sugar, baking powder, baking soda, and salt in large bowl. Cut in butter with pastry blender or two knives until mixture resembles coarse crumbs. Stir in morsels. Stir in buttermilk with a fork just until moistened. Knead 2 or 3 times on floured surface. Pat to ¾-inch thickness. Cut into 2½ x 2½-inch diamonds; place on prepared baking sheets.

BAKE for 12 to 14 minutes or until lightly browned. Remove to wire racks to cool completely.

CUT one shortcake in half horizontally. Spread bottom half with whipped topping; top with strawberries. Cover with shortcake top; layer with more whipped topping and strawberries. Repeat with remaining shortcakes. Serve immediately.

Estimated Times

Preparation: 30 mins

Cooking: 12 mins

Cooling: 15 mins

Chocolate Chip Strawberry Shortcakes

About Toll House

As the popularity of TOLL HOUSE cookies continued to grow, Nestlé looked for ways to make it easier for people to bake. Nestlé began scoring the Semi-Sweet Chocolate Bar, and packaged it with a special chopper for easily cutting it into small morsels. Shortly after, in 1939, we began offering tiny pieces of chocolate in convenient, ready-to-use packages and that is how the first NESTLÉ TOLL HOUSE Real Semi-Sweet Chocolate Morsels were introduced.

Since they were first used by Ruth Wakefield in what would become the most popular cookie of all time, NESTLÉ TOLL HOUSE Semi-Sweet Chocolate Morsels have satisfied the chocolate cravings of millions. Today, they're used to make many of the hundreds of delectable chocolate desserts all across America and around the globe.

Chocolate Cocoa Frosting

This delectable frosting comes together in a snap.

MAKES ENOUGH TO FROST TWO 9-INCH LAYERS OR ONE 13 X 9-INCH SHEET CAKE

INGREDIENTS

½ cup (4 envelopes) Rich Chocolate Flavor NESTLÉ Hot Cocoa Mix

⅓ cup hot water

⅓ cup butter or margarine, softened

1 teaspoon vanilla extract

1 pound powdered sugar

DIRECTIONS

COMBINE cocoa mix and water in large mixer bowl. Beat in butter and vanilla extract. Gradually beat in powdered sugar until smooth and creamy. Add more hot water if frosting is too thick.

Estimated Time

Preparation: 5 mins

Chocolate Cocoa Frosting

Chocolate Cream Cheese Flan

Chocolate Cream Cheese Flan

These flan are rich, smooth, and chocolatey with a luscious caramel sauce.

MAKES 12 SERVINGS

INGREDIENTS

1 cup granulated sugar

½ cup water

1 can (12 fluid ounces) NESTLÉ CARNATION Evaporated Milk

1 can (14 ounces) NESTLÉ CARNATION Sweetened Condensed Milk

1 package (8 ounces) cream cheese, at room temperature

½ cup (1 stick) butter or margarine, softened

2 packets (1 ounce each) NESTLÉ TOLL HOUSE CHOCO BAKE Unsweetened Chocolate Flavor

5 large eggs

1 teaspoon vanilla extract

DIRECTIONS

PREHEAT oven to 350° F.

COMBINE sugar and water in medium saucepan; cook over low heat, stirring constantly, for 3 to 4 minutes or until sugar is dissolved. Increase heat to medium-high; boil, without stirring, for about 15 minutes or until caramel-colored. Quickly pour over bottom and sides of twelve 6-ounce custard cups or ramekins (if syrup hardens, soften over low heat).

PLACE evaporated milk, sweetened condensed milk, cream cheese, butter, Choco Bake, eggs, and vanilla extract in blender; cover. Blend well. Pour mixture into prepared custard cups. Arrange in 1 or 2 large baking pans and fill pan(s) with hot water to 1-inch depth(s).

BAKE for 35 to 45 minutes or until knife inserted near centers comes out clean. Cool in pan(s) on wire rack(s) for 20 minutes. Refrigerate for several hours or overnight. Run knife around rims; gently shake to loosen. Invert onto serving dishes.

Estimated Times
Preparation: 15 mins
Cooking: 55 mins
Cooling: 20 mins
Refrigerating: 3 hrs

Chocolate-Dipped Brandy Snaps

This decidedly adult cookie combines the flavors of chocolate, spiced with cinnamon and ginger, and brandy.

MAKES ABOUT 3 DOZEN COOKIES

INGREDIENTS

½ cup (1 stick) butter
½ cup granulated sugar
⅓ cup dark corn syrup
½ teaspoon ground cinnamon
¼ teaspoon ground ginger
1 cup all-purpose flour
2 teaspoons brandy
1 cup (6 ounces) NESTLÉ TOLL HOUSE Semi-Sweet Chocolate Morsels
1 tablespoon vegetable shortening
⅓ cup finely chopped nuts

DIRECTIONS

PREHEAT oven to 300° F.

COMBINE butter, sugar, corn syrup, cinnamon, and ginger in medium, heavy-duty saucepan. Cook over low heat, stirring until smooth. Remove from heat; stir in flour and brandy. Drop by rounded teaspoon onto ungreased baking sheets about 3 inches apart, baking no more than 6 at a time.

BAKE for 10 to 14 minutes or until deep caramel color. Cool on baking sheets for 10 seconds. Remove from baking sheets and immediately roll around wooden spoon handle; cool completely on wire racks.

LINE baking sheets with wax paper.

MICROWAVE morsels and shortening in medium, uncovered, microwave-safe bowl on HIGH (100%) power for 1 minute; STIR. The morsels may retain some of their original shape. If necessary, microwave at additional 10- to 15-second intervals, stirring just until morsels are melted. Dip cookies halfway in melted chocolate; shake off excess. Sprinkle with nuts; set on prepared baking sheets. Refrigerate for 10 minutes or until chocolate is set. Store in airtight container in refrigerator.

Estimated Times
Preparation: 30 mins
Cooking: 15 mins
Cooling: 15 mins
Refrigerating: 10 mins

Chocolate Gingerbread Boys and Girls

Chocolate Gingerbread Boys and Girls

A classic gets a chocolate twist in these chocolate gingerbread cookies. Fun to make and eat!

MAKES ABOUT 2½ DOZEN COOKIES

INGREDIENTS

2 cups (12-ounce package) NESTLÉ
    TOLL HOUSE Semi-Sweet
    Chocolate Morsels, divided
2¾ cups all-purpose flour
1 teaspoon baking soda
½ teaspoon salt
½ teaspoon ground ginger
½ teaspoon ground cinnamon
3 tablespoons butter or
    margarine, softened
3 tablespoons granulated sugar
½ cup molasses
¼ cup water
1 container (16 ounces) prepared vanilla
    frosting, colored as desired (or colored
    frosting or colored icing in tubes)

DIRECTIONS

MICROWAVE 1½ cups morsels in medium, uncovered, microwave-safe bowl on HIGH (100%) power for 1 minute; STIR. The morsels may retain some of their original shape. If necessary, microwave at additional 10- to 15-second intervals, stirring just until morsels are melted. Cool to room temperature.

COMBINE flour, baking soda, salt, ginger, and cinnamon in small bowl. Beat butter and sugar in large mixer bowl until creamy; beat in molasses and melted chocolate. Gradually add flour mixture alternately with water, beating until smooth. Cover; refrigerate for 1 hour or until firm.

PREHEAT oven to 350° F.

ROLL half of dough to ¼-inch thickness on floured surface with floured rolling pin. Cut dough into gingerbread boy and girl shapes using cookie cutters or a stencil. Place on ungreased baking sheets. Repeat with remaining dough.

BAKE for 5 to 6 minutes or until edges are set but centers are still slightly soft. Cool on baking sheets for 2 minutes; remove to wire racks to cool completely.

PLACE remaining morsels in heavy-duty plastic bag. Microwave on HIGH (100%) power for 30 to 45 seconds; knead. Microwave for an additional 10 seconds; knead until smooth. Cut tiny corner from bag; squeeze to pipe chocolate. Decorate cookies with piped chocolate and prepared frosting or icing.

Estimated Times
Preparation: 45 mins
Refrigerating: 1 hr
Cooking: 7 mins
Cooling: 15 mins

Chocolate Hazelnut Terrine with Raspberry Sauce

This elegant dessert is a chocolate-lover's dream served in a pool of ruby-red raspberry sauce.

MAKES 16 SERVINGS

INGREDIENTS

DARK CHOCOLATE LAYER

2 cups (12-ounce package) NESTLÉ
    TOLL HOUSE Semi-Sweet
    Chocolate Morsels
⅓ cup butter, cut into pieces
¼ cup hazelnut liqueur
1½ cups heavy whipping cream

MILK CHOCOLATE LAYER

1¾ cups (11.5-ounce package) NESTLÉ
   TOLL HOUSE Milk Chocolate Morsels

⅓ cup butter, cut into pieces

RASPBERRY SAUCE

1 package (10 ounces) frozen raspberries
   in syrup, thawed, puréed, and strained

½ cup water

1 tablespoon cornstarch

1 teaspoon granulated sugar

DIRECTIONS

LINE 9 x 5-inch loaf pan with
plastic wrap.

FOR DARK CHOCOLATE LAYER:

MICROWAVE semi-sweet morsels
and butter in medium, uncovered,
microwave-safe bowl on HIGH (100%)
power for 1 minute; STIR. The morsels
may retain some of their original shape.
If necessary, microwave at additional
10- to 15-second intervals, stirring just
until morsels are melted. Stir in liqueur;
cool to room temperature.

WHIP cream in small mixer bowl until
stiff peaks form. Fold 2 cups whipped
cream into chocolate mixture. Spoon
into prepared loaf pan. Refrigerate
remaining whipped cream.

FOR MILK CHOCOLATE LAYER:

MICROWAVE milk chocolate morsels
and butter in medium, uncovered,
microwave-safe bowl on MEDIUM-HIGH
(70%) power for 1 minute; STIR. The
morsels may retain some of their original
shape. If necessary, microwave at
additional 10- to 15-second intervals,
stirring just until morsels are melted.
Cool to room temperature. Stir
remaining whipped cream into
chocolate mixture. Spread over dark
chocolate layer. Cover; refrigerate for
at least 2 hours or until firm.

FOR RASPBERRY SAUCE:

COOK raspberry purée, water, cornstarch,
and sugar in small saucepan over
medium heat, stirring constantly, until
mixture comes to a boil. Boil for
1 minute. Cover; refrigerate.

TO SERVE:

INVERT terrine onto serving platter;
remove plastic wrap. Cut into
½-inch-thick slices. Serve in pool
of Raspberry Sauce.

Estimated Times

Preparation: 30 mins

Cooking: 5 mins

Cooling: 30 mins

Refrigerating: 2 hrs

Chocolate Hazelnut Terrine with Raspberry Sauce

Sweetened Condensed Milk

This newest member of the Nestlé
Carnation line was introduced in
1988. Sweetened condensed milk
is perfect for baking and creating
confectionary delights as well as
sweetening a variety of beverages.
This product gets its sweetness from
removing water and adding sugar.
For example, sweetened condensed
milk is whole milk from which 60
percent of the water has been
removed and is heavily sweetened
with sugar. As a result, this product
is very thick and very sweet. As
the product ages, it may begin to
change color and thicken. Each can
is labeled with a "best before" date.
If your can is within its freshness
date, it is safe to use and should
not affect your recipe performance.

Baking Tip

When melting chocolate, the smallest drop of moisture from a wet spoon, steam from double boiler, or excessive high heat can lead to "seizing," lumpiness or hardening of the chocolate, and cause it not to melt properly. When melting NESTLÉ TOLL HOUSE Semi-Sweet Chocolate Morsels, melt 1 or 2 cups morsels over lowest possible heat. When morsels begin to melt, remove from heat and stir. Return to heat for a few seconds at a time, stirring until smooth. (*Note: This is not recommended for Butterscotch Morsels, Milk Chocolate Morsels, Peanut Butter & Milk Chocolate Morsels, and Premier White Morsels.)

If you're using a double boiler for melting the chocolate morsels, heat in the top of an uncovered double boiler over hot (not boiling) water. When most of morsels are shiny, stir until smooth. To improvise a double boiler, place morsels in a bowl set over a saucepan filled with hot (not boiling) water. Remove bowl from saucepan when morsels are melted.

Chocolate Intensity

Dense chocolate cake is served with a silky-smooth, coffee-spiked crème anglaise for a decadent dessert.

MAKES 12 SERVINGS

INGREDIENTS
CAKE

1 package (8 ounces) NESTLÉ TOLL HOUSE Unsweetened Chocolate Baking Bars, broken into pieces
1½ cups granulated sugar
½ cup (1 stick) butter, softened
3 large eggs
2 teaspoons vanilla extract
⅔ cup all-purpose flour
2 tablespoons powdered sugar

COFFEE CRÈME ANGLAISE

⅓ cup granulated sugar
1 tablespoon NESCAFÉ TASTER'S CHOICE 100% Pure Instant Coffee Granules
1½ cups milk
4 large egg yolks, lightly beaten
1 teaspoon vanilla extract

DIRECTIONS
FOR CAKE:

PREHEAT oven to 350° F. Grease 9-inch springform pan.

MICROWAVE baking bars in medium, uncovered, microwave-safe bowl on HIGH (100%) power for 1 minute; STIR. The bars may retain some of their original shape. If necessary, microwave at additional 10- to 15-second intervals, stirring just until bars are melted. Cool to lukewarm.

BEAT granulated sugar, butter, eggs, and vanilla extract in large mixer bowl for about 4 minutes or until thick and pale yellow. Beat in melted chocolate. Gradually beat in flour. Spread into prepared springform pan.

BAKE for 25 to 28 minutes or until wooden pick inserted in center comes out moist. Cool in pan on wire rack for 15 minutes. Remove side of pan; cool completely. Sprinkle with powdered sugar; serve with Coffee Crème Anglaise.

FOR COFFEE CRÈME ANGLAISE:
COMBINE sugar and coffee granules in medium saucepan; stir in milk. Cook over medium heat, stirring constantly, until mixture comes just to a simmer. Remove from heat. Gradually whisk half of hot milk mixture into egg yolks; return mixture to saucepan. Cook, stirring constantly, for 3 to 4 minutes or until mixture is slightly thickened. Strain into small bowl; stir in vanilla extract. Cover with plastic wrap; refrigerate.

Estimated Times
Preparation: 20 mins
Cooking: 35 mins
Cooling: 1 hr

Chocolate Lover's Chocolate Mousse Pie

Chocolate Lover's Chocolate Mousse Pie

Chocolate crust with a milk chocolate coating, fluffy chocolate filling, whipped cream, and a chocolate drizzle: This pie is not for the faint of heart!

MAKES 12 SERVINGS

INGREDIENTS

1 cup graham cracker crumbs

⅓ cup NESTLÉ TOLL HOUSE Baking Cocoa

¼ cup granulated sugar

⅓ cup butter, melted

2¾ cups (16 ounces) NESTLÉ TOLL HOUSE Semi-Sweet Chocolate Morsels, divided

2 cups heavy whipping cream, divided

2 teaspoons powdered sugar

1 teaspoon vanilla extract

DIRECTIONS

PREHEAT oven to 350° F.

COMBINE graham cracker crumbs, cocoa, and granulated sugar in ungreased 9-inch pie plate. Stir in butter until moistened; press onto bottom and up side of pie plate.

BAKE for 8 to 10 minutes. Sprinkle ½ cup morsels over hot crust. Let stand for 10 minutes or until morsels are shiny. Spread chocolate over bottom and up side of crust. Cool to room temperature.

MICROWAVE 2 cups morsels and ¾ cup cream in large, uncovered, microwave-safe bowl on HIGH (100%) power for 1 minute; STIR. The morsels may retain some of their original shape. If necessary, microwave at additional 10- to 15-second intervals, stirring just until morsels are melted. Cool to room temperature.

BEAT remaining cream, powdered sugar, and vanilla extract in chilled small mixer bowl until soft peaks form. Fold 2 cups whipped cream into chocolate mixture. Spoon into crust; swirl top. Garnish with remaining whipped cream. Refrigerate until firm.

MICROWAVE remaining ¼ cup morsels in heavy-duty plastic bag on HIGH (100%) power for about 30 seconds; knead until smooth. Cut tiny corner from bag; squeeze bag to drizzle chocolate over pie. Let stand a few minutes before serving.

Estimated Times

Preparation: 20 mins

Cooking: 10 mins

Standing: 10 mins

Cooling: 15 mins

Refrigerating: 30 mins

Chocolate Marshmallow Mile-High Squares

Kids will love to make and eat these chocolate-peanut butter-marshmallow concoctions.

MAKES 48 SQUARES

INGREDIENTS

2 cups (12-ounce package) NESTLÉ TOLL HOUSE Semi-Sweet Chocolate Morsels
1⅔ cups (11-ounce package) NESTLÉ TOLL HOUSE Butterscotch Flavored Morsels
½ cup creamy or chunky peanut butter
9 cups (16-ounce package) miniature marshmallows
1 cup dry-roasted peanuts

DIRECTIONS

LINE 13 x 9-inch baking pan with foil.

MICROWAVE semi-sweet morsels, butterscotch morsels, and peanut butter in large, uncovered, microwave-safe bowl on MEDIUM-HIGH (70%) power for 2 minutes; STIR. The morsels may retain some of their original shape. If necessary, microwave at additional 10- to 15-second intervals, stirring just until morsels are melted. Cool for 1 minute. Stir in marshmallows and peanuts.

Chocolate Marshmallow Mile-High Squares

SPREAD into prepared pan. Refrigerate until firm. Cut into squares.

Estimated Times
Preparation: 10 mins
Cooking: 3 mins
Refrigerating: 1 hr

Chocolate Mini Chip Holiday Cookies

These cut-out cookies are dotted with mini chocolate morsels and topped with frosting and a drizzle of melted chocolate for a special treat. Fun to make with kids.

MAKES ABOUT 3 DOZEN COOKIES

INGREDIENTS

1 cup (2 sticks) butter or margarine, softened
½ cup packed brown sugar
⅓ cup granulated sugar
2 teaspoons vanilla extract
½ teaspoon salt
1 large egg yolk
2½ cups all-purpose flour
2 cups (12-ounce package) NESTLÉ TOLL HOUSE Semi-Sweet Chocolate Mini Morsels, divided
1 container (16 ounces) prepared vanilla frosting, colored if desired

DIRECTIONS

BEAT butter, brown sugar, granulated sugar, vanilla extract, and salt in large mixer bowl until creamy. Beat in egg yolk. Gradually beat in flour. Stir in 1½ cups morsels. Divide dough in half. Cover; refrigerate for 1 hour or until firm.

PREHEAT oven to 350° F.

ROLL half of dough to ¼-inch thickness between two sheets of wax paper. Remove top sheet of wax paper. Cut dough into shapes using cookie cutters. Lift from wax paper; place on ungreased baking sheets. Refrigerate for 10 minutes. Repeat with remaining dough.

BAKE for 9 to 11 minutes or until golden brown. Cool on baking sheets for 2 minutes; remove to wire racks to cool completely. Spread with frosting; pipe with melted chocolate.

TO PIPE CHOCOLATE:
PLACE remaining morsels in heavy-duty plastic bag. Microwave on HIGH (100%) power for 45 seconds; knead. Microwave for an additional 10 seconds; knead until

smooth. Cut tiny corner from bag; squeeze bag to pipe chocolate.

Estimated Times
Preparation: 30 mins
Refrigerating: 1 hr, 10 mins
Cooking: 10 mins
Cooling: 15 mins

Chocolate Mudslide Frozen Pie

Take to a party or serve as an after-dinner delight. Chocolate crumb crust is spread with a mixture of sour cream, melted chocolate morsels, and coffee. Cover with a whipped topping and sprinkling of mini chocolate morsels.

MAKES 8 SERVINGS

INGREDIENTS
1 prepared 9-inch (6 ounces) chocolate
   crumb crust
1 cup (6 ounces) NESTLÉ TOLL HOUSE
   Semi-Sweet Chocolate Morsels
1 teaspoon NESCAFÉ TASTER'S CHOICE
   100% Pure Instant Coffee Granules
1 teaspoon hot water
¾ cup sour cream
½ cup granulated sugar
1 teaspoon vanilla extract
1½ cups heavy whipping cream
1 cup powdered sugar
¼ cup NESTLÉ TOLL HOUSE Baking Cocoa
2 tablespoons NESTLÉ TOLL HOUSE
   Semi-Sweet Chocolate Mini Morsels

DIRECTIONS
MELT 1 cup semi-sweet chocolate morsels in small, heavy-duty saucepan over lowest possible heat. When morsels begin to melt, remove from heat; stir. Return to heat for a few seconds at a time, stirring until smooth. Remove from heat; let cool for 10 minutes.

COMBINE coffee granules and water in medium bowl. Add sour cream, granulated sugar, and vanilla extract; stir until sugar is dissolved. Stir in melted chocolate until smooth. Spread into crust; refrigerate.

BEAT cream, powdered sugar, and cocoa in small mixer bowl until stiff peaks form. Spread or pipe over chocolate layer. Sprinkle with mini morsels. Freeze for at least 6 hours or until firm.

Estimated Times
Preparation: 20 mins
Cooking: 3 mins
Cooling: 10 mins
Freezing: 6 hrs

Chocolate Peanut Buddy Bars

Milk chocolate inside peanut butter squares. What could be better?

MAKES 36 BARS

INGREDIENTS
1 cup creamy or chunky peanut butter
6 tablespoons butter or margarine,
   softened
1¼ cups granulated sugar
3 large eggs
1 teaspoon vanilla extract
1 cup all-purpose flour
¼ teaspoon salt
1¾ cups (11.5-ounce package)
   NESTLÉ TOLL HOUSE Milk
   Chocolate Morsels, divided

DIRECTIONS
PREHEAT oven to 350° F.

BEAT peanut butter and butter in large mixer bowl until smooth. Beat in sugar, eggs, and vanilla extract. Beat in flour and salt. Stir in 1 cup morsels. Spread into ungreased 13 x 9-inch baking pan.

BAKE for 25 to 30 minutes or until edges are lightly browned. Sprinkle with remaining morsels. Let stand for 5 minutes or until morsels are shiny; spread evenly. Cool completely in pan on wire rack. Cut into bars.

Estimated Times
Preparation: 15 mins
Cooking: 25 mins
Standing: 5 mins
Cooling: 30 mins

Chocolate Peppermint Wafers

Chocolate Peppermint Wafers

A festive candy treat, these chocolate peppermint wafers are great for parties or just to have around.

MAKES ABOUT 36 PIECES

INGREDIENTS

3 (6-ounce package) NESTLÉ TOLL HOUSE Premier White Baking Bars, broken into pieces

⅓ cup coarsely crushed hard peppermint candies (about 12)

1 cup (6 ounces) NESTLÉ TOLL HOUSE Semi-Sweet Chocolate Morsels

1 tablespoon vegetable shortening

DIRECTIONS

LINE 8-inch-square baking pan with foil. Line baking sheets with wax paper.

MICROWAVE baking bars in medium, uncovered, microwave-safe bowl on MEDIUM-HIGH (70%) power for

1 minute; STIR. The bars may retain some of their original shape. If necessary, microwave at additional 10- to 15-second intervals, stirring just until bars are melted. Stir in candy. Spread thinly in prepared baking pan. Refrigerate for 10 minutes or until firm. Remove foil; break into bite-sized pieces.

MICROWAVE morsels and shortening in small, uncovered, microwave-safe bowl on HIGH (100%) power for 1 minute; STIR. The morsels may retain some of their original shape. If necessary, microwave at additional 10- to 15-second intervals, stirring just until morsels are melted.

DIP candy pieces three-fourths of the way into melted chocolate; shake off excess. Place on prepared baking sheets. Refrigerate until ready to serve.

NOTE: To crush candies, place in a heavy-duty resealable plastic food storage bag; close. Crush with rolling pin or mallet.

Estimated Times

Preparation: 20 mins

Cooking: 3 mins

Refrigerating: 30 mins

Chocolate Rhapsody

This dessert will be music to your taste buds. A thin layer of chocolate separates luscious raspberry mousse and yellow sponge cake. A second layer on top finishes this masterpiece. Garnish with whipped cream and fresh raspberries.

MAKES 8 SERVINGS

INGREDIENTS

CAKE LAYER

⅔ cup all-purpose flour

½ teaspoon baking powder

¼ teaspoon salt

½ cup granulated sugar

6 tablespoons butter or margarine, softened

1 large egg

1 teaspoon vanilla extract

¼ cup milk

CHOCOLATE LAYER

2 cups (12-ounce package) NESTLÉ TOLL HOUSE Semi-Sweet Chocolate Morsels

¾ cup heavy whipping cream

RASPBERRY MOUSSE LAYER

⅓ cup granulated sugar

2 tablespoons water

1 teaspoon cornstarch

2 cups (8 ounces) slightly sweetened or unsweetened frozen raspberries

3 (6-ounce package) NESTLÉ TOLL HOUSE Premier White Baking Bars, broken into pieces

1¾ cups heavy whipping cream, divided

1 teaspoon vanilla extract

Sweetened whipped cream (optional)

Fresh raspberries (optional)

DIRECTIONS

PREHEAT oven to 350° F. Grease 9-inch springform pan.

FOR CAKE LAYER:

COMBINE flour, baking powder, and salt in small bowl. Beat sugar and butter in small mixer bowl until creamy. Beat in egg and vanilla extract. Alternately beat in flour mixture and milk. Spread into prepared springform pan.

BAKE for 15 to 20 minutes or until lightly browned. Cool completely in pan on wire rack.

FOR CHOCOLATE LAYER:

MICROWAVE morsels and cream in medium, uncovered, microwave-safe bowl on HIGH (100%) power for 1 minute; STIR. The morsels may retain some of their original shape. If necessary, microwave at additional 10- to 15-second intervals, stirring just until morsels are melted. Cool completely.

FOR RASPBERRY MOUSSE LAYER:

COMBINE sugar, water, and cornstarch in medium saucepan; stir in raspberries.

Bring mixture to a boil. Boil, stirring constantly, for 1 minute. Cool completely.

MICROWAVE baking bars and ½ cup cream in medium, uncovered, microwave-safe bowl on MEDIUM-HIGH (70%) power for 1 minute; STIR. The bars may retain some of their original shape. If necessary, microwave at additional 10- to 15-second intervals, stirring just until bars are melted. Cool completely. Stir into raspberry mixture.

BEAT remaining cream and vanilla extract in large mixer bowl until stiff peaks form. Fold in raspberry mixture.

TO ASSEMBLE:

REMOVE side of springform pan; dust off crumbs. Grease inside of pan; reattach side. Spread ½ cup chocolate mixture over cake layer; freeze for 5 minutes. Spoon raspberry mousse over chocolate; freeze for 10 minutes. Carefully spread remaining chocolate mixture over raspberry mousse. Refrigerate for at least 4 hours or until firm. Carefully remove side of springform pan. Garnish with whipped cream and raspberries.

Estimated Times

Preparation: 30 mins

Cooking: 20 mins

Cooling: 1 hr

Freezing: 15 mins

Refrigerating: 4 hrs

Chocolate Rhapsody

Baking Tip

For melting chocolate bars, chop about one-third of chocolate to be melted into large chunks and set aside. Chop remaining chocolate into small pieces. (Always melt more chocolate than you'll need for your recipe. You can remelt any leftovers, or use it in another baking recipe.) Place some of the finely chopped chocolate in a fairly large bowl. Place bowl inside another bowl partially filled with very warm water. (If water in larger bowl will touch bottom of smaller bowl, water temp should be 125° F. If smaller bowl will be held above water, then water temp should be 140° F). Prevent water or steam from getting into the chocolate or it will harden and crumble. Stir chocolate as it melts, gradually adding the remaining finely cut pieces. It may be necessary to rewarm the water during the melting process.

Chocolate Treasure Mini Raspberry Cakes

Chocolate and raspberry combine easily to make the perfect dessert.

MAKES 10 SERVINGS

INGREDIENTS
¾ cup granulated sugar
½ cup (1 stick) butter, softened
2 large eggs
¼ cup NESTLÉ CARNATION Evaporated Milk
1 teaspoon vanilla extract
1 cup all-purpose flour
¼ teaspoon salt
1 cup fresh raspberries
10 Chocolate Creme NESTLÉ SIGNATURE TREASURES
Powdered sugar (optional)

DIRECTIONS
PREHEAT oven to 350° F. Grease 10 muffin cups.

BEAT granulated sugar and butter in large mixer bowl until combined. Add eggs, evaporated milk, and vanilla extract; beat until blended. Stir in flour and salt. Gently fold in raspberries. Spoon heaping tablespoon batter into each prepared muffin cup; place 1 Nestlé Treasure in each cup, pressing down slightly. Spoon heaping tablespoon batter over each Nestlé Treasure, covering completely.

BAKE for 20 to 22 minutes or until cakes are golden brown around edges and tops are set. Cool in pan on wire rack for 10 minutes. Run knife around edges to loosen; gently invert onto serving plate. Sprinkle with powdered sugar; serve warm.

Estimated Times
Preparation: 20 mins
Cooking: 20 mins
Cooling: 10 mins

Chocolatey Raspberry Crumb Bars

A thin layer of raspberry jam is all that comes between the brown sugar crust and the nut-flavored topping. Melted chocolate morsels are spread over the top to finish these bars off.

Chocolatey Raspberry Crumb Bars

INGREDIENTS

1 cup (2 sticks) butter or
 margarine, softened
2 cups all-purpose flour
½ cup packed brown sugar
¼ teaspoon salt
2 cups (12-ounce package)
 NESTLÉ TOLL HOUSE Semi-Sweet
 Chocolate Morsels, divided
1 can (14 ounces) NESTLÉ CARNATION
 Sweetened Condensed Milk
½ cup chopped nuts (optional)
⅓ cup seedless raspberry jam

DIRECTIONS

PREHEAT oven to 350° F. Grease
13 x 9-inch baking pan.

BEAT butter in large mixer bowl until
creamy. Beat in flour, sugar, and salt
until crumbly. With floured fingers,
press 1¾ cups crumb mixture onto
bottom of prepared baking pan;
reserve remaining mixture.

BAKE for 10 to 12 minutes or until
edges are golden brown.

MICROWAVE 1 cup morsels and
sweetened condensed milk in medium,
uncovered, microwave-safe bowl on
HIGH (100%) power for 1 minute; STIR.
The morsels may retain some of their
original shape. If necessary, microwave
at additional 10- to 15-second intervals,
stirring just until morsels are melted.
Spread over hot crust.

STIR nuts into reserved crumb mixture;
sprinkle over chocolate filling. Drop
teaspoonfuls of jam over crumb mixture.
Sprinkle with remaining morsels.

BAKE for 25 to 30 minutes or until
center is set. Cool completely in pan
on wire rack. Cut into bars.

Estimated Times
Preparation: 15 mins
Cooking: 35 mins
Cooling: 30 mins

Coconut Cookie Nests

**Too sweet to hide, these fun coconut
cookies are the perfect addition to your
Easter festivities. With delicious egg-
shaped chocolates nestled atop colorful
cookie nests, these easy-to-make treats
are sure to create a "hoppy" Easter.**

INGREDIENTS

2 large egg whites
2 cups shredded sweetened coconut
⅓ cup granulated sugar
2 tablespoons all-purpose flour
½ teaspoon vanilla extract
⅛ teaspoon salt
4 colors of food coloring (optional)
12 NESTLÉ CRUNCH or NESTLÉ
 BUTTERFINGER NestEggs, unwrapped

DIRECTIONS

PREHEAT oven to 325° F. Lightly grease
and flour baking sheet.

WHISK egg whites in medium bowl
until frothy. Stir in coconut, sugar,
flour, vanilla extract, and salt until well
blended. Divide coconut mixture into
4 bowls. Add 1 to 2 drops different
color food coloring to each bowl and
mix until colors are dispersed evenly.
Drop by tablespoonfuls into 12 mounds
1½ inches apart on prepared baking
sheet. Press centers in slightly to
form nests.

BAKE for 20 to 22 minutes or until
set and lightly golden brown. Cool on
baking sheet on wire rack for 10 minutes;
transfer nests to wire rack to cool
completely. Place 1 Nestlé NestEgg
in each nest before serving.

Estimated Times
Preparation: 20 mins
Cooking: 20 mins
Cooling: 20 mins

Coconut Cookie Nests

Cream Cheese Chocolate Chip Pastry Cookies

An enticing dessert and it's easy to make.

MAKES ABOUT 2 DOZEN COOKIES

INGREDIENTS

2 sheets (17.25-ounce package) frozen
    puff pastry, thawed
1 package (8 ounces) cream
    cheese, at room temperature
3 tablespoons granulated sugar
1¾ cups (11.5-ounce package)
    NESTLÉ TOLL HOUSE Milk Chocolate
    Morsels, divided

DIRECTIONS

UNFOLD one puff pastry sheet on lightly floured surface. Roll out to make 14 x 10-inch rectangle. Combine cream cheese and sugar in small bowl until smooth. Spread half cream cheese mixture over puff pastry, leaving 1-inch border on one long side. Sprinkle with half morsels. Roll up starting at long side covered with cream cheese. Seal end by moistening with water. Repeat steps with remaining ingredients. Refrigerate for 1 hour.

PREHEAT oven to 375° F. Lightly grease baking sheets or line with parchment paper.

CUT rolls crosswise into 1-inch-thick slices. Place cut-side-down on prepared baking sheets.

BAKE for 20 to 25 minutes or until golden brown. Cool on baking sheets for 2 minutes; remove to wire racks to cool completely.

Estimated Times
Preparation: 15 mins
Refrigerating: 1 hr
Cooking: 20 mins
Cooling: 15 mins

Creamy Chocolate Pudding

This velvety-soft chocolate pudding will delight 'kids of all ages.' Serve warm or cold!

MAKES 4 SERVINGS

INGREDIENTS

6 tablespoons granulated sugar
¼ cup NESTLÉ TOLL HOUSE
    Baking Cocoa
¼ cup cornstarch
⅛ teaspoon salt
1 can (12 fluid ounces) NESTLÉ
    CARNATION Evaporated Fat Free Milk
½ cup water
1 tablespoon butter or margarine
½ teaspoon vanilla extract

DIRECTIONS

COMBINE sugar, cocoa, cornstarch, and salt in medium saucepan. Add evaporated milk and water; whisk to blend.

Cream Cheese Chocolate Chip Pastry Cookies

Creamy Chocolate Pudding

COOK over medium heat, stirring constantly, for about 7 minutes or until pudding thickens (do not boil). Remove from heat; stir in butter and vanilla extract. Serve warm or cold.

Estimated Times
Preparation: 10 mins
Cooking: 7 mins

Creamy Pear Flan

Imagine a creamy flan with a light pear flavor served in a pool of amber-colored caramel sauce. A delightful, simple, and elegant dessert.

MAKES 8 SERVINGS

INGREDIENTS
¾ cup granulated sugar
1 can (11.5 fluid ounces) pear nectar
1 can (14 ounces) NESTLÉ CARNATION
  Sweetened Condensed Milk

1 package (8 ounces) cream cheese, at
  room temperature and cut into chunks
½ teaspoon vanilla extract
5 large eggs

DIRECTIONS
PREHEAT oven to 350° F.

PLACE sugar in small, heavy-duty saucepan. Cook over medium-high heat, stirring constantly, for 3 to 4 minutes or until sugar is dissolved and golden. Quickly pour into eight 6-ounce custard cups or ramekins.

PLACE nectar, sweetened condensed milk, cream cheese, and vanilla extract in blender or food processor; cover. Blend until smooth. Add eggs; blend until smooth. Pour into prepared custard cups.

Divide cups between two 13 x 9-inch baking pans; fill pans with hot water to 1-inch depths.

BAKE for 35 to 45 minutes or until knife inserted in centers comes out clean. Remove to wire rack to cool for 30 minutes; refrigerate for several hours or overnight.

RUN small spatula around edges of cups; gently shake to loosen. Invert onto serving dishes.

Estimated Times
Preparation: 15 mins
Cooking: 40 mins
Cooling: 30 mins
Refrigerating: 3 hrs

Creamy Pear Flan

Creamy Rice Pudding

Creamy pudding with tender, sweet dried fruit and just a hint of nutmeg.

MAKES 6 SERVINGS

INGREDIENTS

1⅓ cups water
⅔ cup long-grain white rice
1 can (12 fluid ounces) NESTLÉ
   CARNATION Evaporated Milk
½ cup raisins, dried cranberries
   and/or dried cherries
½ cup granulated sugar
1½ teaspoons vanilla extract
½ teaspoon ground nutmeg
¼ teaspoon salt
2 large eggs, lightly beaten

DIRECTIONS

PLACE water and rice in medium saucepan; bring to a boil. Reduce heat to low; cover. Cook for 12 to 15 minutes or until liquid is absorbed.

STIR in evaporated milk, raisins, sugar, vanilla extract, nutmeg, and salt; bring to a boil. Stir a portion of rice mixture into the eggs. Add egg mixture to rice mixture; mix well with wire whisk. Bring to a boil. Cook, stirring constantly, for 2 minutes. Serve warm or chilled.

FOR COCONUT RICE PUDDING:
SUBSTITUTE ½ cup toasted or untoasted flaked coconut for raisins.

Estimated Times
Preparation: 5 mins
Cooking: 20 mins

Creamy Rice Pudding

Crispy Bars Supreme

A dash of cinnamon adds even more rich flavor to these easy bars. Rice cereal makes them crunchy while Raisinets add both a chewy texture and a burst of chocolate in each bite.

MAKES 36 BARS

INGREDIENTS

1 cup all-purpose flour

½ teaspoon baking powder

½ teaspoon ground cinnamon

⅔ cup packed brown sugar

½ cup granulated sugar

½ cup (1 stick) butter or margarine, softened

1 large egg

2 tablespoons water

2 cups oven-toasted rice cereal

1 package (7 ounces) NESTLÉ RAISINETS Milk Chocolate-Covered Raisins

1 cup chopped nuts

DIRECTIONS

PREHEAT oven to 375° F. Grease 13 x 9-inch baking pan.

COMBINE flour, baking powder, and cinnamon in small bowl. Beat brown sugar, granulated sugar, and butter in large mixer bowl until creamy. Beat in

Crispy Bars Supreme

egg and water. Gradually beat in flour mixture. Stir in cereal, Raisinets, and nuts. Spread into prepared baking pan.

BAKE for 12 to 15 minutes or until golden brown. Cool completely in pan on wire rack. Cut into bars.

Estimated Times
Preparation: 15 mins
Cooking: 12 mins
Cooling: 30 mins

Baking Tip

Granulated sugar is most often used for baking. Powdered sugar or confectioners' sugar is also used, especially for frostings. Coarse sugar can be used for garnishing. If you have a hard time finding coarse sugar you can always buy sugar cubes instead. Place the sugar cubes in a plastic bag, seal, and break up the cubes with a rolling pin until you have coarse bits of sugar.

Brown sugar is also sugar but is mixed with molasses which gives it a deep, caramel flavor and color. You can find brown sugar in light, golden, and dark. Golden is best for versatility.

Custard Tart with Fresh Berries

A custard tart with fresh berries will please your family and friends. Sour cream, sweetened condensed milk, and orange juice form a sweet-tart base perfect for showing off any kind of berries.

MAKES 8 SERVINGS

INGREDIENTS

GRAHAM CRACKER CRUST

2 cups graham cracker crumbs

3 tablespoons powdered sugar

6 tablespoons butter or margarine, melted

FILLING

1 container (16 ounces) sour cream

1 can (14 ounces) NESTLÉ CARNATION Sweetened Condensed Milk

½ cup orange juice

2 large eggs

1 teaspoon vanilla extract

GLAZE

1 tablespoon water

1 teaspoon cornstarch

¼ cup raspberry preserves

1 cup fresh berries (e.g., raspberries, blueberries, blackberries, and/or sliced strawberries)

DIRECTIONS

PREHEAT oven to 350° F.

FOR CRUST:

COMBINE graham cracker crumbs and sugar in medium bowl. Stir in butter. Press onto bottom and 1½ inches up side of ungreased 9-inch springform pan. Bake for 8 to 10 minutes.

FOR FILLING:

COMBINE sour cream, sweetened condensed milk, orange juice, eggs, and vanilla extract in large mixer bowl; beat until smooth. Gently pour into crust.

BAKE for 35 to 40 minutes or until center is set. Cool completely in pan on wire rack.

FOR GLAZE:

COMBINE water and cornstarch in small saucepan. Stir in preserves. Bring to a boil over medium-high heat, stirring constantly. Remove from heat; strain to remove seeds. Cool for 10 minutes. Drizzle over filling. Arrange berries on top. Cover; refrigerate. Remove side of springform pan before serving.

Estimated Times

Preparation: 20 mins

Cooking: 45 mins

Cooling: 1 hr

Custard Tart with Fresh Berries

Deluxe Oatmeal Raisin Cookies

Chocolate-covered raisins make these oatmeal cookies deluxe. Treat yourself and your family today!

MAKES ABOUT 4 DOZEN COOKIES

INGREDIENTS

1¼ cups all-purpose flour

1 teaspoon baking soda

¾ teaspoon ground cinnamon

½ teaspoon salt

1 cup (2 sticks) butter or
     margarine, softened

¾ cup granulated sugar

¾ cup packed brown sugar

1 teaspoon vanilla extract

2 large eggs

3 cups quick or old-fashioned oats

1 package (12½ ounces) NESTLÉ
     RAISINETS Milk Chocolate-
     Covered Raisins

1 cup chopped nuts

DIRECTIONS

PREHEAT oven to 375° F.

COMBINE flour, baking soda, cinnamon,
and salt in small bowl. Beat butter,
granulated sugar, brown sugar, and
vanilla extract in large mixer bowl until
creamy. Beat in eggs; gradually beat
in flour mixture. Stir in oats, Raisinets,
and nuts. Drop by rounded tablespoon
onto ungreased baking sheets.

BAKE for 7 to 8 minutes for chewy
cookies, or 9 to 10 minutes for crisp
cookies. Cool on baking sheets for
2 minutes; remove to wire racks to
cool completely.

Estimated Times

Preparation: 15 mins

Cooking: 7 mins

Cooling: 15 mins

Deluxe Toll House Mud Bars

These chewy, chocolate-filled,
chocolate-topped bars also have
nuts in them. Try them for an
afternoon snack.

MAKES 36 BARS

INGREDIENTS

1 cup, plus 2 tablespoons
     all-purpose flour

½ teaspoon baking soda

½ teaspoon salt

¾ cup packed brown sugar

½ cup (1 stick) butter, softened

1 teaspoon vanilla extract

1 large egg

2 cups (12-ounce package)
     NESTLÉ TOLL HOUSE Semi-Sweet
     Chocolate Morsels, divided

½ cup chopped walnuts

DIRECTIONS

PREHEAT oven to 375° F. Grease
9-inch-square baking pan.

COMBINE flour, baking soda, and salt
in small bowl. Beat sugar, butter, and
vanilla extract in large mixer bowl until
creamy. Beat in egg; gradually beat in
flour mixture. Stir in 1¼ cups morsels and
nuts. Spread into prepared baking pan.

Deluxe Toll House Mud Bars

BAKE for 20 to 23 minutes. Remove pan
to wire rack. Sprinkle with remaining
morsels. Let stand for 5 minutes or
until morsels are shiny; spread evenly.
Cool completely in pan on wire rack;
refrigerate for 5 to 10 minutes or until
chocolate is set. Cut into bars.

Estimated Times

Preparation: 20 mins

Cooking: 20 mins

Cooling: 30 mins

Refrigerating: 5 mins

Dirt Cake

Baking Tip

If you usually freeze your unused chocolate bars or morsels, keep in mind, freezing will not significantly increase their shelf life. If frozen, bring the morsels or baking bars to room temperature slowly, or moisture will gather and may cause sugar bloom (i.e., white powdery appearance).

It's recommended that you store the morsels and baking bars in a cool, dry place away from light and at room temperature. They can be refrigerated if wrapped tightly so they don't absorb odors. Airtight wrapping will help prevent moisture from condensing on the chocolate when removed from the refrigerator.

Dirt Cake

This chocolatey kid favorite, topped with gummy worms and chocolate crushed wafers, will keep your gang content.

MAKES 8 SERVINGS

INGREDIENTS

1 package (about 5.9 ounces) chocolate instant pudding and pie filling mix, prepared according to package directions
2 cups crushed chocolate wafer cookies (about 45 to 50 cookies)
⅔ cup Chocolate Flavor NESTLÉ NESQUIK Calcium Fortified Syrup
1 container (8 ounces) frozen whipped topping, thawed
1 package (3 ounces) gummy worms

DIRECTIONS

COMBINE cookie crumbs and Nesquik in medium bowl; reserve ¼ cup.

LAYER half of remaining crumb mixture, half of pudding, and half of whipped topping in large bowl or 8 small bowls. Repeat layers. Sprinkle with reserved crumb mixture; top with gummy worms.

Estimated Time
Preparation: 15 mins

Disappearing Chocolate Bars

Moist and chocolatey, these will be a favorite with the chocolate fans in your family. Ice them for an even more irresistible treat.

MAKES 24 BARS

INGREDIENTS

1¼ cups granulated sugar
1 cup (2 sticks) butter or margarine, softened
⅔ cup NESTLÉ TOLL HOUSE Baking Cocoa
2 large eggs
1 large egg white
2½ teaspoons vanilla extract
½ teaspoon salt
1¼ cups all-purpose flour
⅔ cup (5 fluid-ounce can) NESTLÉ CARNATION Evaporated Milk
1¼ cups chopped walnuts
Creamy Chocolate Icing (recipe follows)

DIRECTIONS

PREHEAT oven to 350° F. Grease 13 x 9-inch baking pan.

COMBINE sugar, butter, cocoa, eggs, egg white, vanilla extract, and salt in large mixer bowl; beat until light and fluffy. Alternately beat in flour and evaporated milk just until blended. Fold in nuts. Spread into prepared baking pan.

BAKE for 20 to 25 minutes or until wooden pick inserted in center comes out clean. Cool completely in pan on wire rack. Frost with Creamy Chocolate Icing.

FOR CREAMY CHOCOLATE ICING:
COMBINE ⅓ cup NESTLÉ TOLL HOUSE Baking Cocoa and 3 tablespoons melted butter or margarine in medium bowl; stir well. Alternately stir in 1 cup sifted powdered sugar and ¼ cup NESTLÉ CARNATION Evaporated Milk. Stir vigorously until icing is smooth.

Estimated Times
Preparation: 15 mins
Cooking: 20 mins
Cooling: 30 mins

Double Chocolate Peanut Butter Thumbprint Cookies

These peanut butter-filled chocolate thumbprint cookies are a must with a tall glass of ice-cold milk.

Double Chocolate Peanut Butter Thumbprint Cookies

MAKES ABOUT 3 DOZEN COOKIES

INGREDIENTS
1½ cups all-purpose flour
⅓ cup NESTLÉ TOLL HOUSE Baking Cocoa
1½ teaspoons baking powder
¼ teaspoon salt
2 cups (12-ounce package) NESTLÉ TOLL HOUSE Semi-Sweet Chocolate Morsels, divided
1 cup granulated sugar
1 cup chunky or creamy peanut butter (not all-natural), divided
⅓ cup butter or margarine, softened
1½ teaspoons vanilla extract
2 large eggs

DIRECTIONS
PREHEAT oven to 350° F.

COMBINE flour, cocoa, baking powder, and salt in small bowl. Melt 1 cup morsels in small, heavy-duty saucepan over low heat; stir until smooth. Beat sugar, ⅓ cup peanut butter, butter, and vanilla extract in large mixer bowl until creamy. Beat in melted chocolate. Add eggs one at a time, beating well after each addition. Gradually beat in cocoa mixture. Stir in remaining morsels. Cover; refrigerate just until firm.

SHAPE dough into 1½-inch balls; press thumb into tops to make about ½-inch-deep depressions. Place 2 inches apart on ungreased baking sheets. Fill each depression with about ½ teaspoon peanut butter.

BAKE for 10 to 15 minutes or until sides are set but centers are still slightly soft. Cool on baking sheets for 2 minutes; remove to wire racks to cool completely.

Estimated Times
Preparation: 45 mins
Refrigerating: 15 mins
Cooking: 10 mins
Cooling: 15 mins

Eggs

When selecting good quality eggs, you need to look for shells that are not shiny. Shells may be white or brown, and yolks may be light or dark. Determine freshness by placing eggs in a bowl of cool water. Discard any that float. Never use eggs that have a doubtful odor, color, or cracked shell, as salmonella can develop under these conditions.

If recipes call for separating eggs, the American Egg Board recommends using an inexpensive egg separator to keep any bacteria on the shell from contaminating the yolk or white. If a bit of yolk gets into the whites, scoop it out with a clean spoon, or else whites won't achieve volume when beaten. Eggs are easier to separate at refrigerated, not room temperature.

Easy Coconut Banana Cream Pie

The smoothness of banana cream pie is complemented with a touch of coconut.

MAKES 8 SERVINGS

INGREDIENTS

1 prebaked 9-inch (4-cup volume)
   deep-dish pie crust
1 can (14 ounces) NESTLÉ CARNATION
   Sweetened Condensed Milk
1 cup cold water
1 package (about 3.4 ounces) vanilla
   or banana cream instant pudding
   and pie filling mix
1 cup flaked coconut
1 container (8 ounces) frozen whipped
   topping, thawed, divided
2 medium bananas, sliced and dipped
   in lemon juice
Toasted or tinted flaked coconut (optional)

DIRECTIONS

COMBINE sweetened condensed milk
and water in large bowl. Add pudding
mix and 1 cup coconut; mix well. Fold
in 1½ cups whipped topping.

ARRANGE single layer of bananas on
bottom of pie crust. Pour filling into
crust. Top with remaining whipped
topping. Refrigerate for 4 hours or until
well set. Top with toasted coconut.

NOTE: To make 2 pies, divide filling between
2 prebaked 9-inch (2-cup volume) pie crusts.
Top with remaining whipped topping.

Estimated Times
Preparation: 20 mins
Refrigerating: 4 hrs

Easy Rocky Road Brownies

The appeal of rocky road is no
surprise. The enduring combination
of marshmallows, chocolate, and nuts
is hard to resist.

MAKES 12 BROWNIES

INGREDIENTS

1 package (18 ounces) NESTLÉ
   TOLL HOUSE Refrigerated Brownie
   Bar Dough
½ cup NESTLÉ TOLL HOUSE Semi-Sweet
   Chocolate Morsels, divided
1 cup miniature marshmallows
¼ cup chopped walnuts

DIRECTIONS

BAKE brownies according to package
directions.

SPRINKLE ¼ cup morsels over hot
brownies. Let stand for 5 minutes or
until morsels are shiny; spread evenly

Easy Rocky Road Brownies

over brownies. Top with marshmallows, remaining morsels, and nuts; press down lightly.

BAKE for an additional 5 minutes or just until marshmallows begin to puff. Cool in pan on wire rack for 20 to 30 minutes. Cut into squares with wet knife.

Estimated Times
Preparation: 15 mins
Cooking: 25 mins
Standing: 5 mins
Cooling: 20 mins

Easy Toffee Candy

Easy and delicious candy for the whole family to enjoy!

Easy Toffee Candy

MAKES 50 PIECES

INGREDIENTS
1¼ cups (2½ sticks) butter, divided
35 to 40 soda crackers
1 cup packed dark brown sugar
1 can (14 ounces) NESTLÉ CARNATION Sweetened Condensed Milk
1½ cups (9 ounces) NESTLÉ TOLL HOUSE Semi-Sweet Chocolate Morsels
¾ cup finely chopped walnuts

DIRECTIONS
PREHEAT oven to 425° F. Line 15 x 10-inch jelly-roll pan with heavy-duty foil.

MELT ¼ cup (½ stick) butter in medium saucepan. Pour into prepared jelly-roll pan. Arrange crackers over butter, breaking crackers to fit empty spaces.

MELT remaining butter in same saucepan; add sugar. Bring to a boil over medium heat. Reduce heat to low; cook, stirring occasionally, for 2 minutes. Remove from heat; stir in sweetened condensed milk. Pour over crackers.

BAKE for 10 to 12 minutes or until mixture is bubbly and slightly darkened. Remove from oven; let cool for 1 minute.

SPRINKLE with morsels. Let stand for 5 minutes or until morsels are shiny; spread evenly. Sprinkle with nuts; press into chocolate. Cool in pan on wire rack for 30 minutes. Refrigerate for about 30 minutes or until chocolate is set. Remove foil; cut into pieces.

Estimated Times
Preparation: 10 mins
Cooking: 15 mins
Standing: 5 mins
Cooling: 30 mins
Refrigerating: 30 mins

Firecracker Fudge Cookies

Made with chocolate morsels and topped with powdered sugar, these fudge cookies are perfect for a holiday get-together.

MAKES ABOUT 3 DOZEN COOKIES

INGREDIENTS

2 cups (12-ounce package) NESTLÉ
  TOLL HOUSE Semi-Sweet
  Chocolate Morsels, divided
1½ cups all-purpose flour
1½ teaspoons baking powder
¼ teaspoon salt
1 cup granulated sugar
6 tablespoons butter or margarine,
  softened
1½ teaspoons vanilla extract
2 large eggs
½ cup powdered sugar

DIRECTIONS

MICROWAVE 1 cup morsels in medium, uncovered, microwave-safe bowl on HIGH (100%) power for 1 minute; STIR. The morsels may retain some of their original shape. If necessary, microwave at additional 10- to 15-second intervals, stirring just until morsels are melted. Cool to room temperature.

COMBINE flour, baking powder, and salt in small bowl. Beat granulated sugar, butter, and vanilla extract in large mixer bowl. Beat in melted chocolate. Add eggs one at a time, beating well after each addition. Gradually beat in flour mixture. Stir in remaining morsels. Cover; refrigerate just until firm.

PREHEAT oven to 350° F.

SHAPE dough into 1½-inch balls; roll in powdered sugar. Place on ungreased baking sheets.

BAKE for 10 to 15 minutes or until sides are set but centers are still slightly soft. Cool on baking sheets for 2 minutes; remove to wire racks to cool completely.

Estimated Times
Preparation: 40 mins
Refrigerating: 15 mins
Cooking: 12 mins
Cooling: 15 mins

French Apple Cobbler

This is sure to become one of your favorite dessert recipes. Serve with scoops of French vanilla ice cream and steaming hot mugs of coffee.

MAKES 6 SERVINGS

INGREDIENTS

2 packages (12 ounces each)
  STOUFFER'S frozen Harvest
  Apples, defrosted*
½ cup all-purpose flour
½ cup granulated sugar
1 large egg, lightly beaten
2 tablespoons butter or
  margarine, softened

French Apple Cobbler

½ teaspoon baking powder

⅛ teaspoon salt

DIRECTIONS

PREHEAT oven to 350° F.

PLACE harvest apples in ungreased 9-inch-square baking pan. Mix flour, sugar, egg, butter, baking powder, and salt in medium bowl until blended.

DROP dough by heaping tablespoons over harvest apples.

BAKE for 25 to 30 minutes or until apples are tender and crust is golden brown.

*DEFROST harvest apples in microwave on MEDIUM (50%) power for 6 to 7 minutes.

Estimated Times
Preparation: 15 mins
Cooking: 25 mins

Frozen Strawberry Hot Chocolate

Your kids will love this chocolate and strawberry-flavored ice cream-like dessert. Perfect for a hot summer day.

MAKES 4 SERVINGS

Frozen Strawberry Hot Chocolate

INGREDIENTS

1 cup hot whole milk

1 cup hot Original NESTLÉ COFFEE-MATE Half & Half

¼ cup (2 envelopes) Rich Chocolate Flavor or Double Chocolate Melt Down Flavor NESTLÉ Hot Cocoa Mix

2 tablespoons Strawberry Flavor NESTLÉ NESQUIK Calcium Fortified Syrup

DIRECTIONS

COMBINE milk, Half & Half, cocoa mix, and Nesquik in medium bowl; divide mixture among two ice cube trays.

Cover with foil; freeze for at least 4 hours or up to 1 week.

PLACE cocoa cubes in food processor or blender; cover. Using on and off turns, process mixture until smooth, scraping sides often. If mixture is too thick to process, add a small amount of whole milk or Half & Half. Serve immediately.

Estimated Times
Preparation: 15 mins
Freezing: 4 hrs

Baking Tip

In baked goods, you can substitute butter for margarine for vegetable shortening cup for cup. However, shortening should not be used in place of butter in fudge or other candy recipes. When measuring raisins or other fruit preserves, nuts, or morsels, place these ingredients into a dry measuring cup to the top only, not to heaping.

To store nuts, their shells protect them from light, heat, moisture, and exposure. If already shelled, store tightly covered in cool, dark, dry place, or in the freezer. Salted nuts are more prone to rancidity than unsalted, so we recommend refrigerating after opening.

Fruit and Chocolate Streusel Squares

Fruit and Chocolate Streusel Squares

A layer of fruit preserves is nestled next to a layer of chocolate in these delectable bar cookies. Oats and almonds give them a chewy texture to offset the sweetness of the filling.

MAKES 36 SQUARES

INGREDIENTS

1½ cups all-purpose flour

1½ cups quick or old-fashioned oats

½ cup granulated sugar

½ cup packed brown sugar

1 teaspoon baking powder

¼ teaspoon salt (optional)

1 cup (2 sticks) butter or
   margarine, softened

¾ cup raspberry, strawberry, or
   apricot preserves

2 cups (12-ounce package)
   NESTLÉ TOLL HOUSE Semi-Sweet
   Chocolate Morsels

¼ cup chopped almonds

DIRECTIONS

PREHEAT oven to 375° F. Grease 9-inch-square baking pan.

COMBINE flour, oats, granulated sugar, brown sugar, baking powder, and salt in large bowl. Cut in butter with pastry blender or two knives. Reserve 1 cup oat mixture for topping. Press remaining oat mixture into prepared baking pan. Spread preserves over crust; sprinkle with morsels.

COMBINE reserved oat mixture with nuts; sprinkle over morsels. Pat down lightly.

BAKE for 30 to 35 minutes or until golden brown. Cool completely in pan on wire rack until chocolate is firm or refrigerate for 30 minutes to speed cooling. Cut into squares.

Estimated Times
Preparation: 20 mins
Cooking: 30 mins
Cooling: 30 mins

Fudgy Chocolate Brownies

This recipe is for those who like their brownies thick, moist, and chocolatey. A must with a glass of cold milk.

MAKES 24 BROWNIES

INGREDIENTS
1⅓ cups all-purpose flour
¼ teaspoon baking soda

¼ teaspoon salt
1⅔ cups granulated sugar
½ cup (1 stick) butter or margarine, melted
4 packets (1 ounce each) NESTLÉ TOLL HOUSE CHOCO BAKE Unsweetened Chocolate Flavor
2 large eggs
2 tablespoons water
1½ teaspoons vanilla extract
½ cup chopped nuts (optional)

DIRECTIONS
PREHEAT oven to 350° F. Grease 13 x 9-inch baking pan.

COMBINE flour, baking soda, and salt in small bowl. Stir in sugar, butter, Choco

Bake, eggs, water, and vanilla extract vigorously in large bowl. Stir in flour mixture. Stir in nuts. Spread into prepared baking pan.

BAKE for 18 to 22 minutes or until wooden pick inserted in center comes out slightly sticky. Cool completely in pan on wire rack. Cut into bars.

Estimated Times
Preparation: 15 mins
Cooking: 18 mins
Cooling: 30 mins

Fudgy Chocolate Brownies

Giant Turtle Treasure Cookies

Giant Turtle Treasure Cookies

Not many people can resist the temptation of chocolate-covered caramel turtles sandwiched between tender sugar cookies.

MAKES 32 COOKIES

INGREDIENTS

2¼ cups all-purpose flour
1 teaspoon baking soda
1 teaspoon salt
¾ cup (1½ sticks) butter or
    margarine, softened
¾ cup granulated sugar
¾ cup packed brown sugar
1 teaspoon vanilla extract
2 large eggs
1 cup chopped pecans
20 NESTLÉ SIGNATURES TURTLES
    Candies, cut in half, divided

DIRECTIONS

COMBINE flour, baking soda, and salt in small bowl. Beat butter, granulated sugar, brown sugar, and vanilla extract in large mixer bowl until creamy. Add eggs one at a time, beating well after each addition. Gradually beat in flour mixture; stir in nuts. Turn dough onto sheet of plastic wrap. Wrap tightly and refrigerate for 2 hours or until firm.

PREHEAT oven to 375° F.

DIVIDE refrigerated dough into 8 equal pieces. Return 6 pieces to refrigerator. Working with 2 pieces at a time, form each piece into a ball; place each on a separate sheet of plastic wrap. Using lightly floured hands, flatten balls into 6-inch circles. Lift one circle with wrap and invert onto ungreased baking sheet; peel off wrap. Arrange 10 Turtle halves on top of circle. Cover with second circle; peel off wrap. Press edges together gently to seal. Repeat with remaining refrigerated dough and remaining Turtle halves to make 3 more cookies.

BAKE for 12 to 15 minutes or until golden brown. Cool on baking sheet for 10 minutes; remove to wire rack to cool completely. Cut each cookie into 8 wedges.

Estimated Times
Preparation: 30 mins
Cooking: 12 mins
Refrigerating: 2 hrs
Cooling: 15 mins

Golden Pound Cake

Create a delicious pound cake that looks as good as it tastes.

Golden Pound Cake

INGREDIENTS

3 cups cake flour

1½ teaspoons baking powder

¼ teaspoon salt

¼ teaspoon mace or ground nutmeg

1½ cups granulated sugar

1 cup (2 sticks) butter or
    margarine, softened

1 teaspoon vanilla extract

3 large eggs

½ cup NESTLÉ CARNATION
    Evaporated Milk

¾ cup chopped walnuts or pecans

DIRECTIONS

PREHEAT oven to 350° F. Grease
9 x 5-inch loaf pan.

COMBINE flour, baking powder, salt,
and mace in medium bowl. Beat sugar,
butter, and vanilla extract in large mixer
bowl until light and fluffy. Add eggs
one at a time, beating well after each
addition. Beat in flour mixture alternately
with evaporated milk. Pour into prepared
loaf pan; sprinkle with nuts.

BAKE for 60 to 70 minutes or until
wooden pick inserted in center comes
out clean. Cool in pan for 10 minutes;
remove to wire rack to cool completely.

Estimated Times
Preparation: 15 mins
Cooking: 1 hr
Cooling: 1 hr

Goober Thumbprint Cookies

**Cocoa-laced thumbprint cookies
filled with creamy peanut butter
and chocolate-covered peanuts.
A popular flavor combination
that endures.**

MAKES ABOUT 1½ DOZEN COOKIES

INGREDIENTS

1½ cups all-purpose flour

⅓ cup NESTLÉ TOLL HOUSE
    Baking Cocoa

1½ teaspoons baking powder

¼ teaspoon salt

1 cup (6 ounces) NESTLÉ TOLL HOUSE
    Semi-Sweet Chocolate Morsels

1 cup granulated sugar

1 cup creamy peanut butter, divided

⅓ cup butter or margarine, softened

1½ teaspoons vanilla extract

2 large eggs

½ cup NESTLÉ GOOBERS Milk
    Chocolate-Covered Peanuts, divided

DIRECTIONS

COMBINE flour, cocoa, baking powder,
and salt in small bowl. Melt morsels in
small, heavy-duty saucepan over lowest
possible heat; stir until smooth. Beat
sugar, ⅓ cup peanut butter, butter, and
vanilla extract in large mixer bowl until
creamy. Beat in melted chocolate. Add
eggs one at a time, beating well after

Goober Thumbprint Cookies

each addition. Gradually stir in flour
mixture. Cover; refrigerate just until firm.

PREHEAT oven to 350° F.

SHAPE into 1-inch balls; press thumb
into tops to make about ½-inch-deep
depressions. Place on ungreased baking
sheets. Fill each depression with about
½ teaspoon peanut butter; press three
Goobers into peanut butter.

BAKE for 10 to 15 minutes or until
sides are set. Cool on baking sheets
for 2 minutes; remove to wire racks
to cool completely.

Estimated Times
Preparation: 30 mins
Refrigerating: 15 mins
Cooking: 10 mins
Cooling: 15 mins

Gooey Baby Ruth Brownies

Lift your brownies out of the ordinary with an extra dollop of richness from cream cheese and BABY RUTH Candy Bars.

MAKES 24 BROWNIES

INGREDIENTS

1 package (18.25 ounces) chocolate brownie mix

3 (2.1 ounces each) NESTLÉ BABY RUTH Candy Bars, chopped

1 package (8 ounces) cream cheese, at room temperature

½ cup granulated sugar

1 large egg

2 teaspoons milk

DIRECTIONS

PREHEAT oven to 350° F. Grease 13 x 9-inch baking pan.

PREPARE brownie batter according to package directions; stir in chopped Baby Ruth. Pour into prepared pan.

BEAT cream cheese and sugar in small mixer bowl until smooth. Beat in egg

Gooey Baby Ruth Brownies

and milk. Using knife or spatula, swirl cream cheese mixture into brownie batter to create a marbling effect.

BAKE for 35 to 40 minutes or until wooden pick inserted in center comes out almost clean. Cool completely in pan on wire rack. Cut into bars using wet knife.

Estimated Times
Preparation: 15 mins
Cooking: 35 mins
Cooling: 30 mins

Great Pumpkin Cookies

Kids will love these yummy and fun cookies! The cookies not only include pumpkin, they have oats and can be decorated with all sorts of goodies like chocolate morsels, icing and candies, or enjoy them plain.

MAKES ABOUT 1½ DOZEN COOKIES

INGREDIENTS
2 cups all-purpose flour
1⅓ cups quick or old-fashioned oats
1 teaspoon baking soda
1 teaspoon ground cinnamon
½ teaspoon salt
1 cup (2 sticks) butter or
 margarine, softened
1 cup packed brown sugar
1 cup granulated sugar
1 cup LIBBY'S 100% Pure Pumpkin
1 large egg
1 teaspoon vanilla extract
¾ cup chopped walnuts
¾ cup raisins
Toppings (e.g., colored icings, NESTLÉ
 TOLL HOUSE Semi-Sweet Chocolate
 Morsels, candies, raisins, nuts)

DIRECTIONS
PREHEAT oven to 350° F. Grease baking sheets.

COMBINE flour, oats, baking soda, cinnamon, and salt in medium bowl. Beat butter, brown sugar, and granulated sugar in large mixer bowl until light and fluffy. Add pumpkin, egg, and vanilla extract; mix well. Add flour mixture; mix well. Stir in nuts and raisins. Drop ¼ cup dough onto prepared baking sheet; spread into 3-inch circle or oval. Repeat with remaining dough.

BAKE for 14 to 16 minutes or until cookies are firm and lightly browned. Cool on baking sheets for 2 minutes; remove to wire racks to cool completely. Decorate with icings, morsels, candies, raisins, and/or nuts, if desired.

Estimated Times
Preparation: 30 mins
Cooking: 14 mins
Cooling: 15 mins

Pumpkin

LIBBY'S 100% Pure Pumpkin and Pumpkin Mix is thoroughly cooked during the canning process so it's ready to use when you open the can. Pumpkin may be stored out of the can, in a sealed plastic container for one week in the refrigerator, and up to three months in the freezer. When freezing, make sure that the pumpkin does not go right to the top of the container because it may expand when frozen. Pumpkin may have a separated appearance when thawed due to air bubbles. This will not affect the pumpkin quality or performance.

With only 40 calories per ½ cup serving, pumpkin is a delicious source of natural vitamins and minerals, including vitamin A with 80 percent as beta carotene. It's also low in fat and high in dietary fiber.

Hidden Treasure Chocolate Soufflés

Want to treat that special someone this Valentine's Day? Tempt them with this tantalizing recipe for chocolate soufflés—a surprisingly simple-to-make delicacy that is sure to please. Savor the intense flavor of the rich chocolate with a creamy caramel secret hidden in the center. It's a sweet treasure to share with the one you love.

MAKES 2 SERVINGS

INGREDIENTS

Nonstick cooking spray
Granulated sugar

Hidden Treasure Chocolate Soufflés

½ cup NESTLÉ TOLL HOUSE Semi-Sweet
   Chocolate Morsels
2 tablespoons butter
1 tablespoon NESTLÉ TOLL HOUSE
   Baking Cocoa
1 large egg, separated
½ teaspoon vanilla extract
2 tablespoons granulated sugar
2 Creamy Caramel NESTLÉ
   SIGNATURE TREASURES
Powdered sugar (optional)

DIRECTIONS

PREHEAT oven to 400° F. Spray two 6-ounce custard cups or ramekins with nonstick cooking spray; coat lightly with granulated sugar.

MICROWAVE morsels, butter, and cocoa in medium, uncovered, microwave-safe bowl on HIGH (100%) power for 45 seconds; STIR. The morsels may retain some of their original shape. If necessary, microwave at additional 10-second intervals, stirring just until morsels are melted. Stir in egg yolk and vanilla extract.

BEAT egg white in small mixer bowl until soft peaks form. Gradually beat in 2 tablespoons granulated sugar until stiff peaks form. Stir one-fourth of egg white mixture into chocolate mixture to lighten. Fold in remaining egg white mixture gently but thoroughly. Spoon into prepared custard cups, filling about three-fourths full. Drop 1 Nestlé Treasure into center of each soufflé; press in slightly. Place soufflés on baking sheet.

BAKE on center oven rack for 16 to 20 minutes or until puffed and center still moves slightly. Sprinkle with powdered sugar. Serve immediately.

Estimated Times
Preparation: 20 mins
Cooking: 17 mins

Honey Nut White Fudge

Treat your taste buds to a rich, creamy delight. Honey roasted peanuts add flavor and crunch to this white fudge recipe.

MAKES 49 PIECES

INGREDIENTS

1½ cups granulated sugar
⅔ cup (5 fluid-ounce can) NESTLÉ
   CARNATION Evaporated Milk
2 tablespoons butter or margarine
2 cups miniature marshmallows
2 cups (12-ounce package) NESTLÉ
   TOLL HOUSE Premier White Morsels
1½ cups honey roasted peanuts, divided
2 teaspoons vanilla extract

DIRECTIONS

LINE 9-inch-square baking pan with foil.

COMBINE sugar, evaporated milk, and butter in medium, heavy-duty saucepan. Bring to a full rolling boil over medium

Honey Nut White Fudge

heat, stirring constantly. Boil, stirring constantly, for 4½ to 5 minutes. Remove from heat.

STIR in marshmallows, morsels, 1 cup peanuts, and vanilla extract. Stir vigorously for 1 minute or until marshmallows are melted. Pour into prepared baking pan. Coarsely chop remaining peanuts. Sprinkle over fudge; press in. Refrigerate for 2 hours or until firm. Lift from pan; remove foil. Cut into 1-inch squares.

Estimated Times
Preparation: 10 mins
Cooking: 5 mins
Refrigerating: 2 hrs

Hoosier Bars

These sweet snack bars have a sweetened meringue-like layer dotted with chocolate morsels and peanuts.

MAKES 36 BARS

INGREDIENTS
1½ cups all-purpose flour
1 teaspoon baking soda
1 cup packed brown sugar, divided
½ cup granulated sugar
½ cup (1 stick) butter or
   margarine, softened
2 large eggs, separated
1 teaspoon vanilla extract
2 cups (12-ounce package)
   NESTLÉ TOLL HOUSE Semi-Sweet
   Chocolate Morsels, divided
¾ cup honey roasted peanuts, divided

DIRECTIONS
PREHEAT oven to 325° F. Grease 13 x 9-inch baking pan.

COMBINE flour and baking soda in small bowl. Beat ½ cup brown sugar, granulated sugar, and butter in large mixer bowl until creamy. Beat in egg yolks and vanilla extract. Gradually beat in flour mixture until crumbly. Stir in 1½ cups morsels and ½ cup peanuts. Press dough onto bottom of prepared baking pan.

BEAT egg whites in small mixer bowl until soft peaks form. Gradually beat in

remaining brown sugar until stiff peaks form; spread over dough. Sprinkle with remaining morsels and remaining peanuts.

BAKE for 35 to 40 minutes or until top is set and lightly browned. Cool in pan on wire rack for 20 minutes. Cut into bars while still warm.

Estimated Times
Preparation: 20 mins
Cooking: 35 mins
Cooling: 20 mins

Baking Tip

Choose a good grade of stick margarine. Avoid tub margarines, spreads, and blends. It's not necessary to soften margarine before adding to dough, but using butter at room temperature is easier when mixing. Or, soften butter in the microwave on MEDIUM-LOW (30%) power for 10 to 15 seconds. Then let stand until ready to use. Butter should be softened just until it yields to light pressure. Melted butter, though it produces cookies that brown evenly, isn't recommended as it produces a flatter cookie with a shiny surface and a slightly crackled appearance. Unsalted butter may be substituted for the same amount of salted butter in most cookie recipes with no other adjustments necessary.

Hot Carameled Apples with Pie Crust Dippers

Remember the smell of a homemade apple pie baking in the oven? Here's a quick and easy way to treat your family to all the flavor and aroma with a fraction of the work.

MAKES 10 SERVINGS

INGREDIENTS

Refrigerated pastry dough for double crust 9-inch pie, rolled to ⅛-inch thickness
½ cup cinnamon-sugar
3 packages (12 ounces each) STOUFFER'S frozen Harvest Apples, prepared according to package directions
⅔ cup caramel syrup or ice cream topping
⅓ cup sour cream

DIRECTIONS

PREHEAT oven to 400° F.

CUT pastry into festive shapes using cookie cutters. Sprinkle with cinnamon-sugar. Place on ungreased baking sheet.

BAKE for 5 to 7 minutes or until lightly browned. Remove to wire rack to cool completely.

COMBINE harvest apples, caramel syrup, and sour cream in medium bowl. Serve warm with pie crust dippers.

Estimated Times
Preparation: 15 mins
Cooking: 5 mins
Cooling: 15 mins

Hot Carameled Apples with Pie Crust Dippers

Iced Pumpkin Blondies

BAKE for 20 to 25 minutes or until wooden pick inserted in center comes out clean. Cool completely in pan on wire rack; spread with Maple Icing. Cut into bars.

FOR MAPLE ICING:
BEAT 6 ounces room temperature cream cheese, 2 tablespoons softened butter or margarine, and 2 cups sifted powdered sugar in small mixer bowl until smooth. Add 1 to 2 teaspoons maple flavoring.

Estimated Times
Preparation: 15 mins
Cooking: 20 mins
Cooling: 30 mins

Iced Pumpkin Blondies

These pumpkin blondies are just the ticket for hungry kids. The addition of pumpkin and brown sugar combined together make this treat extra rich.

MAKES 60 BARS

INGREDIENTS
2¼ cups all-purpose flour
2½ teaspoons baking powder
2 teaspoons ground cinnamon
¼ teaspoon salt
1½ cups packed brown sugar
¾ cup (1½ sticks) butter or
   margarine, softened
1 teaspoon vanilla extract
2 large eggs
1 cup LIBBY'S 100% Pure Pumpkin
Maple Icing (recipe follows)

DIRECTIONS
PREHEAT oven to 350° F. Grease 15 x 10-inch jelly-roll pan.

COMBINE flour, baking powder, cinnamon, and salt in medium bowl. Beat sugar, butter, and vanilla extract in large mixer bowl. Add eggs one at a time, beating well after each addition. Beat in pumpkin. Gradually beat in flour mixture. Spread into prepared pan.

Fruits and Vegetables

Keep the colors of fruit and vegetables bright by altering the acidity. A splash of lemon juice on the cut surfaces of apples, bananas, and avocados will prevent the fruits from browning before they are served.

Indoor S'mores

Indoor S'mores

Unlike traditional campfire s'mores, these can be made ahead of time—in any weather—and they aren't nearly as messy! Have some of these ready the next time all the kids are at your house after school.

MAKES 24 BARS

INGREDIENTS

8 cups (13-ounce box) graham cracker cereal

6 cups (10.5-ounce bag) miniature marshmallows, divided

1½ cups (9 ounces) NESTLÉ TOLL HOUSE Milk Chocolate Morsels

5 tablespoons butter or margarine, cut into pieces

¼ cup light corn syrup (optional)

1 teaspoon vanilla extract

DIRECTIONS

GREASE 13 x 9-inch baking pan. Pour cereal into large bowl.

HEAT 5 cups marshmallows, morsels, butter, and corn syrup in medium, heavy-duty saucepan over low heat, stirring constantly until smooth. Remove from heat. Stir in vanilla extract.

POUR marshmallow mixture over cereal; stir until well coated. Stir in remaining marshmallows. Press

mixture into prepared pan. Refrigerate for 1 hour or until firm. Cut into bars.

MICROWAVE METHOD:

MICROWAVE 5 cups marshmallows, morsels, butter, and corn syrup in large, microwave-safe bowl on HIGH (100%) power for 2 to 3½ minutes, stirring every minute, until smooth. Stir in vanilla extract. Proceed as above.

Estimated Times

Preparation: 10 mins

Cooking: 10 mins

Refrigerating: 1 hr

Island Cookies

The coconut and nut combination give this cookie a tropical flavor!

MAKES ABOUT 3 DOZEN COOKIES

INGREDIENTS

1⅔ cups all-purpose flour

¾ teaspoon baking powder

½ teaspoon baking soda

½ teaspoon salt

¾ cup (1½ sticks) butter or margarine, softened

¾ cup packed brown sugar

⅓ cup granulated sugar

1 teaspoon vanilla extract

1 large egg

1¾ cups (11.5-ounce package) NESTLÉ TOLL HOUSE Milk Chocolate Morsels

1 cup flaked coconut, toasted if desired

1 cup chopped walnuts

DIRECTIONS

PREHEAT oven to 375° F.

COMBINE flour, baking powder, baking soda, and salt in small bowl. Beat butter, brown sugar, granulated sugar, and vanilla extract in large mixer bowl until creamy. Beat in egg. Gradually beat in flour mixture. Stir in morsels, coconut, and nuts. Drop by rounded tablespoon onto ungreased baking sheets.

BAKE for 8 to 11 minutes or until edges are lightly browned. Cool on baking sheets for 2 minutes; remove to wire racks to cool completely.

NOTE: NESTLÉ TOLL HOUSE Semi-Sweet Chocolate Morsels, Semi-Sweet Chocolate Mini Morsels, Premier White Morsels, or Butterscotch Flavored Morsels may be substituted for the Milk Chocolate Morsels.

Estimated Times

Preparation: 15 mins

Cooking: 8 mins

Cooling: 15 mins

Jigglin' Juicy Snacks

You're bound to share a giggle when you handle these jiggly treats.

MAKES ABOUT 2 DOZEN SNACKS

INGREDIENTS

2½ cups Apple LIBBY'S JUICY JUICE Premium 100% Juice

2 packages (6 ounces each) gelatin dessert, any flavor

DIRECTIONS

BRING Juicy Juice to a boil in medium saucepan. Remove from heat. Stir in gelatin until completely dissolved. Pour into 13 x 9-inch baking dish.

Jigglin' Juicy Snacks

REFRIGERATE for 2 hours or until firm. Dip bottom of baking dish in warm water for about 10 seconds. Cut into decorative shapes using cookie cutters. Lift shapes from dish.

LITTLE KITCHEN HELPER HINTS:

Let the kids choose their favorite cookie cutters and cut their own shapes.

Sit in a circle and make up stories with the shapes. See if they can make one continuous story using all the shapes, or just let it be freestyle. Sharing a fun time is what it's all about!

Estimated Times

Preparation: 15 mins

Cooking: 5 mins

Refrigerating: 2 hrs

Lemon Bars

Lemon bars generate thoughts of tall glasses of icy lemonade on a sweltering day. What better baked good to offer with cold or hot drinks than mouth-watering lemon bars.

MAKES 48 BARS

INGREDIENTS

CRUST

2 cups all-purpose flour

½ cup powdered sugar

1 cup (2 sticks) butter or
 margarine, softened

FILLING

1 can (14 ounces) NESTLÉ CARNATION
 Sweetened Condensed Milk

4 large eggs

⅔ cup lemon juice

1 tablespoon all-purpose flour

1 teaspoon baking powder

¼ teaspoon salt

4 drops yellow food coloring (optional)

1 tablespoon grated lemon peel

Sifted powdered sugar (optional)

DIRECTIONS

PREHEAT oven to 350° F.

FOR CRUST:

COMBINE flour and powdered sugar in medium bowl. Cut in butter with pastry blender or two knives until mixture is crumbly. Press lightly onto bottom and

Lemon Bars

halfway up sides of ungreased 13 x 9-inch baking pan.

BAKE for 20 minutes.

FOR FILLING:

BEAT sweetened condensed milk and eggs in large mixer bowl until fluffy. Beat in lemon juice, flour, baking powder, salt, and food coloring just until blended. Fold in lemon peel; pour over crust.

BAKE for an additional 20 to 25 minutes or until filling is set and crust is golden brown. Cool completely in pan on wire rack. Refrigerate for 2 hours. Cut into bars; sprinkle with powdered sugar.

Estimated Times

Preparation: 20 mins

Cooking: 40 mins

Cooling: 30 mins

Refrigerating: 2 hrs

Libby's Famous Pumpkin Pie

The one and only traditional pumpkin pie! Just imagine sinking your teeth into a piece of this warm spice-filled dessert. It's tasty alone or with a decorative dollop of whipped cream.

MAKES 8 SERVINGS

INGREDIENTS

1 unbaked 9-inch (4-cup volume)
   deep-dish pie shell*

¾ cup granulated sugar

1 teaspoon ground cinnamon

½ teaspoon salt

½ teaspoon ground ginger

¼ teaspoon ground cloves

2 large eggs

1 can (15 ounces) LIBBY'S 100%
   Pure Pumpkin

1 can (12 fluid ounces) NESTLÉ
   CARNATION Evaporated Milk

Whipped cream (optional)

DIRECTIONS

PREHEAT oven to 425° F.

COMBINE sugar, cinnamon, salt, ginger, and cloves in small bowl. Beat eggs in large bowl. Stir in pumpkin and sugar-spice mixture. Gradually stir in evaporated milk.

POUR into pie shell.

BAKE for 15 minutes. Reduce temperature to 350° F. Bake for an additional 40 to 50 minutes or until knife inserted near center comes out clean. Cool on wire rack for 2 hours. Serve immediately or refrigerate. Top with whipped cream before serving.

COOKING TIPS

1¾ teaspoons pumpkin pie spice may be substituted for the cinnamon, ginger, and cloves; however, the taste will be slightly different. Do not freeze, as this will cause the crust to separate from the filling.

FOR 2 SHALLOW PIES: Substitute two 9-inch (2-cup volume) pie shells. Bake in preheated 425° F oven for 15 minutes. Reduce temperature to 350° F; bake for an additional 20 to 30 minutes or until pies test done.

**FOR HIGH ALTITUDE BAKING
(3,500 to 6,000 ft.):** Deep-dish pie—extend second bake time to 55 to 60 minutes. Shallow pies—no change.

*If using frozen pie shell, use deep-dish style, thawed completely. Bake pie on baking sheet and increase baking time slightly.

Estimated Times

Preparation: 15 mins

Cooking: 55 mins

Cooling: 2 hrs

Libby's Famous Pumpkin Pie

Pumpkin Pie

When Pilgrims first arrived in the New World, they discovered many new things. One was the Native American's use of pumpkin. Many people associate pumpkin pie with the Pilgrims, but in actuality their first pies were not pies at all. Early Americans would scoop out a pumpkin, fill it with milk and pumpkin flesh, and cook it for hours in hot ashes, often adding spices and syrup to make pudding.

Pumpkin soon became a focal point for the Pilgrims' Thanksgiving festivities, so much so that one early celebration was actually postponed until the arrival of a supply ship carrying molasses—a vital ingredient for baking the much-loved pies.

Early American cooks soon found all kinds of culinary uses for pumpkin. This golden fruit of the vine found its way into breads, puddings, and sauces. Settlers would also dry out slices of pumpkin and store them for later when the snow was high and food was scarce. Pumpkin still remains a staple in American kitchens even to this day.

Libby's Pumpkin Roll

Dazzle family and friends with Libby's Pumpkin Roll—a moist and creamy cake with a tantalizing aroma and beautiful presentation.

MAKES 10 SERVINGS

INGREDIENTS

CAKE
¼ cup powdered sugar (to sprinkle on towel)
¾ cup all-purpose flour
½ teaspoon baking powder
½ teaspoon baking soda
½ teaspoon ground cinnamon
½ teaspoon ground cloves
¼ teaspoon salt
3 large eggs
1 cup granulated sugar
⅔ cup LIBBY'S 100% Pure Pumpkin
1 cup walnuts, chopped (optional)

FILLING
1 package (8 ounces) cream cheese, at room temperature
1 cup powdered sugar, sifted
6 tablespoons butter or margarine, softened
1 teaspoon vanilla extract
Powdered sugar (optional)

DIRECTIONS

FOR CAKE:

PREHEAT oven to 375° F. Grease 15 x 10-inch jelly-roll pan; line with wax paper. Grease and flour paper. Sprinkle a thin, cotton kitchen towel with powdered sugar.

COMBINE flour, baking powder, baking soda, cinnamon, cloves, and salt in small bowl. Beat eggs and granulated sugar in large mixer bowl until thick. Beat in pumpkin. Stir in flour mixture. Spread evenly into prepared pan. Sprinkle with nuts.

BAKE for 13 to 15 minutes or until top of cake springs back when touched. Immediately loosen and turn cake onto prepared towel. Carefully peel off paper. Roll up cake and towel together, starting with narrow end. Cool completely on wire rack.

FOR FILLING:

BEAT cream cheese, powdered sugar, butter, and vanilla extract in small mixer bowl until smooth. Carefully unroll cake; remove towel. Spread cream cheese mixture over cake. Reroll cake. Wrap in plastic wrap and refrigerate for at least 1 hour. Sprinkle with powdered sugar before serving.

COOKING TIPS

Be sure to put enough powdered sugar on the towel when rolling up the cake so it will not stick.

Estimated Times
Preparation: 45 mins
Cooking: 13 mins
Cooling: 30 mins
Refrigerating: 1 hr

Linzer Bars

A dessert to enjoy on almost any occasion.

MAKES 16 BARS

INGREDIENTS
⅓ cup finely chopped almonds
2 tablespoons all-purpose flour
¼ teaspoon ground cinnamon
1 package (18 ounces) NESTLÉ TOLL HOUSE Refrigerated Sugar Cookie Bar Dough, broken into pieces
½ cup seedless raspberry jam

DIRECTIONS

PREHEAT oven to 350° F. Grease 8-inch-square baking pan.

COMBINE nuts, flour, and cinnamon in medium bowl. Add cookie dough; mix well. Reserve ½ cup cookie dough mixture. Press remaining mixture onto bottom of prepared baking pan. Spread jam over dough.

ROLL out reserved dough on lightly floured surface into 8 x 5-inch rectangle. Cut lengthwise into 10 strips. Lay half the strips over jam, about 1 inch apart. Lay remaining strips crosswise over the first strips.

Linzer Bars

BAKE for 30 to 35 minutes or until top is golden brown. Cool in pan on wire rack for 10 minutes. Serve warm or cool completely.

Estimated Times
Preparation: 20 mins
Cooking: 30 mins
Cooling: 10 mins

Macadamia Nut White Chip Pumpkin Cookies

White morsels and crunchy macadamia nuts make a supremely rich cookie. And the pumpkin adds a luscious moistness to these year-round favorites.

MAKES ABOUT 4 DOZEN COOKIES

INGREDIENTS

2 cups all-purpose flour
2 teaspoons ground cinnamon
1 teaspoon ground cloves
1 teaspoon baking soda
1 cup (2 sticks) butter or margarine, softened
½ cup granulated sugar
½ cup packed brown sugar
1 cup LIBBY'S 100% Pure Pumpkin
1 large egg
2 teaspoons vanilla extract
2 cups (12-ounce package) NESTLÉ TOLL HOUSE Premier White Morsels
⅔ cup coarsely chopped macadamia nuts or walnuts, toasted

DIRECTIONS

PREHEAT oven to 350° F. Grease baking sheets.

COMBINE flour, cinnamon, cloves, and baking soda in small bowl. Beat butter, granulated sugar, and brown sugar in large mixer bowl until creamy. Beat in pumpkin, egg, and vanilla extract until blended. Gradually beat in flour mixture. Stir in morsels and nuts.

DROP by rounded tablespoon onto prepared baking sheets; flatten slightly with back of spoon or greased bottom of glass dipped in granulated sugar.

BAKE for 11 to 14 minutes or until centers are set. Cool on baking sheets for 2 minutes; remove to wire racks to cool completely.

Estimated Times
Preparation: 20 mins
Cooking: 11 mins
Cooling: 15 mins

Macadamia Nut White Chip Pumpkin Cookies

Mini Morsel Meringue Cookies

Mini Morsel Meringue Cookies

The contrast of fluffy egg whites with tiny bits of rich chocolate make great cookies to pack and mail as well as elegant fare for parties and luncheons.

MAKES ABOUT 5 DOZEN COOKIES

INGREDIENTS

4 large egg whites
½ teaspoon salt
½ teaspoon cream of tartar
1 cup granulated sugar
2 cups (12-ounce package) NESTLÉ TOLL HOUSE Semi-Sweet Chocolate Mini Morsels

DIRECTIONS

PREHEAT oven to 300° F. Grease baking sheets.

BEAT egg whites, salt, and cream of tartar in small mixer bowl until soft peaks form. Gradually add sugar; beat until stiff peaks form. Gently fold in morsels ⅓ cup at a time. Drop by level tablespoon onto prepared baking sheets.

BAKE for 20 to 25 minutes or until meringues are dry and crisp. Cool on baking sheets for 2 minutes; remove to wire racks to cool completely. Store in airtight containers.

Estimated Times
Preparation: 15 mins
Cooking: 20 mins
Cooling: 15 mins

Mississippi Mud Pie

Outrageous! A chocolate crumb crust layered with a rich chocolate sauce, crunchy nuts, and creamy coffee ice cream. This is a dessert to remember.

MAKES 8 SERVINGS

INGREDIENTS

1 prepared 9-inch (6 ounces) chocolate crumb crust
1 cup powdered sugar
1 cup (6 ounces) NESTLÉ TOLL HOUSE Semi-Sweet Chocolate Morsels
¼ cup (½ stick) butter or margarine, cut into pieces
¼ cup heavy whipping cream
2 tablespoons light corn syrup
1 teaspoon vanilla extract
¾ cup chopped nuts, divided (optional)
2 pints coffee ice cream, softened slightly, divided
Whipped cream (optional)

DIRECTIONS

HEAT sugar, morsels, butter, cream, and corn syrup in small, heavy-duty saucepan over low heat, stirring constantly, until butter is melted and mixture is smooth. Remove from heat. Stir in vanilla extract. Cool until slightly warm.

DRIZZLE ⅓ cup chocolate mixture in bottom of crust; sprinkle with ¼ cup nuts. Layer 1 pint ice cream, scooping thin slices with a large spoon; freeze for 1 hour. Repeat with ⅓ cup chocolate mixture, ¼ cup nuts, and remaining ice cream. Drizzle with remaining chocolate mixture; top with remaining nuts. Freeze for 2 hours or until firm. Top with whipped cream before serving.

Estimated Times

Preparation: 20 mins
Cooking: 5 mins
Cooling: 15 mins
Freezing: 3 hrs

Mocha Mousse

This mocha mousse whips up in a hurry, and your guests will love it. They'll think you slaved for hours.

MAKES 10 SERVINGS

INGREDIENTS

1 can (14 ounces) NESTLÉ CARNATION
   Sweetened Condensed Milk
¼ cup (2 envelopes) Double Chocolate
   Melt Down Flavor NESTLÉ Hot
   Cocoa Mix
3 tablespoons butter or margarine
2 teaspoons NESCAFÉ TASTER'S CHOICE
   100% Pure Instant Coffee Granules,
   dissolved in 2 teaspoons water
2 cups heavy whipping cream
Whipped cream (optional)
Chocolate-covered coffee
   beans (optional)

DIRECTIONS

PLACE sweetened condensed milk, cocoa mix, butter, and coffee mixture in large, microwave-safe bowl. Microwave on HIGH (100%) power for 45 seconds or until butter is melted; stir until combined. Let stand for 15 minutes to cool.

WHIP cream until stiff peaks form. Stir one-fourth whipped cream into cocoa mixture to lighten. Fold in remaining whipped cream. Divide mixture among dessert dishes or place in one large serving dish; cover. Refrigerate for at least 2 hours. Top with whipped cream and chocolate-covered coffee beans before serving.

Estimated Times

Preparation: 15 mins
Cooking: 1 min
Cooling: 15 mins
Refrigerating: 2 hrs

Mocha Mousse

About Nescafé

The beginnings of NESCAFÉ can be traced all the way back to 1930, when the Brazilian government first approached Nestlé. Our coffee guru, Max Morgenthaler, and his team set out immediately to find a way of producing a quality cup of coffee that could be made by adding water, yet would retain the coffee's natural flavor. After seven long years of research in our Swiss laboratories, they found the answer.

The new product was named NESCAFÉ—a combination of Nestlé and café. Nestlé first introduced NESCAFÉ in Switzerland in 1938 and the product was soon exported. Its popularity grew and by the 1950s, coffee had become the beverage of choice for teenagers, who were flocking to coffee houses to hear the new rock 'n' roll music. Today, NESCAFÉ is the number one brand of coffee in the world!

Mocha Shortbread

Classic shortbread gets updated with cocoa and coffee for spectacular results. Eat this delectable holiday bread as is, or use as a garnish for ice cream.

MAKES 16 SERVINGS

INGREDIENTS

1½ cups all-purpose flour

2 tablespoons NESTLÉ TOLL HOUSE Baking Cocoa

4 teaspoons NESCAFÉ TASTER'S CHOICE 100% Pure Instant Coffee Granules

1 teaspoon vanilla extract

¾ cup (1½ sticks) butter, softened

½ cup granulated sugar

¼ teaspoon salt

2 teaspoons granulated sugar

DIRECTIONS

PREHEAT oven to 300° F.

COMBINE flour and cocoa in large bowl. Combine coffee granules and vanilla extract in large mixer bowl. Stir until coffee is dissolved. Add butter, ½ cup sugar, and salt; beat until combined. Add flour mixture; mix just until incorporated. Press dough into ungreased 9-inch tart pan with removable bottom or 9-inch-round cake pan.

BAKE for 55 to 60 minutes or until firm. Sprinkle with 2 teaspoons sugar. Cool in pan on wire rack for 5 to 10 minutes; cut into wedges.

Estimated Times

Preparation: 15 mins

Cooking: 55 mins

Cooling: 5 mins

Moist and Minty Brownies

Delight your guests with chocolate and mint in a terrific brownie!

MAKES 16 BROWNIES

INGREDIENTS

1¼ cups all-purpose flour

½ teaspoon baking soda

¼ teaspoon salt

¾ cup granulated sugar

½ cup (1 stick) butter or margarine

2 tablespoons water

1½ cups (9 ounces) NESTLÉ TOLL HOUSE Semi-Sweet Chocolate Morsels, divided

½ teaspoon peppermint extract

½ teaspoon vanilla extract

2 large eggs

1 container (16 ounces) prepared vanilla frosting

1 tube (4½ ounces) chocolate decorator icing

DIRECTIONS

PREHEAT oven to 350° F. Grease 9-inch-square baking pan.

COMBINE flour, baking soda, and salt in small bowl. Combine sugar, butter, and water in medium saucepan. Bring just to a boil over medium heat, stirring constantly; remove from heat. (Or, combine sugar, butter, and water in medium, microwave-safe bowl. Microwave on HIGH (100%) power for 3 minutes, stirring halfway through cooking time. Stir until smooth.)

ADD 1 cup morsels, peppermint extract, and vanilla extract; stir until smooth. Add eggs one at a time, stirring well after each addition. Stir in flour mixture and remaining morsels. Spread into prepared baking pan.

BAKE for 20 to 30 minutes or until center is set. Cool completely (center will sink) in pan on wire rack.

SPREAD vanilla frosting over brownie. Squeeze chocolate icing in parallel lines over frosting. Drag wooden pick through chocolate icing to feather. Let stand until frosting is set. Cut into bars.

Moist and Minty Brownies

Molasses Spice Cookies

This cookie is spicy and delicious!

MAKES ABOUT 2½ DOZEN COOKIES

INGREDIENTS

1¾ cups all-purpose flour

1 teaspoon baking soda

1 teaspoon ground ginger

1 teaspoon ground cinnamon

¼ teaspoon ground cloves

¼ teaspoon salt

1 cup granulated sugar

¾ cup (1½ sticks) butter or
  margarine, softened

1 large egg

¼ cup unsulphured molasses

2 cups (12-ounce package) NESTLÉ
  TOLL HOUSE Premier White Morsels

1 cup finely chopped walnuts

DIRECTIONS

COMBINE flour, baking soda, ginger, cinnamon, cloves, and salt in small bowl. Beat sugar and butter in large mixer bowl until creamy. Beat in egg and molasses. Gradually beat in flour mixture. Stir in morsels. Refrigerate for 20 minutes or until slightly firm.

Molasses Spice Cookies

PREHEAT oven to 375° F.

ROLL dough into 1-inch balls; roll in nuts. Place on ungreased baking sheets.

BAKE for 9 to 11 minutes or until golden brown. Cool on baking sheets for 2 minutes; remove to wire racks to cool completely.

Estimated Times

Preparation: 25 mins

Refrigerating: 20 mins

Cooking: 9 mins

Cooling: 15 mins

Mrs. Claus' Favorite Oatmeal Cookies

These oatmeal cookies are sure to become your family's favorite. Full of chocolate, oats, cranberries, and nuts, they also make great cookies for giving as gifts.

MAKES ABOUT 3 DOZEN COOKIES

INGREDIENTS

1 cup all-purpose flour

½ teaspoon baking soda

½ teaspoon salt

1¼ cups packed light brown sugar

½ cup (1 stick) butter, softened

¼ cup milk

1 large egg

2 teaspoons vanilla extract

2¾ cups quick oats

20 NESTLÉ CRUNCH or Milk Chocolate
  Jingles, unwrapped and cut in quarters

1 cup sweetened dried cranberries

1 cup chopped nuts (optional)

DIRECTIONS

PREHEAT oven to 375° F.

COMBINE flour, baking soda, and salt in small bowl. Beat sugar, butter, milk, egg, and vanilla extract in large mixer bowl until creamy. Gradually beat in flour mixture. Stir in oats, Nestlé Jingles, cranberries, and nuts. Drop dough by rounded tablespoon onto ungreased baking sheets.

BAKE for 10 minutes or until lightly browned. Cool on baking sheets for 2 minutes; remove to wire racks to cool completely.

Note: Try substituting NESTLÉ CRUNCH Hearts or NestEggs.

Estimated Times

Preparation: 15 mins

Cooking: 10 mins

Cooling: 15 mins

Nerds Cereal Bars

These are fun to serve at a children's party. Just cut fun shapes with cookie cutters.

MAKES 24 BARS

INGREDIENTS

Nonstick cooking spray
4 cups miniature marshmallows
3 tablespoons butter or margarine
6 cups toasted rice cereal
1 to 2 boxes (1.65 ounces each) any
  flavor WONKA NERDS Candies

DIRECTIONS

SPRAY 13 x 9-inch baking pan with nonstick cooking spray.

PLACE marshmallows and butter in large saucepan. Cook over medium heat, stirring frequently, until marshmallows are melted.

STIR in cereal until coated. Spread into prepared baking pan. Sprinkle with Nerds; press in slightly. Cool completely in pan on wire rack; cut into bars.

Estimated Times
Preparation: 10 mins
Cooking: 5 mins
Cooling: 30 mins

Nesquik-Filled Marshmallows

You will start a new tradition when you prepare these easy marshmallow snacks.

SERVINGS VARY

INGREDIENTS

1 bag large marshmallows
Chocolate Flavor NESTLÉ NESQUIK
  Calcium Fortified Syrup

DIRECTIONS

CUT top off of marshmallow. Form a hole in center of marshmallow using your finger. Fill hole with Nesquik. Put top back on marshmallow. Use a wooden pick to hold the top in place if needed. Fix as many as you can eat at one time.

FREEZE or refrigerate for 15 minutes to adhere top of marshmallow to bottom.

Nesquik-Filled Marshmallows

INSERT long campfire-roasting fork or other long fork or skewer into center of marshmallow and slowly roast over the fire to warm the chocolate and turn the marshmallow golden brown. (Do not burn the marshmallow as the chocolate will not have time to heat up and the outside of the marshmallow will slide off.)

Estimated Times
Preparation: 5 mins
Cooking: 2 mins
Freezing: 15 mins

Nesquik Neapolitan Pound Cake

Whether you eat this with a sprinkle of powdered sugar or a dab of whipped topping you will be sure to enjoy this cake.

MAKES 16 SERVINGS

Nerds Cereal Bars

INGREDIENTS

1 package (8 ounces) cream cheese, at room temperature

4 large eggs

1 package (18.25 ounces) white cake mix

¾ cup milk

¾ cup Double Chocolate Flavor NESTLÉ NESQUIK Powder

¾ cup Strawberry Flavor NESTLÉ NESQUIK Calcium Fortified Powder

Powdered sugar (optional)

DIRECTIONS

PREHEAT oven to 350° F. Grease and flour 10-inch, 12-cup fluted tube pan.

BEAT cream cheese and eggs in large mixer bowl until smooth. Beat in cake mix alternately with milk. Beat on high speed for 2 minutes (batter will be thick). Remove 2 cups batter and place in separate bowl; stir in chocolate

Nesquik. Remove 2 more cups white cake batter and place in separate bowl; stir in strawberry Nesquik.

SPOON strawberry batter into prepared pan; tap pan on counter lightly. Spoon white batter over strawberry batter, covering it completely. Spoon chocolate batter over white batter.

BAKE on center oven rack for 55 to 65 minutes or until wooden pick inserted in cake comes out clean. Cool in pan on wire rack for 45 minutes. Loosen edges with butter knife if needed; invert onto wire rack to cool completely. Sprinkle with powdered sugar.

Estimated Times
Preparation: 15 mins
Cooking: 55 mins
Cooling: 1 hr

Nesquik Neapolitan Pound Cake

Nesquik Nibbles

These rich, chocolatey nibbles are best served with a tall glass of cold milk. Plus, each serving of Nesquik Nibbles is a good source of vitamin C.

MAKES ABOUT 2 DOZEN COOKIES

INGREDIENTS

Nonstick cooking spray

1 cup all-purpose flour

¼ teaspoon baking soda

⅛ teaspoon salt

⅔ cup Double Chocolate Flavor NESTLÉ NESQUIK Calcium Fortified Powder

⅓ cup packed brown sugar

5 tablespoons butter or margarine, melted

⅓ cup vanilla or plain lowfat yogurt

1 teaspoon vanilla extract

DIRECTIONS

PREHEAT oven to 350° F. Spray baking sheets with nonstick cooking spray.

COMBINE flour, baking soda, and salt in small bowl; set aside. Combine Nesquik, sugar, and butter in medium bowl until mixture resembles coarse sand. Stir in yogurt and vanilla extract. Stir in flour mixture until combined. Drop by rounded teaspoon onto prepared baking sheets.

BAKE for 8 to 10 minutes or until edges appear done and middles are almost set. Cool on baking sheets for 2 to 3 minutes; remove to wire racks to cool completely.

TWIST IT UP!
Turn these Nibbles into a fun and extra delicious treat with extra protein. Add a spoonful of peanut butter between two Nibbles.

Estimated Times
Preparation: 15 mins
Cooking: 8 mins
Cooling: 15 mins

Nesquik Quivers

You won't mind your kids playing with their food with these fun treats. Nesquik Quivers are a fat free treat and provide an excellent source of calcium.

MAKES ABOUT 8 SERVINGS

INGREDIENTS

2 cups fat free milk
⅔ cup Chocolate Flavor NESTLÉ NESQUIK Calcium Fortified Powder
2 envelopes (7 grams each) unflavored gelatin
Decorative cookie cutters

DIRECTIONS

COMBINE milk, Nesquik, and gelatin in small saucepan. Bring to a boil over medium-high heat, stirring frequently. Pour into 8-inch-square baking dish. Cool to room temperature; cover with plastic wrap.

REFRIGERATE for 3 hours or until firm. Cut out shapes using cookie cutters.

Nesquik Quivers

TWIST IT UP!
Break out the cake decorations— sprinkles, gels, and toppings—and let your kids decorate their own quivers.

Estimated Times
Preparation: 20 mins
Cooling: 30 mins
Refrigerating: 3 hrs

Nesquik Skyscrapers

Constructed with graham cracker "floors," fresh fruit "walls," and yummy Nesquik-flavored cream cheese layers, these delicious towers are as much fun to make as they are to eat.

MAKES 7 SKYSCRAPERS

INGREDIENTS

1 package (8 ounces) nonfat or reduced fat cream cheese, at room temperature
¾ cup Strawberry or Chocolate Flavor NESTLÉ NESQUIK Calcium Fortified Powder
21 honey graham or chocolate graham cracker squares
1 cup sliced strawberries, and/or whole raspberries
1 medium banana, sliced

DIRECTIONS

COMBINE cream cheese and Nesquik in small mixer bowl; beat until smooth

Nesquik Skyscrapers

and creamy. Spread cream cheese mixture evenly over tops of graham crackers. Top 7 frosted crackers evenly with strawberries; top 7 frosted crackers evenly with banana.

STACK banana-topped crackers over top of strawberry-topped crackers. Top with remaining frosted crackers, frosting-side-down. Serve immediately.

TRY MAKING A MEGA SKYSCRAPER:
You will need 20 graham cracker squares.

FROST 5 crackers on one side. Top evenly with strawberries. Frost 5 crackers on both sides; place over strawberries. Top evenly with banana. Frost 5 crackers on both sides; place over banana. Top evenly with strawberries. Frost 5 crackers on one side; place frosting-side-down on strawberries. Makes 5 mega skyscrapers.

Estimated Time
Preparation: 15 mins

Nestlé Crunch Marshmallow Bars

Bake up a delectable dessert or snack with graham cracker crumbs, marshmallow creme, brown sugar, and yummy NESTLÉ CRUNCH Candy Bars.

MAKES 16 BARS

INGREDIENTS

¾ cup all-purpose flour

¾ cup graham cracker crumbs

½ cup (1 stick) butter or margarine, softened

¼ cup granulated sugar

¼ cup packed brown sugar

6 (1.55 ounces each) NESTLÉ CRUNCH Candy Bars, chopped, divided

1 jar (7 ounces) marshmallow creme

DIRECTIONS

PREHEAT oven to 325° F. Grease 9-inch-square baking pan.

BEAT flour, graham cracker crumbs, butter, granulated sugar, and brown sugar in large mixer bowl until mixture resembles fine crumbs. Stir in ½ cup chopped Crunch bars. Press into prepared baking pan.

BAKE for 15 minutes. Remove from oven. Dot with marshmallow creme. Let stand for about 5 minutes to soften; spread evenly over surface.

BAKE for an additional 10 minutes. Remove from oven. Sprinkle with remaining chopped Crunch bars in a single layer. Press in gently with spatula. Cool completely in pan on wire rack. Cut into bars.

Estimated Times
Preparation: 15 mins
Cooking: 25 mins
Standing: 5 mins
Cooling: 30 mins

Nestlé Toll House Chocolate Chip Pie

The sweet, creamy richness of a brown sugar base makes this chocolate chip pie a perfect foil for chopped nuts and whipped or ice cream.

Nestlé Toll House Chocolate Chip Pie

MAKES 8 SERVINGS

INGREDIENTS

1 unbaked 9-inch (4-cup volume) deep-dish pie shell*

2 large eggs

½ cup all-purpose flour

½ cup granulated sugar

½ cup packed brown sugar

¾ cup (1½ sticks) butter, softened

1 cup (6 ounces) NESTLÉ TOLL HOUSE Semi-Sweet Chocolate Morsels

1 cup chopped nuts

DIRECTIONS

PREHEAT oven to 325° F.

BEAT eggs in large mixer bowl on high speed until foamy. Beat in flour, granulated sugar, and brown sugar. Beat in butter. Stir in morsels and nuts. Spoon into pie shell.

BAKE for 55 to 60 minutes or until knife inserted halfway between edge and center comes out clean. Cool on wire rack. Serve warm with sweetened whipped cream or ice cream, if desired.

*If using frozen pie shell, use deep-dish style, thawed completely. Bake pie on baking sheet and increase baking time slightly.

Estimated Times
Preparation: 15 mins
Cooking: 55 mins
Cooling: 15 mins

Oatmeal Crunch Cookies

Crunchy bits of chocolate fill these not-so-traditional oatmeal cookies. They make great snacks to serve after school or add to lunch boxes.

MAKES ABOUT 6 DOZEN COOKIES

INGREDIENTS

2¼ cups all-purpose flour

1½ teaspoons baking soda

¾ teaspoon salt

1½ cups (3 sticks) butter or
   margarine, softened

1¼ cups granulated sugar

1 cup packed brown sugar

1½ teaspoons vanilla extract

3 large eggs

4½ cups quick or old-fashioned oats

6 (1.55 ounces each) NESTLÉ CRUNCH
   Candy Bars, chopped

DIRECTIONS

PREHEAT oven to 375° F.

COMBINE flour, baking soda, and salt in small bowl. Beat butter, granulated sugar, brown sugar, and vanilla extract in large mixer bowl until creamy. Add eggs one at a time, beating well after each addition. Gradually beat in flour mixture. Stir in oats and chopped Crunch bars. Drop by rounded tablespoon onto ungreased baking sheets.

BAKE for 8 to 10 minutes or until very lightly browned. Cool on baking sheets for 2 minutes; remove to wire racks to cool completely.

Estimated Times
Preparation: 15 mins
Cooking: 8 mins
Cooling: 15 mins

Oatmeal Scotchies

The two ingredients that make these extraordinary cookies special are oats and butterscotch morsels. These will disappear from your cookie jar in no time. Enjoy!

MAKES ABOUT 4 DOZEN COOKIES

INGREDIENTS

1¼ cups all-purpose flour

1 teaspoon baking soda

½ teaspoon ground cinnamon

½ teaspoon salt

1 cup (2 sticks) butter or
   margarine, softened

¾ cup granulated sugar

¾ cup packed brown sugar

2 large eggs

1 teaspoon vanilla extract (or grated
   peel of 1 orange)

3 cups quick or old-fashioned oats

1⅔ cups (11-ounce package)
   NESTLÉ TOLL HOUSE Butterscotch
   Flavored Morsels

DIRECTIONS

PREHEAT oven to 375° F.

COMBINE flour, baking soda, cinnamon, and salt in small bowl.

Oatmeal Scotchies

Beat butter, granulated sugar, brown sugar, eggs, and vanilla extract in large mixer bowl. Gradually beat in flour mixture. Stir in oats and morsels. Drop by rounded tablespoon onto ungreased baking sheets.

BAKE for 7 to 8 minutes for chewy cookies or 9 to 10 minutes for crisp cookies. Cool on baking sheets for 2 minutes; remove to wire racks to cool completely.

PAN COOKIE VARIATION:

GREASE 15 x 10-inch jelly-roll pan. Prepare dough as above. Spread into prepared pan. Bake for 18 to 22 minutes or until very lightly browned. Cool completely in pan on wire rack. Makes 4 dozen bars.

Estimated Times
Preparation: 15 mins
Cooking: 7 mins
Cooling: 15 mins

Original Nestlé Toll House Chocolate Chip Cookies

Get your glass of ice cold milk ready! Each cookie, loaded with chocolate morsels and nuts, is a treat worthy of dunking. Try them as pan cookies, cut into brownie-like squares.

Original Nestlé Toll House Chocolate Chip Cookies

MAKES ABOUT 5 DOZEN COOKIES

INGREDIENTS
2¼ cups all-purpose flour
1 teaspoon baking soda
1 teaspoon salt
1 cup (2 sticks) butter or
    margarine, softened
¾ cup granulated sugar
¾ cup packed brown sugar
1 teaspoon vanilla extract
2 large eggs
2 cups (12-ounce package) NESTLÉ
    TOLL HOUSE Semi-Sweet
    Chocolate Morsels
1 cup chopped nuts

DIRECTIONS
PREHEAT oven to 375° F.

COMBINE flour, baking soda, and salt in small bowl. Beat butter, granulated sugar, brown sugar, and vanilla extract in large mixer bowl until creamy. Add eggs one at a time, beating well after each addition. Gradually beat in flour mixture. Stir in morsels and nuts. Drop by rounded tablespoon onto ungreased baking sheets.

BAKE for 9 to 11 minutes or until golden brown. Cool on baking sheets for 2 minutes; remove to wire racks to cool completely.

PAN COOKIE VARIATION:

GREASE 15 x 10-inch jelly-roll pan. Prepare dough as above. Spread into prepared pan. Bake for 20 to 25 minutes or until golden brown. Cool completely in pan on wire rack. Makes 4 dozen bars.

FOR HIGH ALTITUDE BAKING (5,200 FEET):

INCREASE flour to 2½ cups. Add 2 teaspoons water with flour and reduce both granulated sugar and brown sugar to ⅔ cup each. Bake drop cookies for 8 to 10 minutes and pan cookie for 17 to 19 minutes.

Estimated Times
Preparation: 15 mins
Cooking: 9 mins
Cooling: 15 mins

Original Nestlé Toll House Peanut Butter & Milk Chocolate Morsel Cookies

Just when you thought these cookies couldn't be improved upon, we added peanut butter and milk chocolate morsels. Combining these morsels with chopped nuts is a winning ticket!

MAKES ABOUT 5 DOZEN COOKIES

INGREDIENTS

2¼ cups all-purpose flour

1 teaspoon baking soda

1 teaspoon salt

1 cup (2 sticks) butter or
 margarine, softened

¾ cup granulated sugar

¾ cup packed brown sugar

1 teaspoon vanilla extract

2 large eggs

1⅔ cups (11-ounce package)
 NESTLÉ TOLL HOUSE Peanut Butter
 & Milk Chocolate Morsels

1 cup chopped nuts

DIRECTIONS

PREHEAT oven to 375° F.

COMBINE flour, baking soda, and salt in small bowl. Beat butter, granulated sugar, brown sugar, and vanilla extract in large mixer bowl until creamy. Add eggs one at a time, beating well after each addition. Gradually beat in flour mixture. Stir in morsels and nuts. Drop by rounded tablespoon onto ungreased baking sheets.

BAKE for 9 to 11 minutes or until golden brown. Cool on baking sheets for 2 minutes; remove to wire racks to cool completely.

PAN COOKIE VARIATION:

GREASE 15 x 10-inch jelly-roll pan. Prepare dough as above. Spread into prepared pan. Bake for 20 to 25 minutes or until golden brown. Cool completely in pan on wire rack. Makes 4 dozen bars.

FOR HIGH ALTITUDE BAKING (5,200 FEET):

INCREASE flour to 2½ cups. Add 2 teaspoons water with flour and reduce both granulated sugar and brown sugar to ⅔ cup each. Bake drop cookies for 8 to 10 minutes and pan cookie for 17 to 19 minutes.

SLICE AND BAKE COOKIE VARIATION:

PREPARE dough as above. Divide in half; wrap in wax paper. Refrigerate for 1 hour or until firm. Shape each half into 15-inch log; wrap in wax paper. Refrigerate for 30 minutes. Preheat oven to 375° F.

Original Nestlé Toll House Peanut Butter & Milk Chocolate Morsel Cookies

Cut into ½-inch-thick slices; place on ungreased baking sheets. Bake for 8 to 10 minutes or until golden brown. Cool on baking sheets for 2 minutes; remove to wire racks to cool completely. Makes about 5 dozen cookies.

Note: May be stored in refrigerator for up to 1 week or in freezer for up to 8 weeks.

Estimated Times
Preparation: 15 mins
Cooking: 9 mins
Cooling: 15 mins

Outrageous Cookie Bars

These quick and easy cookie snack bars are a perfect treat for a brown-bag lunch.

MAKES 48 BARS

INGREDIENTS

½ cup (1 stick) butter or margarine

1½ cups graham cracker crumbs

1 can (14 ounces) NESTLÉ CARNATION
 Sweetened Condensed Milk

2 cups (12-ounce package)
 NESTLÉ TOLL HOUSE Semi-Sweet
 Chocolate Morsels

1 cup flaked coconut

1 cup chopped walnuts

DIRECTIONS

PREHEAT oven to 350° F.

MELT butter in 13 x 9-inch baking pan in oven; remove from oven. Sprinkle graham cracker crumbs over butter. Stir well; press onto bottom of pan. Pour sweetened condensed milk evenly over crumbs. Sprinkle with morsels, coconut, and nuts; press down firmly.

BAKE for 25 to 30 minutes or until light golden brown. Cool completely in pan on wire rack. Cut into bars.

Estimated Times
Preparation: 10 mins
Cooking: 25 mins
Cooling: 30 mins

Peanut Butter and Chocolate Cookie Cups

Surprise your family with these delicious cookie cups.

MAKES 36 COOKIES

INGREDIENTS
¾ cup (1½ sticks) butter or margarine, softened
⅓ cup granulated sugar
1½ cups all-purpose flour
1⅔ cups (11-ounce package) NESTLÉ TOLL HOUSE Peanut Butter & Milk Chocolate Morsels, divided
2 large eggs

1 can (14 ounces) NESTLÉ CARNATION Sweetened Condensed Milk
1 teaspoon vanilla extract

DIRECTIONS
PREHEAT oven to 350° F. Heavily grease 36 mini-muffin cups.

BEAT butter and sugar in small mixer bowl until creamy. Add flour; beat until mixture is evenly moist and crumbly. Roll rounded teaspoon dough into ball; press onto bottom and halfway up side of prepared muffin cup. Repeat with remaining dough. Place 5 morsels in each cup.

BEAT eggs in medium bowl with wire whisk. Stir in sweetened condensed milk and vanilla extract. Spoon into prepared muffin cups, filling almost to the top of each cup.

BAKE for 15 to 18 minutes or until centers are puffed and edges are just beginning to brown. Remove from oven to wire rack(s). Gently run knife around edges of cookies. Let centers flatten. While still warm, top cookies with half of remaining morsels (they will soften and retain their shape). Repeat with remaining morsels. Cool completely in pans on wire racks. With tip of knife, release cookies from cups.

Estimated Times
Preparation: 45 mins
Cooking: 15 mins
Cooling: 20 mins

Baking Tip

If your chocolate chip cookies often come out of the oven flat, try these tips for best results. Don't omit the nuts, but if you do, add 1 to 2 tablespoons extra flour. Soften butter at room temperature just until it yields to light pressure. If softening butter in the microwave oven, microwave one stick of cold butter on MEDIUM-LOW (30%) power for 10 to 15 seconds. Check; let stand. If not soft enough, rotate butter and microwave 5 to 10 seconds longer. Butter should soften just until it yields to light pressure. When using margarine, do not soften. Use directly from the refrigerator. Use a good grade of margarine, and avoid tub and light margarines. Don't overbeat when mixing. Use ungreased baking sheets. Allow baking sheets to cool between each batch. Baking sheets may be chilled briefly in the refrigerator or freezer to hasten cooling between batches. Wipe baking sheets clean of grease between batches, or wash and dry baking sheets. Add 1 to 2 tablespoons extra flour on humid or rainy days, if desired. Always allow cookies to cool for 2 minutes on baking sheets.

Peanut Butter and Jelly Bars

BAKE for 15 minutes; remove from oven. Dollop jelly by heaping teaspoon over partially baked dough. Let stand for 1 minute; spread to cover. Dollop remaining dough by heaping teaspoon over jelly.

BAKE for an additional 20 to 25 minutes or until edges are set. Cool completely in pan on wire rack. Cut into bars.

Estimated Times
Preparation: 20 mins
Cooking: 35 mins
Cooling: 30 mins

Peanut Butter and Jelly Bars

Treat the peanut butter and jelly fan in your home with these bar cookies. Your favorite jelly is sandwiched between two layers of peanut butter and chocolate dough. Wash them down with a tall glass of milk.

MAKES 48 BARS

INGREDIENTS

1¼ cups all-purpose flour
½ cup graham cracker crumbs
½ teaspoon baking soda
½ teaspoon salt
½ cup (1 stick) butter, softened
½ cup granulated sugar
½ cup packed brown sugar

½ cup creamy peanut butter
1 large egg
1 teaspoon vanilla extract
1¾ cups (11.5-ounce package) NESTLÉ TOLL HOUSE Milk Chocolate Morsels
¾ cup coarsely chopped peanuts
½ cup jelly or jam

DIRECTIONS

PREHEAT oven to 350° F.

COMBINE flour, graham cracker crumbs, baking soda, and salt in small bowl.

BEAT butter, granulated sugar, brown sugar, and peanut butter in large mixer bowl until creamy. Beat in egg and vanilla extract. Gradually beat in flour mixture. Stir in morsels and peanuts. Press three-fourths dough into ungreased 13 x 9-inch baking pan.

Peanut Butter Chocolate Chunk Bars

Bars are a great alternative to cookies. Just spread the dough into a pan, bake, and voilà! A fun and welcome treat to pack into a sack lunch.

Peanut Butter Chocolate Chunk Bars

MAKES 36 BARS

INGREDIENTS

1½ cups all-purpose flour

½ teaspoon baking soda

¾ cup packed brown sugar

¾ cup creamy or chunky peanut butter

½ cup (1 stick) butter or
    margarine, softened

½ cup granulated sugar

1 large egg

1 teaspoon vanilla extract

1¾ cups (11.5-ounce package)
    NESTLÉ TOLL HOUSE Semi-Sweet
    Chocolate Chunks

DIRECTIONS

PREHEAT oven to 350° F.

COMBINE flour and baking soda in
small bowl. Beat brown sugar, peanut
butter, butter, and granulated sugar in
large mixer bowl until creamy. Beat in
egg and vanilla extract. Gradually beat
in flour mixture. Stir in chunks. Press
into ungreased 13 x 9-inch baking pan,
distributing chunks evenly.

BAKE for 18 to 22 minutes or until
center is set. Cool completely in pan
on wire rack. Cut into bars.

Estimated Times

Preparation: 15 mins
Cooking: 18 mins
Cooling: 30 mins

Peanut Butter Chocolate Layer Bars

Peanut Butter Chocolate Layer Bars

These bars will make your taste buds crazy! A must-try treat.

MAKES 24 BARS

INGREDIENTS

2 cups crushed peanut butter sandwich
    cookies (about 20 cookies)

3 tablespoons butter or
    margarine, melted

1¼ cups lightly salted dry-roasted
    peanuts, chopped

1 cup (6 ounces) NESTLÉ TOLL HOUSE
    Semi-Sweet Chocolate Morsels

1 cup flaked coconut

1 can (14 ounces) NESTLÉ CARNATION
    Sweetened Condensed Milk

DIRECTIONS

PREHEAT oven to 350° F. Grease
13 x 9-inch baking pan.

COMBINE cookie crumbs and butter
in small bowl; press onto bottom
of prepared baking pan. Layer peanuts,
morsels, and coconut over crumb
mixture. Drizzle sweetened condensed
milk evenly over top.

BAKE for 20 to 25 minutes or until
coconut is golden brown. Cool
completely in pan on wire rack.
Cut into bars.

Estimated Times

Preparation: 10 mins
Cooking: 20 mins
Cooling: 30 mins

Peanut Butter Ice Cream Pie

A frozen dessert for all the peanut lovers in the world.

MAKES 8 SERVINGS

INGREDIENTS

1 package (18 ounces) NESTLÉ TOLL
    HOUSE Refrigerated Chocolate Chip
    Cookie Bar Dough, softened, divided
½ cup creamy peanut butter, divided

1 pint vanilla ice cream, softened
¼ cup chopped peanuts
3 tablespoons Chocolate Flavor NESTLÉ
    NESQUIK Calcium Fortified Syrup
Chopped peanuts (optional)

DIRECTIONS

PREHEAT oven to 350° F. Grease 9-inch pie plate.

PRESS three-fourths package cookie dough onto bottom and side of prepared pie plate.

BAKE for 15 to 20 minutes or until golden brown. Flatten down cooked dough with back of spoon to form pie shell. Cool completely on wire rack.

SPREAD ¼ cup peanut butter over crust. Mix ice cream, remaining peanut butter, and ¼ cup peanuts in medium bowl. Spoon into cookie crust; spread evenly. Drizzle with Nesquik and additional chopped peanuts. Freeze for at least 2 hours or overnight.

BAKE remaining cookie dough according to package directions. Cool completely on wire rack; crumble baked cookies.

THAW pie for 5 to 10 minutes. Sprinkle cookie crumbs over pie before serving.

Estimated Times
Preparation: 20 mins
Cooking: 30 mins
Cooling: 30 mins
Freezing: 2 hrs

Baking Tip

When removing refrigerated dough from the freezer, thawing is not necessary. Just remove the frozen dough from the wrapper and cut into slices with a sharp knife. Then, follow the baking directions on the package. For best results, check cookies for doneness before minimum cook time. Refrigerated dough can be placed in the freezer for up to two months, if placed there before the "use by" date indicated on the package.

Short on time? Use NESTLÉ TOLL HOUSE Refrigerated Sugar Cookie Bar Dough and your favorite cookie cutters. These quick-fix treats bake in just 7 to 10 minutes! Follow the directions on the package.

Peanut Butter Sleigh Ride Bars

These are the perfect bars for your peanut butter and chocolate lover on your holiday list.

MAKES 16 BARS

INGREDIENTS

¾ cup packed light brown sugar
¾ cup creamy or chunky peanut butter
½ cup (1 stick) butter or margarine,
    softened
½ cup granulated sugar
1 large egg
1 teaspoon vanilla extract
1½ cups all-purpose flour
1 teaspoon baking soda
30 NESTLÉ BUTTERFINGER or NESTLÉ
    CRUNCH Jingles, unwrapped

DIRECTIONS

PREHEAT oven to 350° F.

BEAT brown sugar, peanut butter, butter, and granulated sugar in large mixer bowl until creamy. Beat in egg and vanilla extract. Gradually beat in flour and baking soda. Stir in Nestlé Jingles.

PRESS dough into ungreased 9-inch-square baking pan, distributing Nestlé Jingles evenly.

BAKE for 25 minutes or until golden and wooden pick inserted near center comes out clean. Cool completely in pan on wire rack. Cut into bars.

NOTE: Try substituting NESTLÉ Hearts, NESTLÉ NestEggs, or NESTLÉ SIGNATURE TREASURES.

Estimated Times
Preparation: 15 mins
Cooking: 25 mins
Cooling: 30 mins

Peanut Butterscotch Pretzel Snacks

Turn regular pretzels into a special treat by coating them in a peanut butter and butterscotch mixture.

MAKES 60 SNACKS

INGREDIENTS
1⅔ cups (11-ounce package) NESTLÉ TOLL HOUSE Butterscotch Flavored Morsels
⅓ cup creamy peanut butter
60 (3-inch) twisted pretzels
2 to 3 tablespoons sesame seeds, toasted

DIRECTIONS
MICROWAVE morsels and peanut butter in medium, uncovered, microwave-safe bowl on MEDIUM-HIGH (70%) power for 1 minute; STIR. The morsels may retain some of their original shape. If necessary, microwave at additional

10- to 15-second intervals, stirring just until morsels are melted.

DIP about three-fourths of 1 pretzel in butterscotch mixture; shake off excess. Place on wire rack; sprinkle lightly with sesame seeds. Repeat with remaining pretzels. (If mixture thickens, microwave on MEDIUM-HIGH (70%) power at 10- to 15-second intervals, stirring until smooth.)

REFRIGERATE for 20 minutes or until set. Store in airtight containers or resealable plastic bags.

Estimated Times
Preparation: 25 mins
Cooking: 2 mins
Refrigerating: 20 mins

Peanutty Chocolate Truffles

The classic combination of chocolate and peanut butter is a taste that everyone loves. These delicious truffles will make any party a hit, but don't forget to make a few extra for yourself!

MAKES ABOUT 2 DOZEN TRUFFLES

INGREDIENTS
¾ cup creamy peanut butter
¼ cup (½ stick) butter or margarine, softened

1 teaspoon vanilla extract
1 cup powdered sugar
4 tablespoons (2 envelopes) Rich Chocolate Flavor NESTLÉ Hot Cocoa Mix
1 cup finely chopped cocktail peanuts

DIRECTIONS
LINE baking sheets with wax paper.

BEAT peanut butter, butter, and vanilla extract in medium bowl until creamy. Combine powdered sugar and cocoa mix in small bowl. Stir into peanut butter mixture.

PLACE peanuts in flat dish. Scoop peanut butter mixture into 1-inch balls; roll in peanuts to coat. Place on prepared baking sheets. Refrigerate until firm.

NOTE: Try to make these a day ahead as they hold well and taste even better the day after they are made.

Estimated Times
Preparation: 25 mins
Refrigerating: 30 mins

Peanutty Chocolate Truffles

Peanutty Valentine Cookies

Tempt your sweetie this Valentine's Day with these peanut butter cookies that are full of heart.

MAKES 36 COOKIES

INGREDIENTS
½ cup granulated sugar
½ cup packed brown sugar
½ cup (1 stick) butter or
    margarine, softened
½ cup creamy peanut butter
1 large egg
1 teaspoon vanilla extract
1⅓ cups all-purpose flour
¾ teaspoon baking soda
36 NESTLÉ BUTTERFINGER or NESTLÉ
    CRUNCH Hearts, unwrapped

DIRECTIONS
PREHEAT oven to 375° F.

BEAT granulated sugar, brown sugar, butter, and peanut butter in large mixer bowl until combined. Beat in egg and vanilla extract. Beat in flour and baking soda.

DROP dough by rounded tablespoon into 36 ungreased mini-muffin cups.

BAKE for 8 to 10 minutes. Remove from oven; gently press 1 Nestlé Heart into each cup. Cool in pans on wire racks for at least 10 minutes. Remove cookies from muffin cups with a butter knife. Serve warm or cool completely on wire racks.

NOTE: Try substituting NESTLÉ JINGLES, NESTLÉ CRUNCH Assorted Miniatures, or Peanut Butter NESTLÉ SIGNATURES TREASURES.

Estimated Times
Preparation: 20 mins
Cooking: 8 mins
Cooling: 10 mins

Premier White Lemony Cheesecake

Lemon and white baking bars combine for an elegant and luscious dessert. Try this in the springtime—at Easter or a bridal or baby shower—to rave reviews.

MAKES 12 TO 16 SERVINGS

INGREDIENTS
CRUST
6 tablespoons butter or
    margarine, softened
¼ cup granulated sugar

Peanutty Valentine Cookies

1¼ cups all-purpose flour

1 large egg yolk

⅛ teaspoon salt

CHEESECAKE

2 boxes (6 ounces each) NESTLÉ
   TOLL HOUSE Premier White
   Baking Bars, broken into pieces*

½ cup heavy whipping cream

2 packages (8 ounces each) cream
   cheese, at room temperature

1 tablespoon lemon juice

2 teaspoons grated lemon peel

¼ teaspoon salt

3 large egg whites

1 large egg

DIRECTIONS

PREHEAT oven to 350° F. Grease 9-inch
springform pan.

FOR CRUST:

BEAT butter and sugar in small mixer
bowl until creamy. Beat in flour, egg
yolk, and salt. Press mixture onto bottom
and 1 inch up side of prepared pan.

BAKE for 14 to 16 minutes or until crust
is set.

FOR CHEESECAKE:

MICROWAVE baking bars and cream
in medium, uncovered, microwave-safe
bowl on MEDIUM-HIGH (70%) power
for 1 minute; STIR. The bars may retain
some of their original shape. If necessary,
microwave at additional 10- to 15-
second intervals, stirring just until bars
are melted.

BEAT cream cheese, lemon juice, lemon
peel, and salt in large mixer bowl until
smooth. Gradually beat in melted baking
bars. Beat in egg whites and whole egg.
Pour into crust.

BAKE for 35 to 40 minutes or until
edge is lightly browned. Loosen and
remove side of pan. Cool completely
on wire rack. Refrigerate until firm.
Garnish as desired.

*May use 2 cups (12-ounce package) NESTLÉ
TOLL HOUSE Premier White Morsels instead
of baking bars.

Estimated Times
Preparation: 30 mins
Cooking: 50 mins
Cooling: 1 hr
Refrigerating: 2 hrs

Baking Tip

If you like to bake, you will need to
always keep a ready bag of flour on
hand. Flour gives baked goods their
proper consistency. At the dough or
batter stage, the other ingredients
will always cling to flour. And in the
oven, flour makes sure everything
sticks together. This is because the
starch in flour binds to anything
moist like butter or eggs. Flour,
however, will never completely
harden because of the gluten it
contains. Gluten allows the flour
to swell and become sticky when
kneaded. For all of these reasons and
more, the result is always the same,
a delicious piece of bread or pastry.

Premier White Lemony Cheesecake

Pumpkin Dutch Apple Pie

A layer of crisp, crunchy apples topped with creamy pumpkin and sprinkled with a crumble topping is just what the doctor ordered for those suffering from pumpkin-apple deficiency. Serve with a generous smile and slices of sharp cheddar cheese.

MAKES 8 SERVINGS

INGREDIENTS
APPLE LAYER
1 unbaked 9-inch (4-cup volume) deep-dish pie shell*

2 cups peeled, cored, thinly sliced green apples

¼ cup granulated sugar

2 teaspoons all-purpose flour

1 teaspoon lemon juice

¼ teaspoon ground cinnamon

PUMPKIN LAYER
1½ cups LIBBY'S 100% Pure Pumpkin

1 cup NESTLÉ CARNATION Evaporated Milk

½ cup granulated sugar

2 large eggs, lightly beaten

2 tablespoons butter or margarine, melted

¾ teaspoon ground cinnamon

¼ teaspoon salt

⅛ teaspoon ground nutmeg

CRUMBLE TOPPING
½ cup all-purpose flour

⅓ cup chopped walnuts

5 tablespoons granulated sugar

3 tablespoons butter

DIRECTIONS
PREHEAT oven to 375° F.

FOR APPLE LAYER:
COMBINE apples, sugar, flour, lemon juice, and cinnamon in medium bowl; pour into pie shell.

FOR PUMPKIN LAYER:
COMBINE pumpkin, evaporated milk, sugar, eggs, butter, cinnamon, salt, and nutmeg in medium bowl. Pour over apple mixture.

BAKE for 30 minutes. Remove from oven; sprinkle with Crumble Topping. Bake for an additional 20 minutes or until custard is set. Cool completely on wire rack.

FOR CRUMBLE TOPPING:
COMBINE flour, nuts, and sugar in medium bowl. Cut in butter with pastry blender or two knives until mixtures resembles coarse crumbs.

*If using frozen pie shell, use deep-dish style, thawed completely. Bake pie on baking sheet and increase baking time slightly.

Estimated Times
Preparation: 30 mins

Cooking: 50 mins

Cooling: 30 mins

Pumpkin Spiced and Iced Cookies

These pumpkin cookies offer the moistness of pumpkin pie with the chocolatey sweetness of chocolate morsels. Try these for a Halloween party or a children's dessert at Thanksgiving.

MAKES ABOUT 3 DOZEN COOKIES

INGREDIENTS
2¼ cups all-purpose flour

1½ teaspoons pumpkin pie spice

1 teaspoon baking powder

½ teaspoon baking soda

½ teaspoon salt

1 cup (2 sticks) butter or margarine, softened

1 cup granulated sugar

1 can (15 ounces) LIBBY'S 100% Pure Pumpkin

2 large eggs

1 teaspoon vanilla extract

2 cups (12-ounce package) NESTLÉ TOLL HOUSE Semi-Sweet Chocolate Morsels

1 cup chopped walnuts

Vanilla Glaze (recipe follows)

DIRECTIONS
PREHEAT oven to 375° F. Grease baking sheets.

COMBINE flour, pumpkin pie spice, baking powder, baking soda, and salt in

Pumpkin Spiced and Iced Cookies

medium bowl. Beat butter and sugar in large mixer bowl until creamy. Beat in pumpkin, eggs, and vanilla extract. Gradually beat in flour mixture. Stir in morsels and nuts. Drop by rounded tablespoon onto prepared baking sheets.

BAKE for 15 to 20 minutes or until edges are lightly browned. Cool on baking sheets for 2 minutes; remove to wire racks to cool completely. Drizzle or spread with Vanilla Glaze.

FOR VANILLA GLAZE:
COMBINE 1 cup powdered sugar, 1 to 1½ tablespoons milk, and ½ teaspoon vanilla extract in small bowl; mix well.

Estimated Times
Preparation: 20 mins
Cooking: 15 mins
Cooling: 15 mins

Pumpkin Toffee Cheesecake

This fabulous combination of cream cheese and pumpkin topped with crushed toffee candies is more than a bit 'over the top'—it is the top!

MAKES 16 SERVINGS

INGREDIENTS
CRUST
1¾ cups crushed shortbread cookies (about 14 to 16 cookies)
1 tablespoon butter or margarine, melted

CHEESECAKE
3 packages (8 ounces each) cream cheese, at room temperature
1¼ cups packed brown sugar
1 can (15 ounces) LIBBY'S 100% Pure Pumpkin
⅔ cup (5 fluid-ounce can) NESTLÉ CARNATION Evaporated Milk
2 large eggs
2 tablespoons cornstarch
½ teaspoon ground cinnamon
1 cup crushed toffee candies (about 25 to 30 candies)

TOPPING
1 container (8 ounces) sour cream, at room temperature
2 tablespoons granulated sugar
½ teaspoon vanilla extract
Caramel syrup or ice cream topping (optional)

DIRECTIONS
PREHEAT oven to 350° F.

FOR CRUST:
COMBINE cookie crumbs and butter in small bowl. Press onto bottom and 1-inch up side of ungreased 9-inch springform pan.

BAKE for 6 to 8 minutes (do not allow to brown). Cool on wire rack for 10 minutes.

FOR CHEESECAKE:
BEAT cream cheese and brown sugar in large mixer bowl until creamy. Add pumpkin, evaporated milk, eggs, cornstarch, and cinnamon; beat well. Pour into crust.

BAKE for 60 to 65 minutes or until edge is set but center still moves slightly. Remove from oven; top with toffee candy pieces.

FOR TOPPING:
COMBINE sour cream, sugar, and vanilla extract in small bowl; mix well. Spread over warm cheesecake.

BAKE for 8 minutes. Cool completely in pan on wire rack. Refrigerate for several hours or overnight. Remove side of springform pan. Drizzle with caramel syrup before serving.

Estimated Times
Preparation: 20 mins
Cooking: 1 hr, 15 mins
Cooling: 1 hr, 10 mins
Refrigerating: 3 hrs

Quick Tiramisu

Quick Tiramisu

This easy variation on the classic Italian dessert is a great make-ahead dessert.

MAKES 8 SERVINGS

INGREDIENTS

1 package (18 ounces) NESTLÉ TOLL HOUSE Refrigerated Sugar Cookie Bar Dough

1 package (8 ounces) reduced fat cream cheese, at room temperature

½ cup granulated sugar

¾ teaspoon NESCAFÉ TASTER'S CHOICE 100% Pure Instant Coffee Granules, dissolved in ¾ cup cold water, divided

1 container (8 ounces) frozen whipped topping, thawed

1 tablespoon NESTLÉ TOLL HOUSE Baking Cocoa

DIRECTIONS

PREHEAT oven to 325° F.

DIVIDE cookie dough into 20 pieces. Shape into 2½ x 1-inch oblong shapes. Place on ungreased baking sheets.

BAKE for 10 to 12 minutes or until light golden brown around edges. Cool on baking sheets for 1 minute; remove to wire racks to cool completely.

BEAT cream cheese and sugar in large mixer bowl until smooth. Beat in ¼ cup coffee. Fold in whipped topping. Layer 6 cookies in ungreased 8-inch-square baking dish. Sprinkle each cookie with 1 teaspoon coffee. Spread one-third cream cheese mixture over cookies. Repeat layers 2 more times with 12 cookies, remaining coffee and remaining cream cheese mixture. Cover; refrigerate for 2 to 3 hours. Crumble remaining cookies over top. Sift cocoa over cookies.

Estimated Times
Preparation: 20 mins
Cooking: 10 mins
Cooling: 15 mins
Refrigerating: 2 hrs

Raisin Bread Pudding

Brown sugar, cinnamon, and nutmeg will fill your kitchen with sweet aromas and sweet memories of happy faces around your table. Serve with whipped cream or milk for breakfast for a change of pace.

MAKES 8 SERVINGS

INGREDIENTS

16 slices bread, cubed

1 cup raisins

2 cans (12 fluid ounces each) NESTLÉ CARNATION Evaporated Milk

4 large eggs, slightly beaten

¾ cup packed brown sugar

¼ cup (½ stick) butter, melted

2 teaspoons vanilla extract

1 teaspoon ground cinnamon

½ teaspoon ground nutmeg

Caramel syrup or ice cream topping (optional)

DIRECTIONS

PREHEAT oven to 350° F. Grease 12 x 8-inch baking dish.

COMBINE bread and raisins in large bowl. Combine evaporated milk, eggs, sugar, butter, vanilla extract, cinnamon, and nutmeg in medium bowl. Pour egg mixture over bread mixture; combine well. Pour mixture into prepared baking dish. Let stand for 10 minutes.

BAKE for 35 to 45 minutes or until knife inserted in center comes out clean. Drizzle with caramel syrup before serving.

Estimated Times
Preparation: 20 mins
Cooking: 35 mins
Standing: 10 mins

Raisinet Spiders

This is the perfect snack that the kids can help assemble, and they are sure to be a hit at any Halloween party.

MAKES 10 SPIDERS

INGREDIENTS
⅓ cup peanut butter
20 round crackers
80 thin pretzel sticks
20 NESTLÉ RAISINETS Milk
   Chocolate-Covered Raisins

DIRECTIONS
SPREAD about 2 teaspoons peanut butter over top of 10 crackers. Press 8 pretzels into peanut butter, arranging 4 on each side to resemble legs. Top with remaining crackers. Dab top of cracker sandwiches with 2 peanut butter dots. Place 1 Raisinet on each dot to resemble eyes.

Estimated Time
Preparation: 20 mins

Raisinets Oatmeal Bars

A great treat to bring hiking or camping for an instant energy boost.

MAKES 24 BARS

INGREDIENTS
1½ cups all-purpose flour
1 teaspoon baking soda
¾ teaspoon ground cinnamon
½ teaspoon salt
1 cup packed brown sugar
¾ cup (1½ sticks) butter or
   margarine, softened
1½ teaspoons vanilla extract
1 large egg
1 package (12½ ounces) NESTLÉ
   RAISINETS Milk Chocolate-
   Covered Raisins
1¾ cups quick or old-fashioned
   oats, divided

DIRECTIONS
PREHEAT oven to 350° F. Grease 13 x 9-inch baking pan.

COMBINE flour, baking soda, cinnamon, and salt in small bowl. Beat sugar, butter, and vanilla extract in large mixer bowl until creamy. Beat in egg; gradually beat in flour mixture. Stir in Raisinets and 1½ cups oats. Spread into prepared baking pan. Sprinkle with remaining oats.

Raisinets Oatmeal Bars

BAKE for 18 to 20 minutes or until golden brown. Cool completely in pan on wire rack. Cut into bars.

Estimated Times
Preparation: 10 mins
Cooking: 18 mins
Cooling: 30 mins

About Raisinets

RAISINETS are sun-ripened, plump raisins coated with milk chocolate. It was first introduced in 1927 by the Blumenthal Chocolate Company. Nestlé acquired the brand in 1984. You can find RAISINETS at your local grocery store, drug or convenience store as well as enjoy them during your next trip to the movie theatre. Try mixing RAISINETS with popcorn, and you'll create a sweet and salty treat!

Raspberry Twinkles

Raspberry Twinkles

NESTLÉ CRUNCH and raspberry jam combine to make these tasty holiday cookies. These also make the perfect snack to leave out for a hungry Santa and his helpers.

MAKES ABOUT 3½ DOZEN COOKIES

INGREDIENTS

COOKIES

1 cup (2 sticks) butter, softened

⅔ cup granulated sugar

½ teaspoon vanilla extract

2 cups all-purpose flour

½ cup raspberry jam

1 package (13 ounces) NESTLÉ CRUNCH or Milk Chocolate Jingles, unwrapped

GLAZE

1 cup powdered sugar

1 tablespoon butter, softened

1 tablespoon milk or water

DIRECTIONS

FOR COOKIES:

BEAT butter, sugar, and vanilla extract in large mixer bowl until creamy. Gradually beat in flour. Cover; refrigerate for 1 hour.

PREHEAT oven to 350° F.

SHAPE dough into 1-inch balls; place 2 inches apart on ungreased baking sheets. Press thumb into tops to make ½-inch-deep depressions (dough will crack around edges). Fill each depression with about ¼ teaspoon jam.

BAKE for 14 to 16 minutes or until edges are lightly browned. Immediately press 1 Nestlé Jingle into center of each cookie. Cool on baking sheets for 2 minutes; remove to wire racks to cool completely.

FOR GLAZE:

COMBINE powdered sugar, butter, and milk in small mixer bowl; whisk until smooth. Add more milk if needed. Drizzle over tops of cookies.

NOTE: Try substituting NESTLÉ Hearts or NESTLÉ NestEggs.

Estimated Times

Preparation: 40 mins

Refrigerating: 1 hr

Cooking: 14 mins

Cooling: 15 mins

Rich Chocolate Cupcakes

Super-creamy, super-rich, and ultra-decadent, these luscious cupcakes with their buttery frosting will make you cry for more!

MAKES 20 CUPCAKES

INGREDIENTS

CUPCAKES

1½ cups all-purpose flour

⅔ cup NESTLÉ TOLL HOUSE
    Baking Cocoa

1 teaspoon baking soda

½ teaspoon salt

1½ cups granulated sugar

½ cup (1 stick) butter or
    margarine, softened

2 large eggs

1 teaspoon vanilla extract

1 cup milk

MILK CHOCOLATE FROSTING

1¾ cups (11.5-ounce package) NESTLÉ
    TOLL HOUSE Milk Chocolate Morsels

6 tablespoons butter or
    margarine, softened

½ teaspoon salt

2½ cups sifted powdered sugar

¼ cup milk

1 teaspoon vanilla extract

DIRECTIONS

PREHEAT oven to 350° F. Paper-line
20 muffin cups.

FOR CUPCAKES:
COMBINE flour, cocoa, baking soda, and salt in small bowl. Beat sugar, butter, eggs, and vanilla extract in large mixer bowl. Gradually beat in flour mixture alternately with milk. Spoon ¼ cup batter into each prepared muffin cup.

BAKE for 18 to 20 minutes or until wooden pick inserted in centers comes out clean. Cool in pans for 5 minutes; remove to wire racks to cool completely. Frost with Milk Chocolate Frosting.

FOR MILK CHOCOLATE FROSTING:
MICROWAVE morsels, butter, and salt in medium, uncovered, microwave-safe bowl on MEDIUM-HIGH (70%) power for 1 minute; STIR. The morsels may retain some of their original shape. If necessary, microwave at additional 10- to 15-second intervals, stirring just until morsels are melted. Transfer to large mixer bowl. Gradually beat in sugar alternately with milk. Stir in vanilla extract.

Estimated Times

Preparation: 20 mins

Cooking: 20 mins

Cooling: 15 mins

Rich Chocolate Cupcakes

Rich Chocolate Pound Cake

Classic pound cake gets a chocolate boost in this rich dessert that's finished with a decorative drizzle of melted chocolate.

MAKES 16 SERVINGS

INGREDIENTS

2 cups (12-ounce package) NESTLÉ TOLL HOUSE Semi-Sweet Chocolate Morsels, divided

3 cups all-purpose flour

1 tablespoon baking powder

½ teaspoon salt

2 cups packed light brown sugar

1 cup (2 sticks) butter, softened

1 tablespoon vanilla extract

4 large eggs, at room temperature

½ cup milk

DIRECTIONS

PREHEAT oven to 350° F. Grease 10-inch Bundt pan.

MICROWAVE 1½ cups morsels in medium, uncovered, microwave-safe bowl on HIGH (100%) power for 1 minute; STIR. The morsels may retain some of their original shape. If necessary, microwave at additional 10- to 15-second intervals, stirring just until morsels are melted. Cool to room temperature.

COMBINE flour, baking powder, and salt in medium bowl. Beat sugar, butter, and vanilla extract in large mixer bowl until creamy. Add eggs one at a time, beating well after each addition. Beat in melted chocolate. Gradually beat in flour mixture alternately with milk. Spoon into prepared Bundt pan.

BAKE for 55 to 65 minutes or until wooden pick inserted in cake comes out clean. Cool in pan for 30 minutes. Invert onto wire rack to cool completely.

MICROWAVE remaining morsels in heavy-duty plastic bag on HIGH (100%) power for 45 seconds; knead. Microwave at additional 10- to 15-second intervals, kneading until smooth. Cut tiny corner from bag; squeeze bag to drizzle chocolate over cake.

Estimated Times

Preparation: 15 mins

Cooking: 57 mins

Cooling: 1 hr

Rich Chocolate Pound Cake

Rich Peanut Butterscotch Brownies

Rich Peanut Butterscotch Brownies

Peanut butter and butterscotch combine for a new taste sensation in this variation of the brownie. Perfect for dessert or a snack—kids and adults will love them.

MAKES 48 BROWNIES

INGREDIENTS

1 package (18.5 ounces) devil's food or chocolate cake mix
¾ cup chopped peanuts
½ cup (1 stick) butter or margarine, melted
⅔ cup (5 fluid-ounce can) NESTLÉ CARNATION Evaporated Milk
1⅔ cups (11-ounce package) NESTLÉ TOLL HOUSE Butterscotch Flavored Morsels, divided
½ cup creamy peanut butter

DIRECTIONS

PREHEAT oven to 350° F. Grease 13 x 9-inch baking pan.

COMBINE cake mix and peanuts in large bowl; stir in butter. Stir in evaporated milk (batter will be thick). Spread half of batter into prepared baking pan.

BAKE for 15 minutes.

MICROWAVE 1⅓ cups morsels and peanut butter in medium, uncovered, microwave-safe bowl on MEDIUM-HIGH (70%) power for 1 minute; STIR. The morsels may retain some of their original shape. If necessary, microwave at additional 10- to 15-second intervals, stirring just until morsels are melted. Spread mixture over baked layer. Drop remaining batter by heaping teaspoon over butterscotch mixture.

BAKE for 20 to 25 minutes (top layer will be soft). Cool completely in pan on wire rack.

PLACE remaining morsels in small, heavy-duty plastic bag. Microwave on MEDIUM-HIGH (70%) power for 30 seconds; knead. Microwave at additional 10- to 15-second intervals, kneading until smooth. Cut tiny corner from bag; squeeze bag to drizzle chocolate over brownies. Cut into bars.

Estimated Times
Preparation: 15 mins
Cooking: 40 mins
Cooling: 30 mins

Scotcheroos

Scotcheroos

Need sticky, chewy, and chocolatey all in one bite? These no-bake bar cookies have it all!

MAKES 30 BARS

INGREDIENTS

Nonstick cooking spray

1½ cups creamy peanut butter

1 cup granulated sugar

1 cup light corn syrup

6 cups toasted rice cereal

1⅔ cups (11-ounce package)
NESTLÉ TOLL HOUSE Butterscotch
Flavored Morsels

1 cup (6 ounces) NESTLÉ TOLL HOUSE
Semi-Sweet Chocolate Morsels

DIRECTIONS

COAT 13 x 9-inch baking pan with nonstick cooking spray.

COMBINE peanut butter, sugar, and corn syrup in large saucepan. Cook over medium-low heat, stirring frequently, until melted. Remove from heat. Add cereal; stir until thoroughly coated. Press onto bottom of prepared baking pan.

MICROWAVE butterscotch morsels and semi-sweet morsels in large, uncovered, microwave-safe bowl on HIGH (100%) power for 1 minute; STIR. The morsels may retain some of their original shape. If necessary, microwave at additional 10- to 15-second intervals, stirring just until morsels are melted. Spread over cereal mixture.

REFRIGERATE for 15 to 20 minutes or until topping is firm. Cut into bars.

Estimated Times
Preparation: 5 mins
Cooking: 5 mins
Refrigerating: 15 mins

S'mores that CRUNCH!

For family fun indoors or out, treat yourself and your kids to S'mores that Crunch! These treats are an exciting version of the old campfire classic. This simple and tasty recipe combines a unique crunchy chocolate with a warm, roasted marshmallow between two golden graham crackers.

MAKES 2 SERVINGS

INGREDIENTS

2 large marshmallows

4 honey graham cracker squares

1 (1.55 ounces) NESTLÉ CRUNCH
Candy Bar, cut in half

DIRECTIONS

FOR OUTDOOR S'MORES:

THREAD marshmallows onto skewers. Toast over flame, turning frequently, until golden. Place 1 marshmallow on each of 2 graham cracker squares. Top each marshmallow with 1 Crunch square and remaining graham cracker square.

FOR INDOOR S'MORES:

PLACE 2 graham cracker squares on microwave-safe plate. Top each square with 1 marshmallow.

MICROWAVE on HIGH (100%) power for 10 to 15 seconds or until marshmallows expand. Top each marshmallow with 1 Crunch square and remaining graham cracker square.

Estimated Times
Preparation: 5 mins
Cooking: 1 min

S'mores that CRUNCH!

Spiderweb Munch

This crispy snack is topped with a layer of chocolate and then decorated with a thin piping of peanut butter. A candy spider on top would complete the image for a creepy Halloween treat!

MAKES 12 SERVINGS

INGREDIENTS

2 cups (12-ounce package) NESTLÉ TOLL HOUSE Semi-Sweet Chocolate Morsels
1 cup creamy peanut butter, divided
⅓ cup powdered sugar
3 cups toasted rice cereal

DIRECTIONS

HEAT morsels and ¾ cup peanut butter in small, heavy-duty saucepan over low heat, stirring constantly until smooth. Remove from heat. Add sugar; stir vigorously until smooth.

PLACE cereal in large bowl. Add 1 cup chocolate mixture; stir until evenly coated. Place on ungreased baking sheet. Using small metal spatula, shape into 10-inch circle with slightly raised 1-inch-wide border. Pour remaining chocolate mixture in center of circle; spread to border.

FOR SPIDERWEB:
PLACE remaining peanut butter in small, heavy-duty plastic bag. Cut tiny corner from bag; squeeze bag to pipe concentric circles on top of chocolate. Using wooden pick or tip of sharp knife, pull tip through peanut butter from center to border. Refrigerate for 30 minutes or until firm. Cut into wedges.

Estimated Times
Preparation: 20 mins
Cooking: 5 mins
Refrigerating: 30 mins

Spring Fruit Tart

Celebrate the sweetness of Spring with this stunning tart, bursting with the flavor of fresh, seasonal fruit such as red raspberries, sliced mango, and kiwifruit. This recipe is a breeze to make.

MAKES 8 SERVINGS

INGREDIENTS

1 package (18 ounces) NESTLÉ TOLL HOUSE Refrigerated Sugar Cookie Bar Dough
1 package (8 ounces) cream cheese, at room temperature
⅓ cup granulated sugar
½ teaspoon vanilla extract
1½ cups fruit (e.g., raspberries, sliced mango, kiwifruit, bananas)

DIRECTIONS

PREHEAT oven to 325° F. Grease bottom and side of 9-inch fluted tart pan with removable bottom.*

Spring Fruit Tart

PRESS cookie dough evenly into prepared pan.

BAKE for 22 to 27 minutes or until lightly golden and wooden pick inserted in center comes out clean. Cool completely in pan on wire rack.

BEAT cream cheese, sugar, and vanilla extract in small mixer bowl until smooth. Spread evenly over cooled cookie crust to within ½ inch of edge.

ARRANGE fruit as desired on top of cream cheese mixture. Refrigerate for 1 hour. Remove rim of pan; slice into wedges.

*If tart pan is not available, press cookie dough onto greased pizza pan or baking sheet to measure an 8-inch circle. Bake for 16 to 18 minutes or until lightly golden.

Estimated Times
Preparation: 15 mins
Cooking: 22 mins
Cooling: 30 mins
Refrigerating: 1 hr

Baking Tip

Enjoy baking but just don't have the time? No problem. With NESTLÉ TOLL HOUSE Refrigerated Cookie and Brownie Bar Dough, you can enjoy the authentic scratch-baking taste in minutes. Each flavor is homemade delicious and sure to satisfy your craving to bake!

Baking sugar cookies has never been so simple and convenient. Each package contains 20 prescored squares. Simply break apart and bake. Or, easily roll out the dough and use your favorite cookie cutters. Each square piece of dough magically transforms into delicious round cookies.

Stained Glass Window Cookies

Stained Glass Window Cookies

Create your own excitement with these unique treats. They make an exceptional holiday cookie!

MAKES ABOUT 15 COOKIES

INGREDIENTS

1 package (18 ounces) NESTLÉ
    TOLL HOUSE Refrigerated
    Sugar Cookie Bar Dough

All-purpose flour
About ½ cup finely crushed hard candy

DIRECTIONS

PREHEAT oven to 350° F. Line baking sheets with foil.

CUT dough in half; refrigerate one half. Sprinkle about 1 tablespoon flour onto working surface. Sprinkle additional flour over remaining half. Roll out dough to ¼-inch thickness, using additional flour as needed to prevent sticking.

CUT into desired shapes with 2½-inch cookie cutters. Transfer cookies to prepared baking sheets with spatula, placing about 2 inches apart. Cut out small shapes in cookie centers. Spoon candy into each center to fill holes. Pierce hole at top of shape if cookie is going to be hung. Repeat with remaining dough.

BAKE for 7 to 8 minutes or until edges are light golden brown. Cool on baking sheets for 1 minute; slide foil with cookies to wire racks to cool completely. Store tightly covered.

Estimated Times
Preparation: 30 mins
Cooking: 7 mins
Cooling: 15 mins

Star of David Chocolate Cookies

These sweet, buttery cookies are sure to become a holiday favorite! Add a few drops of food coloring to the frosting for a festive touch.

MAKES ABOUT 3 DOZEN COOKIES

INGREDIENTS
2 cups all-purpose flour
½ cup NESTLÉ TOLL HOUSE Baking Cocoa
¼ teaspoon salt

1 cup (2 sticks) butter or margarine, softened
1 cup powdered sugar
1 teaspoon vanilla extract
1 package (16 ounces) prepared vanilla frosting

DIRECTIONS
PREHEAT oven to 350° F.

COMBINE flour, cocoa, and salt in small bowl. Beat butter, sugar, and vanilla extract in large mixer bowl until creamy. Gradually beat in cocoa mixture. Shape dough into 2 balls.

ROLL each ball of dough between 2 sheets of wax paper to ¼-inch thickness. Remove top sheet of wax paper. Cut with 2-inch star-shaped cookie cutter. Place on ungreased baking sheets; pierce with fork.

BAKE for 8 to 10 minutes or until set. Cool on baking sheets for 2 minutes; remove to wire racks to cool completely. Decorate with frosting.

Estimated Times
Preparation: 30 mins
Cooking: 8 mins
Cooling: 15 mins

Star of David Chocolate Cookies

Sticks & Stones Candy Bark

Salty and sweet together make for a tasty snack.

MAKES ABOUT 36 PIECES

INGREDIENTS

1⅔ cups (11-ounce package) NESTLÉ
  TOLL HOUSE Butterscotch Flavored
  Morsels, divided
1½ cups (9 ounces) NESTLÉ TOLL
  HOUSE Milk Chocolate Morsels
½ cup creamy peanut butter
2 cups pretzel sticks
2 cups dry-roasted peanuts
1⅓ cups NESTLÉ RAISINETS Milk
  Chocolate-Covered Raisins

DIRECTIONS

BUTTER 13 x 9-inch baking pan.

MICROWAVE 1⅓ cups butterscotch morsels, semi-sweet morsels, and peanut butter in large, uncovered, microwave-safe bowl on HIGH (100%) power for 1 minute; STIR. The morsels may retain some of their original shape. If necessary, microwave at additional 10- to 15-second intervals, stirring just until morsels are melted.

ADD pretzels, peanuts, and Raisinets; stir well to coat. Spread into prepared baking pan.

Sticks & Stones Candy Bark

PLACE remaining butterscotch morsels in small, heavy-duty plastic bag. Microwave on MEDIUM-HIGH (70%) power for 30 seconds; knead. Microwave at additional 10- to 15-second intervals, kneading until smooth. Cut tiny corner from bag; squeeze bag to drizzle over candy.

REFRIGERATE for 1 hour or until firm. Break into bite-sized pieces.

Estimated Times
Preparation: 10 mins
Cooking: 2 mins
Refrigerating: 1 hr

Strawberries & Creme Cheesecake

A delicious way to treat your special someone, this dreamy cheesecake features a decadent combination of traditional cheesecake with strawberries & creme candies.

MAKES 12 SERVINGS

INGREDIENTS

CRUST

1½ cups chocolate graham
  cracker crumbs
¼ cup (½ stick) butter or
  margarine, melted

CHEESECAKE

1 package (12 ounces) Strawberries
  & Creme NESTLÉ SIGNATURES
  TREASURES
3 packages (8 ounces each) cream
  cheese, at room temperature
1 cup granulated sugar
1 tablespoon vanilla extract
3 large eggs

TOPPING

1 container (16 ounces) sour cream
¼ cup granulated sugar
1 teaspoon vanilla extract

DIRECTIONS

PREHEAT oven to 350° F.

FOR CRUST:
GREASE bottom and side of 9-inch springform pan.

COMBINE graham cracker crumbs and butter in medium bowl. Press onto bottom of prepared pan. Place in freezer for 5 minutes.

FOR CHEESECAKE:

SET aside 12 Nestlé Treasures to use for garnish. Unwrap and cut remaining Nestlé Treasures in quarters.

BEAT cream cheese and sugar in large mixer bowl until fluffy. Beat in vanilla extract. Beat in eggs one at a time, beating well after each addition. Sprinkle cut Nestlé Treasures over bottom of crust to ½ inch from edge. Pour filling into crust.

BAKE for 50 minutes or until center is set and edges begin to crack. Cool on wire rack for 2 minutes before adding sour cream topping.

FOR TOPPING:

COMBINE sour cream, sugar, and vanilla extract in medium bowl; mix well.

Strawberries & Creme Cheesecake

Spread over surface of warm cheesecake. Bake for 5 minutes. Remove from oven; cool completely on wire rack.

REFRIGERATE for several hours or overnight. Remove side of springform pan. Garnish each slice with 1 unwrapped whole Nestlé Treasure.

Estimated Times
Preparation: 20 mins
Freezing: 5 mins
Cooking: 55 mins
Cooling: 1 hr
Refrigerating: 3 hrs

Strawberry Almond Chocolate Tart

This tart makes a beautiful presentation and it tastes wonderful!

MAKES 8 SERVINGS

INGREDIENTS

Refrigerated pastry dough for 9-inch pie
¼ cup strawberry jam
1 cup (6 ounces) NESTLÉ TOLL HOUSE Semi-Sweet Chocolate Morsels
⅔ cup NESTLÉ CARNATION Sweetened Condensed Milk
1 tablespoon amaretto liqueur (or ½ teaspoon almond extract)
2 cups sliced strawberries
3 tablespoons toasted almonds

DIRECTIONS

PREHEAT oven to 425° F.

PLACE unfolded pastry on ungreased baking sheet. Turn edges under ½ inch and flute. Prick pastry with tines of a fork.

BAKE for 10 to 12 minutes or until golden brown. Cool completely on baking sheet on wire rack. Spread with jam.

MICROWAVE morsels and sweetened condensed milk in medium, uncovered, microwave-safe bowl on HIGH (100%) power for 1 minute; STIR. The morsels may retain some of their original shape. If necessary, microwave at additional 10- to 15-second intervals, stirring just until morsels are melted. Stir in liqueur. Pour over jam; spread to edges. Refrigerate for 1 hour or until chocolate is set.

ARRANGE strawberries over chocolate; sprinkle with nuts. Serve immediately.

Estimated Times
Preparation: 20 mins
Cooking: 10 mins
Cooling: 30 mins
Refrigerating: 1 hr

Chocolate

Here's some tips on how to temper (cool) chocolate. Pour some of the melted chocolate into another bowl and cool slightly. Reserve the rest of the melted chocolate over warm water, adding more warm water as needed. Add several of the large chunks of solid chocolate to the melted, slightly cooled chocolate. Stir constantly and continue to lower the temperature until chocolate reaches 90° F for semi-sweet or bittersweet chocolate, and 88° F for milk or white chocolate. Immediately remove what is left of the large chunks and set them aside.

Always test the temper of your chocolate before you start molding or dipping. To test, spread a dab of your tempered chocolate on a small piece of wax paper or foil. Within about 5 minutes (in a cool room), the chocolate should harden and take on a semi-shiny gloss. When it is broken, you should clearly hear a 'snap.' If this test fails the first time, cool the chocolate one or two degrees and repeat the test. If it continues to fail, warm the chocolate to 120° F and repeat the cooling (tempering) process.

Strawberry Cheesecake Pie

The perfect dessert for a sunny day. Fresh strawberries are kept shiny with a fruit-sweetened glaze.

MAKES 8 SERVINGS

INGREDIENTS

1 prepared 9-inch (6 ounces) graham cracker crumb crust
⅔ cup (5 fluid-ounce can) NESTLÉ CARNATION Evaporated Fat Free Milk
1 package (8 ounces) fat free cream cheese, at room temperature
1 large egg
½ cup granulated sugar
2 tablespoons all-purpose flour
1 teaspoon grated lemon peel
1½ to 2 cups halved fresh strawberries
3 tablespoons strawberry jelly, warmed

DIRECTIONS

PREHEAT oven to 325° F.

PLACE evaporated milk, cream cheese, egg, sugar, flour, and lemon peel in blender; cover. Blend until smooth. Pour into crust.

BAKE for 35 to 40 minutes or until center is set. Cool completely in pan on wire rack. Arrange strawberries on top of pie; drizzle with jelly. Refrigerate for 2 hours before serving.

Estimated Times
Preparation: 10 mins
Cooking: 35 mins
Cooling: 1 hr
Refrigerating: 2 hrs

Super Candy Bar Cookie Pops

Send your kids to cookie heaven with these sweet and yummy cookies on a stick.

MAKES 20 COOKIES

INGREDIENTS

1 package (18 ounces) NESTLÉ TOLL HOUSE Refrigerated Chocolate Chip Cookie Bar Dough
20 wooden craft sticks
½ cup NESTLÉ TOLL HOUSE Semi-Sweet Chocolate Morsels
1 tablespoon creamy peanut butter
2 (1.5 to 2.1 ounces each) NESTLÉ CRUNCH, BABY RUTH, and/or BUTTERFINGER Candy Bars, chopped

Super Candy Bar Cookie Pops

DIRECTIONS

PREHEAT oven to 350° F.

BREAK dough along prescored lines. Roll each square into a ball. Place six balls at a time onto ungreased baking sheet. Insert sticks into each ball to resemble a lollipop; flatten dough slightly.

BAKE for 10 to 12 minutes or until golden. Cool on baking sheets for 2 minutes; gently remove to wire racks to cool completely.

MICROWAVE morsels and peanut butter in small, uncovered, microwave-safe bowl on HIGH (100%) power for 30 seconds; STIR. Microwave at additional 10-second intervals, stirring until smooth.

SPREAD about 1 teaspoon chocolate mixture over each pop. Sprinkle each pop with chopped candy bars. Refrigerate for about 15 minutes or until chocolate has set.

Estimated Times

Preparation: 30 mins
Cooking: 10 mins
Cooling: 15 mins
Refrigerating: 15 mins

Super-Easy Rocky Road Fudge

Super-Easy Rocky Road Fudge

Rich and truly divine fudge! Each piece is made with a smooth mixture of chocolate morsels, sweetened condensed milk, marshmallows, and walnuts. Easy to make and bring along to all of your holiday parties!

MAKES 48 PIECES

INGREDIENTS

2 cups (12-ounce package) NESTLÉ TOLL HOUSE Semi-Sweet Chocolate Morsels
1 can (14 ounces) NESTLÉ CARNATION Sweetened Condensed Milk
1 teaspoon vanilla extract
3 cups miniature marshmallows
1½ cups coarsely chopped walnuts

DIRECTIONS

LINE 13 x 9-inch baking pan with foil; grease lightly.

MICROWAVE morsels and sweetened condensed milk in large, uncovered, microwave-safe bowl on HIGH (100%) power for 1 minute; STIR. The morsels may retain some of their original shape. If necessary, microwave at additional 10- to 15-second intervals, stirring just until morsels are melted. Stir in vanilla extract. Fold in marshmallows and nuts.

PRESS mixture into prepared baking pan. Refrigerate until ready to serve. Lift from pan; remove foil. Cut into pieces.

Estimated Times

Preparation: 10 mins
Cooking: 2 mins
Refrigerating: 1 hr

Baking Tip

Shiny aluminum baking sheets with only one or two sides work best for baking cookies. For best results, make sure your baking sheets fit your oven properly. Baking sheets that are too large or placed off-center in the oven cause heat to build-up underneath, producing cookies that get too dark or burn on the bottom. Choose baking sheets with at least a one- or two-inch clearance all the way around, and make sure sheets do not touch the sides, front, or back of the oven.

Swirl of Chocolate Cheesecake Triangles

Elegant white swirls decorate these rich cheesecake bars. They're great for picnics or birthday parties—easy to handle and no implements needed!

MAKES 30 TRIANGLES

INGREDIENTS

CRUST
2 cups graham cracker crumbs

½ cup (1 stick) butter or margarine, melted

⅓ cup granulated sugar

FILLING
2 packages (8 ounces each) cream cheese, at room temperature

1 cup granulated sugar

¼ cup all-purpose flour

1 can (12 fluid ounces) NESTLÉ CARNATION Evaporated Milk

2 large eggs

1 tablespoon vanilla extract

1 cup (6 ounces) NESTLÉ TOLL HOUSE Semi-Sweet Chocolate Morsels

DIRECTIONS
PREHEAT oven to 325° F.

FOR CRUST:
COMBINE graham cracker crumbs, butter, and sugar in medium bowl.

Press graham cracker mixture onto bottom of ungreased 13 x 9-inch baking pan.

FOR FILLING:
BEAT cream cheese, sugar, and flour in large mixer bowl until smooth. Gradually beat in evaporated milk, eggs, and vanilla extract.

MICROWAVE morsels in medium, uncovered, microwave-safe bowl on HIGH (100%) power for 1 minute; STIR. The morsels may retain some of their original shape. If necessary, microwave at additional 10- to 15-second intervals, stirring just until morsels are melted. Stir 1 cup cream cheese mixture into chocolate. Pour remaining cream cheese mixture over crust. Pour chocolate mixture over cream cheese mixture. Swirl mixtures with spoon, pulling plain cream cheese mixture up to surface.

BAKE for 40 to 45 minutes or until set. Cool completely in pan on wire rack; refrigerate until firm. Cut into 15 rectangles; cut each rectangle in half diagonally to form triangles.

Estimated Times
Preparation: 30 mins

Cooking: 45 mins

Cooling: 30 mins

Refrigerating: 1 hr

Three Milk Cake— Pastel Tres Leches

This rich and intriguing cake is a combination of tasty flavors and whipped cream.

MAKES 12 SERVINGS

INGREDIENTS

CAKE
6 large egg whites

½ cup granulated sugar, divided

6 large egg yolks

1 cup all-purpose flour, sifted

CREAM
1 can (14 ounces) NESTLÉ CARNATION Sweetened Condensed Milk

1 can (7.6 fluid ounces) NESTLÉ Media Crema or 1 cup heavy whipping cream

⅔ cup (5 fluid-ounce can) NESTLÉ CARNATION Evaporated Milk

¼ cup brandy

1 teaspoon vanilla extract

TOPPING
1 cup heavy whipping cream

2 tablespoons granulated sugar

½ teaspoon vanilla extract

DIRECTIONS
PREHEAT oven to 375° F. Grease and flour 9-inch springform pan.

FOR CAKE:
BEAT egg whites and ¼ cup sugar in

Three Milk Cake—Pastel Tres Leches

small mixer bowl until stiff peaks form. Combine egg yolks and remaining sugar in medium bowl; beat until light yellow in color. Fold egg white mixture and flour alternately into egg yolk mixture. Pour into prepared pan.

BAKE for 15 to 20 minutes or until just golden and wooden pick inserted in center comes out clean. Remove from oven to wire rack.

FOR CREAM:
COMBINE sweetened condensed milk, media crema, evaporated milk, brandy, and vanilla extract in medium bowl; stir well. Prick top of cake thoroughly with wooden pick. Pour 2 cups cream over cake. Spoon excess cream from side of pan over top of cake. Let stand for 30 minutes or until cake absorbs cream. Remove side of pan.

FOR TOPPING:
BEAT cream, sugar, and vanilla extract in small mixer bowl until stiff peaks form. Spread over top and side of cake. Serve immediately with remaining cream.

Estimated Times
Preparation: 30 mins
Cooking: 15 mins
Standing: 30 mins

Traditional Cheesecake

For an elegant dessert, try this scrumptious cheesecake. It won't disappoint you!

MAKES 12 SERVINGS

INGREDIENTS

CRUST

1½ cups graham cracker crumbs

⅓ cup butter, melted

¼ cup granulated sugar

CHEESECAKE

3 packages (8 ounces each) cream
   cheese, at room temperature

1 can (14 ounces) NESTLÉ CARNATION
   Sweetened Condensed Milk

4 large eggs

¼ cup all-purpose flour

2 tablespoons lemon juice

1 tablespoon grated lemon peel

1 cup (8 ounces) sour cream

Fruit pie filling or fruit topping (optional)

DIRECTIONS

PREHEAT oven to 350° F.

FOR CRUST:

COMBINE graham cracker crumbs, butter, and sugar in small bowl. Press onto bottom and 1 inch up side of ungreased 9-inch springform pan.

BAKE for 6 to 8 minutes. Cool on wire rack for 10 minutes.

Traditional Cheesecake

FOR CHEESECAKE:

BEAT cream cheese and sweetened condensed milk in large mixer bowl. Beat in eggs, flour, lemon juice, and lemon peel. Pour into crust.

BAKE for 50 minutes. Remove from oven; spread with sour cream.

BAKE for 10 minutes or until edge is set but center still moves slightly. Cool completely in pan on wire rack. Refrigerate for several hours or overnight. Garnish with fruit topping.

Estimated Times
Preparation: 20 mins
Cooking: 1 hr, 6 mins
Cooling: 1 hr, 10 mins
Refrigerating: 3 hrs

Turtle Brownie Dessert

This is for the candy lover!

MAKES 20 BROWNIES

INGREDIENTS

1 package (18.25 ounces) German chocolate cake mix
¾ cup (1½ sticks) butter or margarine, melted
7 tablespoons NESTLÉ CARNATION Evaporated Milk, divided

1 cup chopped pecans
1 cup (6 ounces) NESTLÉ TOLL HOUSE Semi-Sweet Chocolate Morsels
20 NESTLÉ SIGNATURES TURTLES Candies

DIRECTIONS

PREHEAT oven to 375° F. Grease 13 x 9-inch baking pan.

COMBINE cake mix, butter, and 5 tablespoons evaporated milk in large bowl; stir until blended. Stir in nuts. Spread half of cake mix mixture onto bottom of prepared pan.

BAKE for 12 minutes. Cool in pan on wire rack for 10 minutes.

MICROWAVE morsels and remaining evaporated milk in small, uncovered, microwave-safe bowl on HIGH (100%) power for 1 minute; STIR. The morsels may retain some of their original shape. If necessary, microwave at additional 10- to 15-second intervals, stirring just until morsels are melted. Gently spread over cake layer. Place Turtles on chocolate layer; drop remaining cake mix mixture by heaping teaspoon between Turtles.

BAKE for 16 to 18 minutes. Cool completely in pan on wire rack. Cut into squares.

Estimated Times
Preparation: 15 mins
Cooking: 30 mins
Cooling: 40 mins

Baking Tip

If your cookie recipe calls for semi-sweet chocolate morsels, try replacing them with homemade mint-flavored morsels. Place 2 cups (12-ounce package) NESTLÉ TOLL HOUSE Semi-Sweet Chocolate Morsels in a medium, heavy-duty plastic bag or container. Add ¼ teaspoon pure peppermint extract; seal bag or cover container. Shake to coat. Store for 24 hours. Allow sufficient time for morsels to absorb the mint extract.

If you don't have overnight, add ½ teaspoon pure peppermint extract to the same amount of morsels. Seal bag or cover container; shake to coat. The mint-flavored morsels can be added directly to your recipe or melted according to morsel package directions.

Turtle Brownie Dessert

Turtle Cheesecake

A finalist in the 2001 Nestlé Toll House "Share the Very Best" recipe contest, this family favorite is a marbled cheesecake topped with a decadent combination of pecans, chocolate morsels, and caramel and chocolate syrups.

MAKES 14 SERVINGS

INGREDIENTS

CRUST

1¾ cups chocolate graham
   cracker crumbs

⅓ cup butter or margarine, melted

FILLING

3 packages (8 ounces each) cream
   cheese, at room temperature

1 can (14 ounces) NESTLÉ CARNATION
   Sweetened Condensed Milk

½ cup granulated sugar

3 large eggs

3 tablespoons lime juice

1 tablespoon vanilla extract

1½ cups (9 ounces) NESTLÉ TOLL
   HOUSE Semi-Sweet Chocolate Morsels

2 tablespoons Chocolate Flavor NESTLÉ
   NESQUIK Calcium Fortified Syrup

2 tablespoons caramel syrup or ice
   cream topping

½ cup coarsely chopped pecans

¼ cup NESTLÉ TOLL HOUSE Semi-Sweet
   Chocolate Mini Morsels

DIRECTIONS

PREHEAT oven to 300° F. Grease 9-inch springform pan.

FOR CRUST:

COMBINE graham cracker crumbs and butter in medium bowl. Press onto bottom and 1 inch up side of prepared pan.

FOR FILLING:

BEAT cream cheese and sweetened condensed milk in large mixer bowl until smooth. Add sugar, eggs, lime juice, and vanilla extract. Beat until combined.

MICROWAVE 1½ cups semi-sweet morsels in medium, uncovered, microwave-safe bowl on HIGH (100%) power for 1 minute; STIR. The morsels may retain some of their original shape. If necessary, microwave at additional 10- to 15-second intervals, stirring just until morsels are melted. Stir 2 cups of cheesecake batter into melted morsels; mix well. Alternately spoon batters into crust, beginning and ending with yellow batter.

BAKE for 70 to 75 minutes or until edge is set and center moves slightly. Cool in pan on wire rack for 10 minutes; run

Turtle Cheesecake

knife around edge of cheesecake. Cool completely. Drizzle Nesquik and caramel syrup over cheesecake. Sprinkle with nuts and mini morsels. Refrigerate for several hours or overnight. Remove side of pan.

Estimated Times
Preparation: 30 mins
Cooking: 1 hr, 10 mins
Cooling: 1 hr, 10 mins
Refrigerating: 3 hrs

Ultimate Chocolate Chocolate Chip Cookies

Here's the ultimate chocolate, chocolate chip cookie.

MAKES ABOUT 4 DOZEN COOKIES

INGREDIENTS
4 cups (two 12-ounce packages) NESTLÉ TOLL HOUSE Semi-Sweet Chocolate Morsels, divided
2⅔ cups all-purpose flour
1 teaspoon baking soda
1 teaspoon salt
1 cup (2 sticks) butter or margarine, softened
1 cup packed brown sugar
½ cup granulated sugar
1 teaspoon vanilla extract
3 large eggs

Ultimate Chocolate Chocolate Chip Cookies

DIRECTIONS
PREHEAT oven to 375° F.

MELT 2 cups morsels in small, heavy-duty saucepan over low heat; stir until smooth. Remove from heat.

COMBINE flour, baking soda, and salt in medium bowl. Beat butter, brown sugar, granulated sugar, and vanilla extract in large mixer bowl. Add eggs one at a time, beating well after each addition. Beat in melted chocolate. Gradually beat in flour mixture. Stir in remaining morsels. Drop by rounded tablespoon onto ungreased baking sheets.

BAKE for 8 to 9 minutes or until cookies are puffed. Cool on baking sheets for 2 minutes; remove to wire racks to cool completely.

Estimated Times
Preparation: 15 mins
Cooking: 10 mins
Cooling: 15 mins

Ultimate Ice Cream Sandwiches

Create the perfect summer escape with this incredible recipe for Ultimate Ice Cream Sandwiches. With large, soft, chewy cookie sides, each full of delicious premium toppings, ranging from macadamia nuts to peanut butter cups, this fun-to-eat treat is the "ultimate" indulgence for kids and adults alike.

MAKES 6 SANDWICHES

INGREDIENTS

1 package (18 ounces) NESTLÉ TOLL HOUSE ULTIMATES Refrigerated Cookie Bar Dough (e.g., Chocolate Chip Lovers, Chocolate Chips & Chunks with Pecans, White Chip Macadamia Nut, or Peanut Butter Cups, Chips & Chunks)

3 cups vanilla or chocolate ice cream, slightly softened

NESTLÉ TOLL HOUSE Semi-Sweet Chocolate Mini Morsels (optional)

DIRECTIONS

PREPARE cookies according to package directions. Cool completely.

PLACE ½ cup ice cream on flat side of each of 6 cookies; top with flat side of remaining cookies to make sandwiches. Roll sides of sandwiches in morsels. Wrap tightly in plastic wrap; freeze for at least 1 hour before serving.

Estimated Times

Preparation: 30 mins
Cooking: 17 mins
Cooling: 15 mins
Freezing: 1 hr

Ultimate Ice Cream Sandwiches

Valentine Cheesecake

This cheesecake makes a delicious, elegant dessert for that special Valentine dinner.

MAKES 12 SERVINGS

INGREDIENTS

CRUST

1½ cups chocolate graham cracker crumbs

¼ cup (½ stick) butter or margarine, melted

CHEESECAKE

36 NESTLÉ BUTTERFINGER or Milk Chocolate Hearts

3 packages (8 ounces each) cream cheese, at room temperature

1 cup granulated sugar

1 tablespoon vanilla extract

3 large eggs

TOPPING

1 container (16 ounces) sour cream

¼ cup granulated sugar

1 teaspoon vanilla extract

DIRECTIONS

PREHEAT oven to 350° F. Grease bottom and side of 9-inch springform pan.

Valentine Cheesecake

FOR CRUST:

COMBINE graham cracker crumbs and butter in medium bowl. Press onto bottom of prepared pan. Place in freezer for 5 minutes.

FOR CHEESECAKE:

SET aside 12 Nestlé Hearts to use for garnish. Unwrap and cut remaining Nestlé Hearts in quarters.

BEAT cream cheese and sugar in large mixer bowl until fluffy. Beat in vanilla extract. Add eggs one at a time, beating well after each addition. Sprinkle cut Nestlé Hearts over bottom of crust to ½ inch from edge. Pour filling into crust.

BAKE for 50 minutes or until center is set and edges begin to crack. Cool for 2 minutes before adding sour cream topping.

FOR TOPPING:

COMBINE sour cream, sugar, and vanilla extract in medium bowl. Mix well. Spread over surface of warm cheesecake. Bake for 5 minutes. Remove from oven; cool completely on wire rack.

REFRIGERATE for several hours or overnight. Remove side of springform pan. Garnish each slice with one unwrapped Nestlé Heart.

NOTE: Try substituting NESTLÉ Jingles or NESTLÉ NestEggs.

Estimated Times
Preparation: 30 mins
Freezing: 5 mins
Cooking: 50 mins
Cooling: 1 hr
Refrigerating: 3 hrs

Pie Crusts

With most pie recipes, you can use a homemade crust, a refrigerated pie crust, pie crust mix, or a frozen pie crust. If you have problems with burning crust, here's a tip for preventing the crust from getting too brown. Cut a 9-inch circle in the center of a square piece of aluminum foil and place the square piece over the edge of the crust, leaving filling exposed. Continue baking until the filling is done.

Here's what to expect in volume when filling pie crusts: 9-inch deep-dish pie crust holds four cups. 9-inch shallow pie crust holds two cups. A frozen 9-inch deep-dish or shallow pie crust may be used. The crust typically does not need to be defrosted before baking. However, if preparing and freezing a homemade pie crust ahead of time and the crust is frozen in a glass pie plate, defrost before using; otherwise, it may shatter in a hot oven. Graham cracker crusts are not recommended because they burn easily.

Warm Mocha Pudding Cake

Warm Mocha Pudding Cake

Warm and steamy mocha pudding cake topped off with fluffy whipped cream and seasonal berries speaks the language of elegance and taste.

MAKES 8 SERVINGS

INGREDIENTS

1 cup all-purpose flour

1 cup packed brown sugar, divided

4 tablespoons NESTLÉ TOLL HOUSE Baking Cocoa, divided

2 tablespoons NESCAFÉ TASTER'S CHOICE 100% Pure Instant Coffee Granules, divided

1 teaspoon baking powder

⅛ teaspoon salt

⅓ cup milk

5 tablespoons butter or margarine, melted

1 large egg

2 teaspoons vanilla extract

¾ cup boiling water

Whipped cream (optional)

Fresh assorted berries (optional)

DIRECTIONS

PREHEAT oven to 350° F. Grease 8-inch-round cake pan.

COMBINE flour, ½ cup sugar, 2 tablespoons cocoa, 1 tablespoon coffee granules, baking powder, and salt in small bowl. Beat milk, butter, egg, and vanilla extract in medium bowl until blended. Add flour mixture; stir until combined. Spoon batter into prepared pan.

COMBINE remaining sugar, remaining cocoa, and remaining coffee granules in small bowl. Sprinkle evenly over batter. Pour water evenly over batter.

BAKE for 20 to 25 minutes or until wooden pick inserted in center comes out clean. Cool for 5 minutes in pan on wire rack. Invert onto serving plate or serve from pan. Serve warm with whipped cream and berries.

Estimated Times
Preparation: 15 mins
Cooking: 20 mins
Cooling: 5 mins

White Chip Chocolate Cookies

A stylish cookie—make sure you eat one right out of the oven!

MAKES ABOUT 5 DOZEN COOKIES

INGREDIENTS

2¼ cups all-purpose flour

⅔ cup NESTLÉ TOLL HOUSE Baking Cocoa

1 teaspoon baking soda

¼ teaspoon salt

1 cup (2 sticks) butter or margarine, softened

¾ cup granulated sugar

⅔ cup packed brown sugar

1 teaspoon vanilla extract

2 large eggs

2 cups (12-ounce package) NESTLÉ TOLL HOUSE Premier White Morsels

DIRECTIONS

PREHEAT oven to 350° F.

COMBINE flour, cocoa, baking soda, and salt in small bowl. Beat butter, granulated sugar, brown sugar, and vanilla extract in large mixer bowl until creamy. Add eggs one at a time, beating well after each addition. Gradually beat in flour mixture. Stir in morsels. Drop by well-rounded teaspoon onto ungreased baking sheets.

BAKE for 9 to 11 minutes or until centers are set. Cool on baking sheets for 2 minutes; remove to wire racks to cool completely.

Estimated Times
Preparation: 15 mins
Cooking: 9 mins
Cooling: 15 mins

White Chip Meringue Dessert Bars

Brown sugar-sweetened meringue gives these dessert bars a delicate texture.

MAKES 24 BARS

INGREDIENTS

CRUST

2 cups all-purpose flour

½ cup powdered sugar

1 cup (2 sticks) butter, softened

TOPPING

2 cups (12-ounce package) NESTLÉ TOLL HOUSE Premier White Morsels

1¼ cups coarsely chopped nuts, divided

3 large egg whites

1 cup packed brown sugar

DIRECTIONS

PREHEAT oven to 375° F.

FOR CRUST:

COMBINE flour and powdered sugar in medium bowl. Cut in butter with pastry blender or two knives until mixture is crumbly. Press evenly onto bottom of ungreased 13 x 9-inch baking pan.

BAKE for 10 to 12 minutes or until set.

FOR TOPPING:

SPRINKLE morsels and 1 cup nuts over hot crust.

BEAT egg whites in medium mixer bowl until frothy. Gradually add brown sugar. Beat until stiff peaks form. Carefully spread meringue over morsels and nuts. Sprinkle with remaining nuts.

BAKE for 15 to 20 minutes or until golden brown. Serve warm or cool completely.

Estimated Times

Preparation: 15 mins

Cooking: 25 mins

White Chip Meringue Dessert Bars

White Chip Orange Cookies

The white morsels and orange blend together and create marvelous effects in this cookie.

MAKES ABOUT 3½ DOZEN COOKIES

INGREDIENTS

2¼ cups all-purpose flour

¾ teaspoon baking soda

½ teaspoon salt

1 cup (2 sticks) butter or margarine, softened

½ cup granulated sugar

½ cup packed light brown sugar

1 large egg

2 to 3 teaspoons grated orange peel

2 cups (12-ounce package) NESTLÉ TOLL HOUSE Premier White Morsels

DIRECTIONS

PREHEAT oven to 350° F.

COMBINE flour, baking soda, and salt in small bowl. Beat butter, granulated sugar, and brown sugar in large mixer bowl until creamy. Beat in egg and orange peel. Gradually beat in flour mixture. Stir in morsels. Drop by rounded tablespoon onto ungreased baking sheets.

BAKE for 10 to 12 minutes or until edges are light golden brown. Cool on baking sheets for 2 minutes; remove to wire racks to cool completely.

Estimated Times

Preparation: 15 mins

Cooking: 10 mins

Cooling: 15 mins

more resources

Simply put, water is the beverage of life. While you may survive for six weeks without food, you won't live longer than a week or so without water. It's the most abundant substance in the human body as well as the most common substance on Earth. An average adult body is 55-75 percent water (about 10-12 gallons). It's found in every cell, tissue and organ, and almost every life sustaining body process needs water to function.

nutrition
water balance

In healthy people, water intake and water loss balance out. If you consume more than you need, your kidneys simply excrete the extra. To see if you're drinking enough fluid, check your urine. A small amount of dark-colored urine indicates that you aren't getting enough fluid. Almost clear urine means you're drinking enough.

drink before you get thirsty
When you don't consume enough fluids, your body may trigger a sensation of thirst. Although thirst signals the need for fluids, you actually need fluids long before you become thirsty. This is especially important for seniors, children, and for anyone during illness, hot weather, or strenuous physical activity. If you wait until you feel thirsty to drink then this probably means that you're already deficient by two or more cups of body fluids.

how much is enough?
The average adult loses about two quarts (about 8 cups) of water daily through perspiration, urination, bowel movements, and breathing. This water needs to be replaced because the body doesn't store an extra supply. How much water the body needs depends on the amount of calories used as well as body weight, level of physical activity, diet, exposure to dry air, pregnancy, and illness.

To keep your body well hydrated, drink 8 to 12 cups of water throughout the day. Because milk, juice, and other beverages are mostly water, they can count toward your daily water intake. Caffeinated and alcoholic beverages are not the best sources of fluid since caffeine and alcohol are diuretics, causing the body to lose water through increased urination.

water vs. sports drinks

Sports drinks are an excellent choice for people who are engaged in physical activity lasting over 90 minutes. These products contain sugars, sodium, potassium, and other nutrients that are lost during strenuous physical activity. If you exercise less than 90 minutes, plain water is best to replenish body fluids.

tips to increase your water intake:

- Invest in a 32-ounce sports bottle. Fill it with ice water and keep it handy throughout the day. Drink two of these each day.
- Water down your meals and snacks. Complement food with water, milk, or juice. Occasionally start your meals with soup.
- Refresh yourself at snack time with juice, milk, or sparkling water.
- Before, during, and after any physical activity, drink water, especially in hot weather. Consume 4 to 8 ounces of water every 15 to 20 minutes while you exercise. Don't wait until you feel thirsty.
- Add a lemon, lime, or orange slice to jazz up your glass of water.

trim fat not flavor

Love to improve your waistline, cholesterol, or blood pressure? What's in your kitchen cabinet can be more important than what is in your medicine cabinet. Eating plenty of whole grains, fruits, and vegetables is a good start, but exercising some lowfat cooking skills can also make a big difference. Try these easy tips to trim some fat without sacrificing flavor.

add flavor to cooking liquids

Prepare rice, couscous, potatoes, and other vegetables with fat free chicken or vegetable broth instead of water. You won't need butter or margarine for flavor.

blend in beans

Puree a can of kidney beans or pinto beans in a food processor and add to ground beef for meatloaf, meatballs, or tacos. Bean puree is also a great thickener for soups and stews. It's a delicious way to add a hefty dose of fiber.

choose skinny sauces

Barbecue sauce, chili sauce, chutney, Dijon mustard, salsa, soy sauce, teriyaki sauce, tomato sauce, and Worcestershire sauce all add flavor without fat.

cook with foil

Wrap skinless poultry or seafood, sliced vegetables, and fresh or dried herbs in heavy-duty aluminum foil packets and bake in the oven. Foods come out moist and flavorful with virtually no fat or clean up!

give ground beef a bath

Rinse cooked ground beef with hot water before adding to recipes. You'll get rid of an extra 2 to 5 grams of fat per three-ounce serving.

get more greens

Low in calories and loaded with antioxidants and vitamins, greens add color and flavor to a variety of dishes. Add spinach to salads and kale, collards or chard to pasta, rice and stir-fry dishes.

grate on flavor

Add big flavor with small amounts of rich ingredients. Use a grater to top vegetables and pasta with a thin layer of extra-sharp cheddar or Parmesan cheese instead of butter or margarine. A sprinkling of grated chocolate adds a deluxe touch to skinny desserts.

pick the right pork

When a recipe calls for bacon, substitute lean ham or Canadian bacon. It will give you the smoky flavor you want, with less fat.

pucker up

Use citrus juices to marinate meat, poultry, and seafood. Add fresh herbs and just a drizzle of oil to orange, lemon, or lime juice for zesty, lowfat flavor.

sauté without fat

Instead of cooking vegetables in oil or butter, use a little liquid—defatted broth, fruit juice, or wine. You'll save 120 calories and 13 grams of fat for each tablespoon of fat you skip.

food and nutrition tips

Here's some helpful advice from a nutritionist on a variety of food and nutrition-related topics from Meals.com and Lean Cuisine.

Q: I have recently become lactoovovegetarian. I've been enjoying Lean Cuisine Roasted Potatoes, Broccoli, and Cheese Sauce for lunch. I use your products at least three times a week. Can you tell me which other meals are meatless?

A: Here are some more meatless products, Angel Hair Pasta, Cheese Cannelloni, Cheese Lasagna Casserole, Cheese Pizza, Cheese Ravioli, Classic Five Cheese Lasagna, Fettuccine Alfredo, Macaroni & Cheese, Penne Pasta, Three Bean Chili, Vegetable Eggroll, Vegetable Lasagna, and Three Cheese Stuffed Rigatoni.

Q: What products help me control my diabetes?

A: Eating a diet that is balanced, full of variety, and with moderation may help stabilize blood glucose levels. This is very important along with your medication. I suggest that you meet with your registered dietitian who can help you identify specific products that fit into your lifestyle and preferences.

Q: When trying to lose weight, what is more important to count: calories or fat grams?

A: When concerned about weight control and weight loss, it is more important to reduce calories than fat content (i.e., 3500 calories = 1 pound of body fat). If you only reduce fat intake you need to make sure you don't increase protein or carbohydrates which would increase the total calorie amount.

Q: How about developing some products with less carbs? The fat content is great but so many of the products have such high carb counts I can't eat them since I have trouble with my blood glucose.

A: Most health organizations agree that about half of your daily calories should come from carbohydrates. The meal planner on the Lean Cuisine website can help you plan for balanced fat, carbohydrate, and protein meals. Did you know there are 15 Lean Cuisine meals that have less than 30 grams of carbohydrates?

Q: Do your products contain transfatty acids?

A: Transfatty acids are typically found in hydrogenated fats, which are used in only a few Lean Cuisine items in very small amounts. Many of the products primarily use liquid canola oil, which is transfat free. Total fat content is more important to monitor for many health reasons and all Lean Cuisine items are low in total fat.

Q: When I get my cholesterol checked I get four numbers. What do they mean, and what can I do to affect each individual number?

A: Most likely, you received a blood cholesterol level, high-density lipoprotein (HDL) cholesterol, low-density lipoprotein (LDL), and triglycerides (TG). Your cholesterol level is affected by two sources, one being the amount your liver produces and the second source is from the foods you consume. Cholesterol is found only in the fats of animal products such as milk, meat, etc. The effect of dietary cholesterol on your blood cholesterol levels is also affected by other components of your diet such as saturated fat intake. High-density lipoprotein (HDL) cholesterol is considered the "good cholesterol" which is associated with a reduced risk of heart disease. You can increase this by exercise. Low-density lipoprotein (LDL) cholesterol is considered the "bad cholesterol" and increased levels increase your risk of heart disease. Both HDL and LDL are not found in foods, but your LDL can be affected by the amount of fat and cholesterol in your diet. Triglycerides are fatty acids, which are the form of fat storage in the body. To reduce this amount in your blood—reduce intake of refined carbohydrates such as sweets as well as alcohol. Overall, decrease the amount of fat in your diet by focusing on eating lowfat plant foods like grains, beans, vegetables, and fruits. Use fat free dairy products and small servings of lean meats. This may help you in maintaining healthy blood fat levels.

Q: How can I get used to eating certain types of foods? It seems I can never lose any weight, only around 10–15 pounds then I gain it back again. After eating fixed food portions I am still hungry.
A: The best way to lose weight and keep it off long term is to follow a well-balanced meal plan combined with regular activity. Lean Cuisine entrées can be part of a balanced meal plan, but keep in mind they are not intended to be full meals. Round out your Lean Cuisine entrées with foods such as fruits, vegetables, and dairy products.

Q: What is the difference between sodium and salt?
A: "Salt" usually refers to table salt, technically known as sodium chloride. Salt contains about 40 percent sodium and 60 percent chloride. It is sodium, not salt, which is usually studied in relation to health issues.

Q: How much sodium does a teaspoon of salt have?
A: Table salt consists of sodium and chloride. A teaspoon of table salt has 2300 milligrams of sodium. Many people think of sodium as a non-nutritious dietary element, but sodium is an essential nutrient, a mineral that the body cannot store or manufacture by itself. Sodium is needed by the body for proper functioning of nerves and

muscles, and regulates blood pressure and blood volume.

Q: How much sodium should I consume?
A: The average intake in the United States is between 4,000 and 5,000 milligrams of sodium per day. The Daily Reference Value is 2400 milligrams of sodium per day. Each person's need for sodium differs. It is recommended that healthy individuals consume a diet with moderate levels of sodium. If you have health concerns, I suggest you see a registered dietitian who can customize your diet according to your individual needs.

Q: How is a "serving size" determined?
A: The Food and Drug Administration defines serving size as the amount of food customarily eaten at one time. The serving sizes that appear on food labels are based on FDA-established lists of "Reference Amounts Customarily Consumed per Eating Occasion." These reference amounts, which are part of the regulations, are broken down into 139 food categories, including 11 groups of foods specially formulated or processed for infants or children. They list the amounts of food typically consumed per eating occasion for each category, based primarily on national food consumption surveys.

Q: Your package no longer has the diet exchanges on them and I could not find them on your website?
A: The diet exchange information can now be found on the Lean Cuisine website under the "Find Your Favorite section, Nutrition Details."

Q: I would like to add a serving/glass of wine to my evening meal. What is a "serving" of wine and how many calories in a serving?
A: A serving of wine is considered five ounces and 100 calories.

Q: What constitutes two servings of vegetables?
A: Based on USDA's Food Guide pyramid, most vegetables are measured as a ½ cup serving.

Q: What is the importance of potassium in our diet?
A: Potassium is an electrolyte found in our intracellular fluid and is involved in regulating the neuromuscular activity of the skeletal, cardiac, and smooth muscle. It also helps maintain normal blood pressure. You can find potassium in many fruits and vegetables such as broccoli, carrots, mushrooms, bananas, raisins, and oranges.

special cuisines

simply italian

Italian food, for the most part, is simple food. From the golden hills of Tuscany to the blue waters of the Adriatic Sea, each area in Italy has its food traditions, and nearly all of them come from what has traditionally been available in that region. In the agriculturally rich North, for instance, the pasta is made with rich egg yolks and the sauces incorporate butter. In the arid South, pasta is made with water, and is therefore harder and chewier; it is made into small shapes and used with stronger sauces, using more tomatoes and olive oil.

This tradition of working with fresh pastas, artisan breads, and fresh seafood and vegetables allows the dishes of Italy to focus on flavorful ingredients rather than complex techniques. With a few of these simple, age-old ideas, you can make authentic Italian dishes a delicious part of your everyday cooking.

planning an Italian meal

In Italian cooking, according to Marcella Hazan, a guru of Italian cookery in America, there is no "main course," but a succession of small courses that complement one another.

First the antipasti is served, which can be anything from cured meats to roasted vegetables to shrimp. The first course, or primi, comes next, and is usually pasta, risotto, or soup. The second course, or secondi, is usually a meat or fish dish served with side vegetables. The meal is finished off with a light green salad, and then fruit or sweets.

the Italian pantry

For Italians, the garden is as important as the pantry. If you don't have your own garden, try to buy fresh herbs and vegetables when they are in season and therefore less expensive.

Always keep your pantry full of extra virgin olive oil and balsamic vinegar. Select fresh garlic and onions, and try canned capers and anchovies for rich, flavorful sauces.

Look for fresh herbs like basil for pesto and use in salads and sauces; flat-leaf or Italian parsley and marjoram are best fresh. Also, black pepper and nutmeg are standbys. It is important to keep dried herbs available such as: oregano, bay leaf, rosemary, and sage. These herbs hold their flavor when dried, but use whole leaves, not powdered. Beans, either canned or dry, like fava beans, cranberry beans, garbanzo beans, lentils, or the traditional cannellini bean (white kidney bean) are also important in meals.

Keep dry pasta, e.g. spaghetti, linguine, rotini, and lasagna on hand since they are economical and easy to prepare. Cooking with bread crumbs is also essential. Try saving stale bread and crumble when it is very dry for coating meats, tossing with pasta, topping for vegetables, or using in meatballs. You can make your own broth very inexpensively. Nothing is complete without the right cheese. Parmesan, mozzarella, ricotta, and Romano are among the favorites. And, when looking for canned tomatoes, make sure they are whole, peeled plum tomatoes with no sauce, only a bit of juice. Find a brand that has good flavor without being too sweet.

building a delectable dish

A few fundamentals make all the difference in cooking Italian meat sauces, risottos, and soups. First, create a "foundation" for flavor by sautéing a battuto, which means "to strike"— and it contains olive oil or butter, and diced onion, parsley, garlic, and celery or carrot.

healthy Italian desserts

Italy has a history of creating delectable desserts that have become all the rage around the world. When we think of Italian desserts, creamy (and high-fat) delights such as tiramisu and zabaglione come to mind. But the range of desserts with an Italian heritage is mind boggling—and many of them are relatively low in fat and calories. We have a few lowfat versions of some Italian favorites, as well as some traditional desserts that are light on calories but not on flavor.

spice up dessert with fruit and nuts

At the end of the everyday Italian meal, fruit is the usual dessert. Truly ripe pears, plums, or melons are as sweet as any sugary concoction. The practice of macerating fruit, or soaking it in lemon juice and sugar, sometimes with wine or vinegar, was imported to Italy from Macedonia, a region in southeastern Europe. So recipes such as Melon Macedonia or Strawberries with Candied Pine Nuts are called macedonias. Soaking the fruit makes it sweeter and creates a compote-like

sauce that can be spooned over ice cream or cake.

Another popular technique is poaching or steaming. Steamed Honey Pears are cooked with very little water, and the sweet combination of dried fruits and honey makes a rich sauce that is poured on top. Gingered Figs and Pistachio Berry Vineyard Pears are poached until they are softened.

Spiced nuts are a great complement to poached or macerated fruit. Sugared Walnuts or Roast Chestnuts are often served at the end of a meal with cheese and fruit.

luscious light cakes, tarts, and cookies

So you still want a slice of that creamy tiramisu? Quick Tiramisu or Frozen Tiramisu made with ice cream and fresh raspberries can be made lowfat by using lower fat ice cream, pudding, and whipped cream. But other mouth-watering cakes shouldn't go unnoticed. Tarts with nut crusts, then filled with fruit and topped with a dollop of light whipped cream are also ancient treats; try our Rustic Plum-Walnut Tart. Homemade biscotti are surprisingly easy to make a light and tasty dessert when served with ice cream or gelato and coffee: Chocolate Almond Biscotti or Walnut Biscotti. For the desserts mentioned here that are not featured in the book, please visit Meals.com for more recipe selections.

mexican foods

Latino Salsa

A true fusion of foods, Nuevo Latino (New Latin) is a craze that is not likely to say "hasta la vista" any time soon. For centuries, Latin American cuisines have blended Aztec and African, Incan, and Italian and other traditions into a melting pot stirred with a Spanish spoon. Even now, as people keep moving around the world, we continue to meld old ideas and techniques with new ways of cooking and eating.

Fresh and fast, salsas are a great way to add a Latino zing to your cooking. They're easy to make, and the possibilities are limited only by your imagination. Tomatoes, garlic, and peppers are just the beginning. Fruit salsas made with mango, peaches, or pineapple complement grilled chicken or pork chops. A quick sauce of fresh garden vegetables, onions, garlic, and dried or fresh herbs is an easy addition to traditional Latino fare such as tacos or fajitas.

spice up both surf and turf

A great seafood dish to try is ceviche (sah-vee-chay). The freshest seafood is tossed with onion, tomato, parsley, hot peppers, and lime or lemon juice to "cook" the seafood. Every coastal region of Mexico, Cuba, and the Caribbean has its specialty, from tilapia (a firm white fish) to pulpo (octopus). Use one of our salsas as the base for a ceviche. Refreshing as an appetizer or a light lunch, ceviche can also be paired with slices of fresh avocado and a green salad for a hot-summer-night supper.

The carnivores dish of preference is the Argentinean parillada mixta (mixed grill) that displays the pride of the cattle ranchers grilled fast over a high flame and served with a tangy chimichurri sauce, a sort of spicy parsley pesto. The Brazilian churrasco is similar, but adds lamb, pork, chicken, and even goat cooked on skewers.

don't need a recipe?

If basic ingredients are all you need for inspiration, here's how a few traditional salsas are put together in different parts of the Latin universe.

Cuba's salsa mojo

This spicy salsa is on every table in Cuba. Traditionally made with fresh juice of the sour orange, now fresh lime, grapefruit, or pineapple juices are often used. Blend with olive oil, garlic, and cumin and cook briefly and you have a brightly colored dressing, similar to vinaigrette. Sprinkle over meats and fish, or stir into soups.

Argentina's chimichurri

Argentineans smother delectable grilled meats with this tangy sauce that includes fresh or dried herbs. Mix olive oil, red wine vinegar, onion, parsley, garlic, oregano, and pepper to add an extra zing to basic grilled chicken breast.

Mexico's salsa cruda

This simple cold salsa can be made in endless variations. Start with fresh tomatoes, onion, chiles, and cilantro. Add avocado, jicama, black beans, mangoes, lime, or any fresh fruit or vegetable you have on hand to brighten up grilled meats and fish. Serve on fish tacos or as a dip for chips.

salsa ranchera

A smooth, cooked red sauce made with chiles and tomatoes is commonly used on huevos rancheros (country-style eggs).

tortillas

It's not Mexican without tortillas. Fresh flour and corn tortillas may be found in the refrigerated section as well as near the Mexican canned products, unrefrigerated, at your supermarket. Whichever type you buy, serve them hot.

Try the oven, and wrap the tortillas in foil and place in a 350° F oven for 10 to 15 minutes. You can also microwave tortillas by laying four or five tortillas on a damp paper towel and cover with another damp paper towel. Microwave on high about one minute. Live gas flame is a great way to create the freshly made flavor of tortillas by heating directly over a low gas flame, turning them almost constantly until warm.

key ingredients

- Seasonings: Chile powder, cilantro, cinnamon, cumin, Mexican oregano, and dried chiles.
- Fruits and vegetables: Tomatoes, tomatillos, avocados, papayas, mangoes, jicama, lemons, limes, and fresh chiles.
- Beans: Black, pinto, and kidney beans are staples of Mexican cooking as well as rice.

guacamole

Avocados are the base for the popular Mexican dip, guacamole.

Avocados should be slightly soft when served. If you're not using avocados within a day or two, choose ones that are firm. Store in a paper bag at room temperature until ripe. Check your supermarket for frozen guacamole if fresh avocados are not available.

One way to access the rich flesh for guacamole is to insert a sharp knife at the top of the avocado until it hits the pit. Then slice all the way around the pit. Separate the halves. Insert the tip of a knife into the pit enough to use as a handle and twist the pit out. Scoop out the flesh with a spoon and place in a shallow bowl. Mash with a dinner fork or potato masher. To prevent browning, add lemon juice to the mashed avocado.

Green Chile Guacamole

More zip as you dip; the green chiles make this guacamole a real crowd pleaser.

MAKES 8 SERVINGS

INGREDIENTS

2 medium very ripe avocados, pitted, peeled and mashed

1 can (4 oz.) diced green chiles or jalapeños

2 large green onions, chopped

2 tablespoons olive oil

1 teaspoon lime juice

1 clove garlic, finely chopped

¼ teaspoon salt

DIRECTIONS

COMBINE avocados, chiles, green onions, oil, lime juice, garlic and salt in medium bowl. Cover; refrigerate for at least 1 hour. Serve with tortilla chips, if desired.

Estimated Times

Preparation: 10 mins
Refrigerating: 1 hr

For more great recipes on Latin American cuisine and other dishes from around the world visit Meals.com.

entertaining
party planning

Whether you volunteered, or by the nature of relations inherited the job, you are in charge of having a party to celebrate a graduation or a wedding. Think positive. This is supposed to be fun. We'll help. If you've done it many times or never ever before, read on.

Today there are many types of parties to choose from: brunch, lunch, tea, cocktail party, dessert party, buffet, sit down dinner, potluck, soup and sandwich buffet, picnic, or BBQ, to name a few. You decide which style will be most comfortable and doable for you.

leave your super-hostess apron on the hook

Creative is good, but be realistic. Do the party basics, and then concentrate on what you enjoy about parties the most. For example, you might have a flair for food presentation or complicated desserts or decorating. Keep your favorite activity in mind when selecting your type of party, theme, and menu.

happy helpers

Create a list of jobs you feel comfortable doling out. When someone asks, "What can I do to help?" you'll have an answer. When planning a large important event, get a definite commitment or hire outside professionals to fill in the gaps you won't be able to handle.

A job you might not have thought about is that of designated food timekeeper, who will take food away during parties when left out too long, so you can concentrate on enjoying your guests.

the right menu mentality

Fit the menu to the guests. Gourmet might be perfect to impress the boss but a gaggle of teens would probably

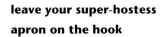

protest. Fit the menu to your kitchen and to your capabilities. How many you will be feeding is very important, and what you can realistically accomplish. How much refrigerator, oven, and counter space do you need to accomplish each task?

danger zone for food safety

It is imperative that hot food is kept at 140° F and above and cold at 40° F or below. Consider renting large chafing dishes to hold hot food at the correct serving temperature especially if it is a very large party. Two hours is the maximum that food should be left out at room temperature, this includes the time spent out of refrigeration for preparation. After two hours, announce that the food is being moved to the refrigerator. This is where the designated timekeeper comes in handy.

Don't set out perishable foods until guests start arriving. Remember the two-hour limit. Have snacks like a relish tray, nuts, or other dry snacks available for early guests. Offer first guests beverages and bring out perishable food after most have arrived.

It is a good idea to make small trays of food so they can be swapped out. A smaller, fresh tray of food is more appealing than a half-empty, large tray anyway. Do not mix the old with the fresh food.

the best chilling trick in the world

For big serving bowls, freeze smaller water-filled plastic bowls with lids, which can fit in the bottom of the big serving bowl and be hidden by a small plate or food during the party. Or freeze a re-sealable freezer bag of water in a serving bowl for a perfect fit if the bowl is freezer safe. When frozen, remove the bowl from the freezer and return the frozen bag. At party-time place the frozen bag in the bottom of the serving bowl and cover it with a small plate, which fits neatly into the bowl. For platters, freeze water-filled, resealable freezer bags laid out flat in the freezer to place under platters. They will last anywhere from two to four hours at about a half- to three-quarters-inch thick.

a little detailing makes all the difference

Prevent last minute stage fright by setting out the serving dishes a day or so ahead and make a mental or written note of what will go in each dish. This way you will know if you have enough dishes and serving utensils. Also, check for cleanliness, if they have been stored for some time.

Don't scrimp on paper plates or plasticware. Sturdy disposables can prevent a potential mess from collapsing paper plates.

Even the dullest food can appear enticing with some thought to presentation. Look at the colors, textures, and flavors when setting the food table. Platters are better than bowls for presentation purposes. A few minutes spent designing well-chosen fruit or vegetable garnishes can make a difference. Parsley has been done and there are so many other easy garnishes made from stuff in your refrigerator, like lemons or carrots.

maximize refrigerator space

Prep all of the food you can in advance and store in separate plastic bags that stack easily in the refrigerator and require no cleanup. Label each bag carefully as you may have identical foods in different recipes. Group recipe ingredient bags together in plastic grocery sacks for help with last minute assembly.

be gracious to grateful guests

You worked hard on this party. Accept praise graciously, by saying, "You're so welcome, thank you for coming," and take notes if you want to make your next party even better.

kitchen notes

kitchen notes

kitchen notes

kitchen notes

index

Acknowledgments

The publisher would like to thank the entire Nestlé family for their tireless work, guidance, and effort in helping to bring this book to fruition, and some special thanks to Jeremy Barron, Amy Hiestand, Christine Garboski, Jenny Harper, Barb Sypen, Ava Baffoni, and Bridgette Vega.

Editorial and Design Team:
Text and original recipes created by Meals.com
Design and Art Direction: Elizabeth Watson
Production: Patty Holden
Project Editor: Lisa M. Tooker
Food Writer and Editor: Ann Beman

Photo Credits:
Diane Padys Food Photography,
www.limagemagick.com: cover and back cover, 28 (bottom), 47, 172, 209, 211, 237, 246 (top), 252 (top), 266 (bottom), 267, 280

Special thanks to Pete Gent and Tim Sutton for additional food photography.

ISBN 1-930603-88-6

Printed in Hong Kong